# VICTORIAN GIRLS

# Victorian Girls

## *Lord Lyttleton's Daughters*

Sheila Fletcher

Hambledon and London
London and New York

Published by Hambledon and London 2001

102 Gloucester Avenue, London, NW1 8HX
838 Broadway, New York, NY 10003–4812

ISBN 1 85285 150 3 (cased)
    1 85285 333 6 (paper)

A description of this book is available from
the British Library and from the Library of Congress.

Typeset by Carnegie Publishing, Chatsworth Road, Lancaster

Printed on acid-free paper and bound in
Great Britain by Cambridge University Press

# Contents

# Illustrations

# Preface

I first encountered the fourth Lord Lyttelton many years ago in the course of research for *Feminists and Bureaucrats* (1979), a book concerned with Commissioners appointed in 1868 to reform the old grammar schools, who used their power – against fierce opposition – to launch the first grammar schools for *girls*. Lyttelton, who headed this Endowed Schools Commission, would have thought it comic that its dusty papers should be raked over a hundred years later; though had he lived long enough it would have pleased him to see how its fruits swelled the efflorescence of girls' schools and colleges for women in the last years of the nineteenth century. That some girls then went on to the suffrage; worse, that a student from the first women's college ever to be established in Oxford turned her mind to the Anglican priesthood (my *Maude Royden*, 1989) would have shocked him. For he was not another John Stuart Mill. Despite his work for girls' education, there is no sign that Lyttelton envisaged major changes in the status quo regarding the relations of men and women.

His daughters teased him for having given them the kind of 'slip-sloppy' education which he officially castigated; but they were certainly not 'new women'. In 1867 Lucy wrote in her diary that the subject of female suffrage, 'odious and ridiculous notion as it is', was beginning to be spoken of without laughter, 'as if it was an open question. I trust we are not coming to that'. In 1889 she and her sisters signed the anti-women's suffrage petition organised by Mrs Humphrey Ward. The roles they took at home fit our stereotype of Victorian family life, where the main duty of the female members was to succour and advance the men; a role enhanced here since Lady Lyttelton, the mother of the family, had died, leaving eight boys, and four girls to take charge. But stereotypes rarely survive close contact. The Lyttelton sisters' diaries and letters seduce us from this all too simple picture by the one they create of an enchanting Hagley, a father who held their admiring affection by somehow never demanding it, a religious faith that assuaged disaster without suppressing a sense of fun.

I owe a tremendous debt of gratitude to Lord Lyttelton's great-great-grandson, Viscount Cobham, for his kindness in giving me access over several years to the Archives at Hagley; and to Stanley Hodkinson, Hagley's archivist, who spared no effort to find what I wanted and from his own great knowledge and interest backed my project from the beginning. Two other great-great-grandchildren played a crucial part in the book's completion: Charles Talbot of Falconhurst in Kent, who most generously made available photographs from a family album which supply the bulk of the illustrations; and his sister, Joanna Smith, who had the originals photographed. A great-grandson, Sir John Stephenson, was kind enough to talk to me at length and to lend me his own account of the family. Dame Anne Warburton, then the President of Lucy Cavendish College, Cambridge, most hospitably gave me access to the relevant archives there, while Sir Neville Lyttelton's family papers, at Queen Mary and Westfield College, London, were put at my disposal with the friendly assistance of the College Archivist, Anselm Nye. The staff of the Clwyd County Record Office, which houses the Gladstone-Glynne Papers, and those at the Centre for Kentish Studies, which holds the Talbot Papers, have been most kind. Quotations from the diary of Lady Frederick Cavendish, which belongs to the Devonshire Collections at Chatsworth, are made by kind permission of the Chatsworth Trustees.

Rare must be the book which has not drawn on the bottomless support of friends and I dare not try to assess the gratitude I owe in this direction. No one was spared, but Julia Bush, Cecily Coales, Pamela Hawker and Gill Sutherland are those who have now most cause to breathe a sigh of relief. Finally, I want to express warm thanks to Martin Sheppard of the Hambledon Press. He is a most unusual publisher, giving his books all the thought and attention which their authors think they deserve but in today's world never think they'll get.

Berkhamsted                                            Sheila Fletcher

*To my grandchildren*

*Edward, Nicholas, Jessica, Charlotte, Anna, Matthew and Rebecca*

1

# *Hagley*

'We came safely home to the dear
snug quietness of green summer Hagley.'

Lucy Lyttelton, Diary, 29 July 1859

The mid-Victorian period in England – roughly, the years between the
1850s and the 1870s (the span of this book) – was very prosperous: a
time when Britain was well able to exploit her position as the world's
first industrial nation and, with high confidence, set out her stall at the
Great Exhibition of 1851. Thanks to the *Illustrated London News*, we can
go round the Crystal Palace (itself a technological marvel) and see such
triumphs of engineering as the 700 horse-power engines built by Messrs
Boulton & Watt, Whitworth's planing and drilling tools, and the new
vertical printing press which threw off *Illustrated* sheets so fast that
Queen Victoria could be given a copy she had just seen fed in as blank
paper.

The years which followed the Exhibition brought substantial and
increasing wealth. Britain was the 'Workshop of the World' indeed –
but not yet an industrial nation in the modern sense of that term. There
were main-line railways, but travel by road was still confined to the
speed of a horse. There were thousands of industrial and factory
workers, but rather more people still employed in farm labour and
domestic service. Industrial cities were growing fast, and the census of
1851 showed that more people now lived in towns than in the country.
But the difference was slight. Almost half the nation, in fact, still
belonged to a rural society, supervised – if not in the forms, then in
the spirit of feudal times – by a landed aristocracy.

'What a mighty space', wrote one observer, 'lies between the palace
and the cottage in this country!'[1] He had in mind, not a royal palace,
but the great mansions on great estates: the ducal palaces, for example,

scattered through the length and breadth of England and unbelievably more luxurious than the dwellings of other people. Of course, the contrast was taken for granted, not only in both palace and cottage but at every level of tenant farmer and country gentleman in between. For this was a country of deference; and even those near the top of the tree could be overawed by the scale and splendour of ducal palaces such as Chatsworth, where Lord Lyttelton's daughter, Lucy, had much trouble to find her room in 1864 – among miles of passages, several staircases 'and turns and twists innumerable'. She had grown up with something smaller (though not small, for Hagley Hall, the Lyttelton seat in Worcestershire, was a substantial Palladian mansion). She had certainly grown up with much less money and a great many fewer servants. In fact, her father and the Duke of Devonshire, though distant cousins, represented – in terms of the income they could command – opposite poles of the aristocracy.

About £10,000 a year is thought to have been the *minimum* income necessary at this time to support an aristocratic lifestyle in the country, along with customary participation in the pleasures of the London Season which occurred between May and July.[2] Most of this income would have come from land, and since the usual rent was £1 an acre, 10,000 acres would have been needed. At the time he married in 1839 George William, fourth Baron Lyttelton, seems to have had only £7000 a year; and to have been paying off a debt of £1300 a year on the estate.[3] Strikingly, by 1872 (when the one and only official return of estates was made) the land at Hagley was estimated at barely more than a thousand acres and the rents at just over £1000 p.a. The same return gives the land at Chatsworth (which was only one of the Duke's estates) as approaching 84,000 acres and the rental as £83,000 p.a.[4] (This, of course, takes no account of the Duke of Devonshire's industrial interests, which were very considerable).

From the start then, Lyttelton was poor for a nobleman. If wealth had been the qualification for a Lord Lieutenancy, the obvious candidate – in Worcestershire – would have been Lord Ward (later Earl of Dudley), a man whose wife's wedding dress was said to have cost £3000. There is no reason at all to suppose that Lord Ward was ever considered. In any case, the fact that his fortune came from iron and coal, and not from land, would have told against him. Whereas Lord Lyttelton, whose forbears had held land in Worcestershire from the middle ages, might well claim (as he did on one occasion, to his brother-in-law, William Gladstone) that his estate was 'of very great antiquity'.

He took pride in being Lord Lieutenant: an office which was more important then than it is today, for at that time there was no other form of county government. County Councils had not been thought of, and central government had only just made its first and bitterly resented incursion into the affairs of the localities with the New Poor Law of 1834. Otherwise, rural England presented a governmental vacuum to be filled by local magnates, whose authority was taken as a matter of course; and, in the case of such as Lyttelton, discharged with great conscientiousness: the more, he once said, as 'I have never had, and am never likely to have the means' to spend what others might have spent on the county.[5] Routine duties of his office included chairing the magistrates at Quarter Sessions and dining the judges of Assize. But it was up to the Lord Lieutenant to take the lead in any emergency (as Lyttelton's father had done, for instance, in the first cholera epidemic); also, as Colonel of the Yeomanry, to assist in quelling any serious threat to the maintenance of law and order. Lyttelton was twenty when his father died, and so came young into all the business of establishing himself in the county: serious-minded, and in the midst of a very brilliant career at Cambridge; brusque in manner and inclined to deafness. In 1839, aged twenty-three, he married Mary Glynne, the younger daughter of Sir Stephen Glynne, of Hawarden in Cheshire, at a double wedding where her sister, Catherine, married Gladstone, the future Prime Minister. Mary's beauty, grace and awareness of 'all the little civil things' due to neighbours eased Lyttelton's path. But he was more at home on the hunting field than in the ballroom: an eager huntsman and a fearless rider, yet content, if they were drawing blank, to gossip happily with local squires.

Twelve children were born over seventeen years: eight sons and four daughters. The *Peerage*, in those days, did not trouble with the birth dates of girls, since these could not affect the succession. So Meriel, Lucy, Lavinia and May huddle, dateless, at the foot of the column; though the actual pattern of his children's births (two girls, four boys; two girls, four boys) seemed to their father rather striking, and turned out to be important later. From 1840 there were always babies and toddlers in the nursery; where, as Lucy recalled, an ornamental pin-cushion lay in a drawer, along with the christening cap and powder-box, ready for the next arrival. Theirs was the first rumbustious young family ever to occupy Hagley Hall: an austere mansion with a tower at each corner, built to replace an earlier one by the first Lord Lyttelton in 1760. He had also redesigned the park according to the canons of 'natural' landscape just then coming into fashion, and it became famous. The cognoscenti travelled great distances to see it; the celebrated

Horace Walpole thrilled over its cascades and vistas and its tributes to antiquity – the Doric temple and Roman rotunda, the obelisk and 'ruined' castle – placed so judiciously against a background of exceeding natural beauty.

All this of course meant nothing much to the young Lytteltons of later years – busy digging caves and damming streams, riding, climbing and hunting rabbits. In their eyes, certainly, the cricket pitch was more important than the Doric temple, for they were all obsessed with cricket. On high days and holidays, their father liked to open the park to local people, so visitors were just as likely to be part of an outing from the Stourbridge glass-works as a party of connoisseurs. With Stourbridge three miles off, and Birmingham twelve, Hagley could not be called remote (even with a park of two hundred acres); and the long view in that direction had changed a little since Walpole's time. The glow of foundries was just perceptible from high ground in the sky at night, a faint reminder that these leafy hills were on the verge of the Black Country.

Such things probably played a part in shaping Lyttelton's earnest mind. 'A strong, righteous man, incessantly busied in useful work for others', as one son remembered,[6] he had come of age at a time when the idea that education must be provided for the working masses began to be taken seriously. His busyness had much to do with that, for he regarded education – especially in its aspect of moral training – as the first duty of a Christian parent; gave himself to it, with his own children, and spent a great deal of time and effort promoting schools for the children of the poor. In all this, as in every duty, he felt the driving force of religion; for his was also a generation reacting strongly against the slackness of the Church of England in the eighteenth century. John Keble's famous sermon, 'National Apostasy', preached at Oxford in 1833 in protest against what he regarded as state interference in Church matters, gave that Church a new view of itself as 'more than a merely human institution', possessing sacraments and a ministry which had their origins in Christ. This was the start of the Oxford Movement, to which Lyttelton was drawn at Cambridge and through the influence of his brother-in-law, Gladstone. Its beliefs and observances, harking back to the Catholic roots of the Church of England, came to be labelled Anglo-Catholic. Chief among them was a sense that the sacrament of Communion lay at the very heart of worship.

So the church at Hagley, close to the Hall, where Lyttelton was Patron and his brother was Rector, itself became 'High Church' or 'Anglo-Catholic'. Communion was celebrated every Sunday; and, in common with other Anglo-Catholic gentry, Lyttelton planned to improve the interior (as soon as he was able to find the money) so as to give a clear view of the altar. The children took an interest in all these changes but it did not dampen their love of cricket. All of them, down to the next to youngest, went to church regularly – twice on Sundays and once on saints' days (for with High Church people, saints had come into their own again). 'There can never be too many Sundays, even in the longest life', said Lucy (though much later). She was very devout, and her cricketer brothers would not all have agreed with that. But they would have challenged Lord Melbourne's assumption that devoutness precluded gaiety. 'Nobody is gay now, they are so religious', he had complained to Queen Victoria. This was very far from the case at Hagley, where summer visitors were pushed to decide whether the main influence was church or cricket; and memories of childhood were as much connected with Lyttelton's uproarious sense of fun, and his napkin fights with the boys, as with his piety and sense of duty.

'I should imagine that life at Hagley was much the same as that at many other country houses', one of the sons reflected later:

> 'We dwelt among our own people', we entertained our neighbours in a rather formal fashion, we knew most of the villagers, played cricket with the boys, and all our interests were local.[7]

But Lucy, who became the family chronicler at thirteen, thought Hagley unique; and felt its troop of children secure – not only in the love of God, but in the loving care of parents who were close to them and close to each other. 'Mamma taught us our Bible when we were little and Papa as we grew older', she wrote, 'and we had them always to help us by their example as well as training'. She describes how schoolroom life was enlivened 'by Papa's visits to Mamma and hers to him; our room being the passage between them'.

> We were never interrupted by this, for one got so thoroughly accustomed to it, and it was seldom that either took any notice of us, beyond a smile from Mamma and 'You little pigs', or 'Absurd monkeys', from Papa. But it always gave me a happy feeling when I heard Mamma's little cough, or saw her tall and graceful figure passing through the room.

'As I grew older and understood more and more what our happiness was; thought of our unclouded home, of the exceeding blessing to us of such parents as ours . . . I trust I grew year by year more grateful, while at times there would mingle with the happiness, a feeling that it could not last.'[8] And of course it did not. They met the calamity

Victorian families faced and dreaded, for their mother's death in August 1857 changed their family life for ever.

Meriel, the eldest of all the children, who was just seventeen at the time, took charge of Hagley for the next three years. When she married, Lucy took over. And when she married, her sister Lavinia, though only fifteen, carried things on. The peculiar symmetry of the Lyttelton family turned out to be a blessing then. It would have been a different story had the four daughters all been infants. As things were, although irrelevant to family survival in the eyes of the *Peerage*, to its survival in another sense – a family's struggle to retrieve itself after disablement – the girls were essential.

Plainly, their mother's early death changed the nature of young ladyhood at Hagley. 'My young lady life was a very short one', Meriel wrote later, looking back to the time when she had nervously taken on the business of running that large household: ordering dinners, instructing servants, making things comfortable for her father; and, in regard to the younger children ('especially the boys', for whom her example had always been reckoned of great importance), exercising the moral authority which until then had been her mother's.

This book is not much about the Lyttelton sons (though they made their mark in the history of cricket, and several were distinguished in public life) but about the daughters: how they coped with the role that was thrust upon them, and their relationships with their father – one of the most idiosyncratic characters in the Victorian aristocracy. The Lytteltons, like others in the leisured classes, kept regular diaries; and corresponded on a scale which seems remarkable today. Though nothing like all of what they wrote survives, through such sources a door is opened on the threshold of their private lives. Meriel's indeed is intensely private (though she is revealed a good deal by others). In contrast, Lucy, with her gift for writing and wit, and readiness to pour things out, habitually fills a large canvas and, more than anyone else, conveys the strength and warmth of family feeling which, even in a family-minded age, seems to have been notable among the Lytteltons. Lavinia's writing is quite consistent with her having been the only sister who found the taking charge of Hagley easy; and May's with her having been the only one whose succession to that task was forestalled by her father's unexpected remarriage. May's diary shows her often frustrated, and very much in need of a role (at a time when significant roles were rare for intellectual, unmarried daughters, scrappily equipped with education and lacking even the thought of employment).

But all this lay well in the future in 1857 when their mother died.

## 2

# An Eloquent Death

'The memory of her life and the eloquence of her
death will be all of your mother that you have left.'

Johnny Talbot to Meriel Lyttelton, 30 November 1857

Nobody expected her to die in August. February had been the month
to dread – for those who knew that Dr Locock, London's eminent
obstetrician, thought the birth would endanger her life. Naturally none
of the children knew that. Even the eldest, Meriel and Lucy, nearly
seventeen and fifteen, who shared the anxiety, did not realise how great
was the risk. 'Dim before us lies the Eternal Future', Lucy declaims on
the opening page of her diary for 1857. 'Vainly we strive to pierce its
unknown gloom, Vainly to fathom its Profundity.'[1] But she probably
meant nothing prophetic, for she was inclined to greet every New Year
with a touch of devout apprehension. And on this particular New Year's
Day, as soon as the Gladstone cousins arrived, Hagley Hall was awash
with children (eighteen children under seventeen) and in the minds of
all but the youngest there was only one thought: the play.

'The PLAY is to come off on the 7th,' wrote Lucy, 'rehearsals are
ceaseless, lessons droop.' They had to build a Magician's Cave and
Fisherman's Cottage in the gallery and this involved much spangling
of paper, 'pasting, hanging . . . fetching, carrying . . . pinning, nailing . . . gilding, silvering . . . scientific piling of rocks and shells'. The
great day came and, despite the fact that the couch with the fairy queen
(Agnes Gladstone) was wheeled on with its back to the audience, the
performance was reckoned extremely good by the Lyttelton and Gladstone parents and the gathering of local guests. Only Meriel, who rather
nobly had taken the invisible role of pianist, was unable to share the
applause. 'Buried alive behind the Fairies' Grotto . . . this most unfortunate individual', wrote Lucy, 'saw nothing of the whole concern.'

Her mother, she considered, stood up well to all the bustle and noise that night: 'I only hope it won't tell upon her later'. But at least one guest, on returning home, expressed a fear that her days were numbered. Such thoughts were not current at Hagley Hall till the week after the servants' ball when Mary Lyttelton began to get nose bleeds. 'Mamma so poorly, alas,' writes Lucy, 'that she could not come down to dinner.' The Gladstones had gone away by now but, at this frightening news of her sister, Catherine Gladstone at once came back and was at hand for the next alarm when it was decided to get Mary to London. Lucy describes their rushed departure, her mother looking wretchedly ill and 'Auntie Pussy' (as they called Mrs Gladstone) obviously consumed with worry. George Lyttelton followed, while those at Hagley passed through a dreadful day of suspense, fearing what they might hear by telegraph.

But nothing happened. When Meriel and Lucy themselves arrived in St James's Square they found their mother a little better with Mrs Gladstone in loving attendance. Which, with Parliament sitting again and William Gladstone a leading figure, involved her in a good deal of shuttling between her own house and her sister's. 'She cannot bear being away from Mamma whose nose has been bleeding again', wrote Lucy. It seemed to signal a new decline. 'Everything seems failing her by degrees.' And the spirits of the rest were failing. Mrs Talbot, a family friend who was often there and as much devoted as if she too were Lady Lyttelton's sister, seemed depressed to the greatest degree. 'There is a gloom deepening', Lucy wrote.

Yet on the morning of 7 February the servant who came to wake Lucy whispered that the baby was expected soon, and she had barely time to dress when Mrs Gladstone came in eagerly: '"The Baby's born!". I was stricken with astonishment, I never expected it . . . to happen at once . . . "Oh Auntie Pussy! – boy or girl?" "Oh, a boy – never mind what it is!" "Oh how is she?" "So quiet and well."'[2] Then there was weeping, relief, confusion and people rushing past each other on the stairs. Meriel and Miss Smith, the governess, fetched ice and water which somebody wanted. Then they all raced to Lord Lyttelton's room and Lucy told him. 'He made a curious pucker with his mouth, opened his eyes wide and said, "A boy! Why, I was never told!" and stamped upstairs with a terrible noise . . . On the top he said . . . with a delighted chuckle, "Another boy! What in the world shall we do with another boy!" and went into the room.' The rest of them sat outside on the stairs and Lucy heard her mother say, 'Oh, what a darling!' as the baby was put into her arms.

The christening took place at the end of March. It was a great disappointment to Lucy not to be a godmother (she was not yet confirmed) but no prayers more eager than hers can have ascended from around the font at that great moment when the sign of the cross marked Alfred Lyttelton Christ's soldier and servant. Later on the baby was taken to Hagley while the rest of the party left for Brighton where Mary's real convalescence began. An ex-dragoon wheeled her basket chair up and down the Parade every day. 'It is a great comfort to think of your dear Mammy in the oxygen gaining strength', wrote Sarah, the dowager Lady Lyttelton ('the General Granny', as she called herself).[3] She also liked to think that her granddaughters were able to help their mother so much. 'A *very great* difference you and Lucy do make in one's account of the state of things', she wrote to Meriel; and Mrs Talbot evidently took this view, for, when the family left Brighton in May to stay with her at her house in Kent, it was to Meriel that she gave advice concerning Mary Lyttelton's journey. 'Remind your Papa to send beforehand to the Station Master at Brighton to bespeak a comfortable carriage for her.'[4] And Meriel must check that her mother's maid knew how her mother's egg flip was done. For there were different ways of making it 'and it would be as well', wrote Mrs Talbot, 'that she should have exactly what she has been used to'.

Later, this holiday at Falconhurst ranked as their last happy time together, despite the attack of breathlessness with which Mary was seized one night. 'The first toll of the knell', her husband recalled.[5] But Dr Locock had been reassuring. When Mrs Talbot went to London to see him he said it was of no importance, wrote Lucy. She herself was in the seventh heaven. Falconhurst – New Falconhurst as it was called, for the new mansion had been completed just after Mr Talbot's death – seemed magical in that golden spring. She enlarged on the beauty of the house, the church, the woods, the walks and especially on the birds' nests. Witherby the butler showed them a linnet's nest; they found a thrush's with five eggs in it, a chaffinch's, a robin's in the roots of an oak with a cuckoo's egg in it (which Lucy removed to save the lives of the unborn young). They picnicked in the woods and lit a fire; they fished and Lucy caught a carp which would have been served up for dinner had it not been dropped by the cook. Even Meriel who, though not seventeen, was effectively out of the schoolroom, joined in all this.

Their mother too seemed to be regaining her vitality and some of the girlish pleasure in things (she was forty-three) which was part of her charm. She joined in a shopping trip to Tunbridge Wells ('peering about as briskly as anyone'), though not in the Canterbury expedition

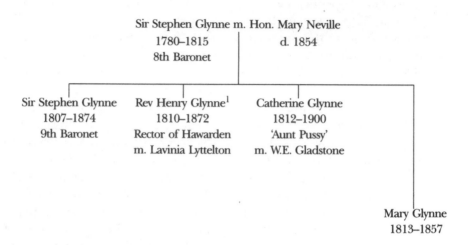

Sir Stephen Glynne m. Hon. Mary Neville
1780–1815       d. 1854
8th Baronet

Sir Stephen Glynne      Rev Henry Glynne[1]      Catherine Glynne
1807–1874           1810–1872           1812–1900
9th Baronet        Rector of Hawarden     'Aunt Pussy'
              m. Lavinia Lyttelton     m. W.E. Gladstone

Mary Glynne
1813–1857

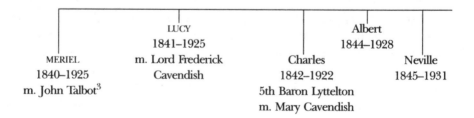

               LUCY                      Albert
              1841–1925                1844–1928
MERIEL      m. Lord Frederick      Charles         Neville
1840–1925       Cavendish        1842–1922       1845–1931
m. John Talbot[3]                  5th Baron Lyttelton
                        m. Mary Cavendish

1   Appears twice
2   Née Clive, widow of Humphrey Francis Mildmay M.P.
3   Elder son of Mrs Caroline Talbot ('Ganma')
4   Younger son of Mrs Caroline Talbot ('Ganma')

## The Lyttelton Family

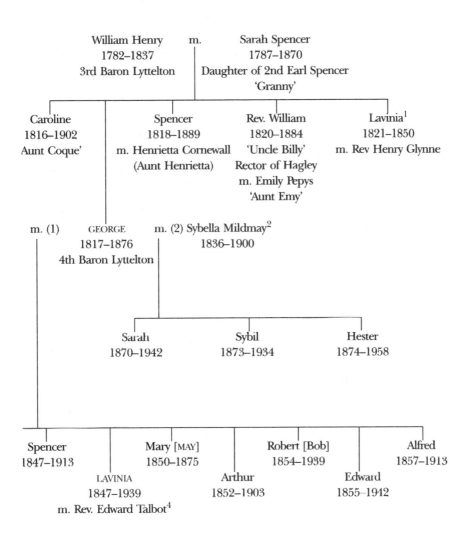

William Henry
1782–1837
3rd Baron Lyttelton

m.

Sarah Spencer
1787–1870
Daughter of 2nd Earl Spencer
'Granny'

Caroline
1816–1902
Aunt Coque'

Spencer
1818–1889
m. Henrietta Cornewall
(Aunt Henrietta)

Rev. William
1820–1884
'Uncle Billy'
Rector of Hagley
m. Emily Pepys
'Aunt Emy'

Lavinia[1]
1821–1850
m. Rev Henry Glynne

m. (1)

GEORGE
1817–1876
4th Baron Lyttelton

m. (2) Sybella Mildmay[2]
1836–1900

Sarah
1870–1942

Sybil
1873–1934

Hester
1874–1958

Spencer
1847–1913

Mary [MAY]
1850–1875

Robert [Bob]
1854–1939

Alfred
1857–1913

LAVINIA
1847–1939
m. Rev. Edward Talbot[4]

Arthur
1852–1903

Edward
1855–1942

her husband organised for Meriel and Lucy and Mrs Talbot's sons: which was just as well, for he set out with so little cash that they almost came to pawning their watches in order to pay for the meal that day. All such escapades delighted Lucy, but her thoughts by now were on a great event – for 4 June was the day marked out for her Confirmation, in the church at Penshurst, by the Archbishop of Canterbury. That her entry through this mystical gateway into the community of Christ's Church should be in her mother's presence she had hardly dared hope. She describes the quiet drive ('nice and stilling'), and the bells ringing out as they reached the church. 'I had Papa on one side, Mamma on the other.'[6]

> I seem to remember nothing very distinctly till I went up and knelt on that altar step, feeling the strangest thrill as I did so . . . And I know how I waited breathlessly for my turn, with the longing for it to be safe done, half feeling that something might yet prevent it.

Afterwards she wrote, 'The new Life has begun'. And on 6 June, 'All my thoughts, all my existence are now with tomorrow'. On that next day, she made her First Communion, and found the happiness of the Confirmation was as nothing to the joy of that. A few days later, they all left Falconhurst.

> I saved a daisy from among my Confirmation ones which were all expanding in water, stuffed the beautiful little nest of the chaffinch into my pocket, with the cuckoo's egg in it, and we all set off.

At first, to London. 'We have left a bright blessed time behind us.'[7]

The journey to Mrs Talbot's house in London was easy, and after a few days' rest Mary Lyttelton was ready to embark on the longer one to Worcestershire. Mrs Talbot, cautious as ever, checked that Dr Locock saw no objection, and Mary reached Hagley, in Lucy's account, 'not seeming over-tired and so glad to be at home again'. She herself felt, as always on return, 'the old firm links, as old as myself, that are so lovingly connected with Hagley' and rushed to see Alfred, now four months old – only to find he had lost all his hair and did not look as sweet as she expected. 'Tea and talks and a walk and then up to the little bedroom and small white bed . . . where I now lie down, full of thankfulness and peace for the Hand which has led us safe through all the distress.'[8]

Heat was a major problem that June; especially on Sundays, for Hagley church was in process of being restored and the nearby barn which they used instead was far too hot to be endured by Mary. Everybody sought means to relieve her. Currents of air were contrived by Lucy so that afternoon service could be held in the house. A little pony carriage with gentle springs in which the invalid could take airings appeared through the kindness of Mrs Talbot, and carriage horses were lent by the Gladstones. Funds at Hagley did not run to such things. 'Remember, Papa and Mamma are not rich', Mary had written once to Meriel when she had carelessly lost her slate. Now she was delighted to be borne aloft into the breeze on the top of Clent Hill. 'We turned her round with her face to [the wind] and . . . she came back . . . with new life in her.'[9] That her mother should trust her to drive was a source of great pride to Lucy.

The great heat lessened in early July. When the day came for the Flower Show which was always held in the park,

> that naughty Mammie . . . actually drove out . . . into the thick of it, saw the people and the flowers and delighted everyone. It is now such a time since she has seen the neighbours. She was looking well and enjoyed it, especially the prize giving, which Papa did, with much joking, so that everyone was bursting, and which Mamma witnessed, sitting on a hard backless bench![10]

Later that week Lucy drove her mother to inspect the church restoration, in which she showed great interest. But the heat grew worse and Mary's breathless fits more frequent; in fact she laboured so on the stairs that they had begun to carry her up. July 14th, one week from the Flower Show, was the last day that she ever came down.

The doctor they summoned spoke of heart disease. George Lyttelton was away in London and Sarah, his mother, awaited his return, dreading the shock this would be to him. 'He had inferred nothing like the truth from letters and we really *could not* tell him all.'[11] For fear he should not bear it, perhaps. He had the family's depressive streak and Sarah was not the only one whose first thought was to shield him from trouble. Still, the point had come where he must be told. 'God bless and help him! He looks so ill and low', she wrote.

Catherine Gladstone and Mrs Talbot ('the two lady nurses', as Sarah called them) now came back, and a sofa bed was made up in Mary's dressing room for their use on alternate nights. The illness was erratic, however. After the heavy dark days came good ones. 'She is in great spirits, making jokes with the girls!' Sarah noted on 20 July. 'When Meriel asked her, "Did you eat that arrowroot?" "Every man Jack of it!" was her answer.'[12] Next day, 'Mary had a blessed long good night'.

And the next, which was her birthday, passed off well. She kept saying, 'So comfy, feel in Paradise'. There had been Paradise in past Julys with the return of her schoolboy sons but now as the date of their arrival approached it was decided that the stress of reunion would be too much and they must not see her yet. A glimpse of them coming in by the back way, and so quietly, gave their grandmother 'my worst throat lump since George's shock'.[13]

So July wore on to its end. 'The changes, if any, from day to day are so trifling there is little to be noted . . . George is gone in his uniform to a Yeomanry Review at Worcester', his mother wrote.[14] Two days earlier he had dined with his tenants. 'He has done all such duties steadily.' And others of which she was equally proud. Her son's distinction as a classical scholar always evoked her admiration and she said now that he was busy with letters, having received 'much praise from high authority' for *Oenone*, his recent translation into Greek verse of Tennyson's poem. 'Poor darling!' When they were alone together he was sometimes silent and low. 'And I can't help him'. But in general he was cheerful: which is the impression given by his letters at this time to Gladstone, his fellow scholar and brother-in-law. They suggest a man still hedged from reality by social duty and scholarly habit. 'Mary has been considerably worse, but they have changed the treatment, which I hope may answer', he ends a note on 17 July. On the 28th, another – and longer one – is devoted to an article of Gladstone's on Homer.

By now 'the crammed fulness' of Hagley Hall, as Sarah put it, was beginning to tell. For all her unusual vitality at seventy, 'the crowds of children, the worn-out servants, the army of ladies' maids' were trying.[15] Outside the baize door which protected Mary the life of the busy house went on. 'But under all this fair appearance there still . . . lurks danger . . . a cloud is hovering over us.' For her at least it was not dispelled on 4 August when the doctor told them that Lady Lyttelton was out of danger – though there were one or two hopeful signs. Mary sat up and even stood for a moment. She played 'proverbs' with some of the children and another time asked that they should sing for her. This was 'very throat-lumpy' in their granny's account. 'A fine loud mellow sweet volume . . . went up and we opened the poor dear piano-forte wide.' Unluckily, as the windows were shut, very little of it reached the bedroom.[16]

The claustrophobic atmosphere grew worse in August, since by now there was no coming and going beyond what seemed unavoidable. Lyttelton, with the doctor's authority, kept a two-day engagement in Birmingham. Mrs Talbot ('much missed', wrote Sarah) had to make a brief visit to town which threw the burden on Catherine Gladstone. Perhaps on that account Sarah herself gave up all thought of paying visits and gazed from within on the fine weather and on a spectacle which must have looked like a distant army preparing a siege: 'an amazing pleasure excursion from Stourbridge filling all the upper part of the Park'.

> Many tents on the Castle Terrace, bands and a huge crowd, 20,000 people. Oh the beauty of the Park glittering with crowds, many colored flags, every kind of dress scattered over Milton's Hill![17]

And – which amused her – her grandson, Charles, watching an ill-played cricket match with a very critical air.

All this faded before fresh anxiety. 'We have had sad minutes since the week before . . . I cannot say her strength continues . . . Tomorrow she will be prayed for in the service. We are afraid Mr Johnstone may hardly utter it.'[18] Lyttelton returned on 14 August to be met with this terrible change: Mary's breathlessness so much worse; her lips so cold. 'It needs no doctor to tell us how ill she is', Sarah wrote.

> George is able to command himself wonderfully when with her, and can nurse her a good deal. I . . . left them together and he was moistening her lips . . . and then rubbing her poor arms which grow cold when left alone.[19]

This, he later wrote, in the record which he composed of Mary's death from the recollections of those present, was the moment when he felt that she was going to die. 'On the 15th I slept not a wink.' At three in the morning she sent for him and asked if she was dying. He had to tell her ('softening it however a little') that the doctor gave only faint hope. So in the small hours of 16 August the first stage of their leave-taking began.

William Gladstone, on a flying visit in the thick of the Divorce Bill debate, spoke to her later on that day and was profoundly impressed by her calm: 'She seemed as one preparing for an ordinary journey'.[20] She had had much experience of ordinary journeys and of the partings they entailed, especially of partings from her children. Close as she was to every one of them, much as she savoured their idiosyncrasies and loved their company, there were always partings – provoked by the Season, by her confinements, by spells in Brighton for convalescence or visits to Rockingham, Althorp, Hawarden and other houses of the family connection: partings from all the children, or some – depending

on the needs of the case. Ordinary journeys led to places from which
she instantly showered them with letters. Meriel, as eldest, was her chief
correspondent and from early childhood her lieutenant at Hagley,
through whom her presence, by remote control, reached out into the
nursery and schoolroom.

'I hope Lucy holds her back up, I forgot to ask Miss P. to let her
use the backboard a little.'[21] 'I don't think Charles's ringworm will
matter.' 'Wear your straw bonnet, the hat is so shabby.' 'Does Lucy
grind her teeth at night?' 'I hope you say your prayers quite thoroughly
and that you go directly into bed after saying them, that no thoughts
of play may make you forget what you have just been praying for.'
Incidents of all kinds bring her response: 'Only think of you getting
pale and red over roly poly pudding, you odd children!' 'Only think
of your fall! Well they say no one is a good rider till they have had
one.' 'Poor darling, how your double tooth must have hurt!' And there
was always news for them, often about the latest baby ('Poor tiny Lavinia
has a very bad cold . . . she is so angry at her nose being wiped') but
also of glittering and grand occasions: the Drawing Rooms, or the
visit she made with Auntie Pussy to the House of Commons to hear
Uncle William's Budget Speech. 'Auntie Pussy desires me to be smart
because she hopes all the great people will come up and congratulate
her.' Which of course they did. 'Going out with Auntie Pussy is like
being with a Queen, everyone comes up . . . and her hand aches with
shakes.'

She missed the children. 'I think much of you all and wish I could
open the door and have a look at you.' 'I wish I could kiss you all, my
dearies!' 'I wish I could have been with you on your birthday.' 'I do
hope when we get home to go those pretty walks with you.' It was hard
on them, as she understood, that she was not always back when expected, for only a few days' extra parting give a sad taste of what parting
can be. 'You will hate to see my handwriting . . . as you will guess what
is the reason which is that Papa *cannot* go away from town on account
of the H. of Lords so I shall stay with him till Tuesday.' 'Do not count
the days, dear, for me to get to you, as I may not be allowed to travel.'
She suffered often from rheumatism and, after her later confinements,
neuralgia. She also became very easily tired. 'I am very weak [so] do
not be disappointed at our not returning tomorrow.' 'Of course my
heart is with you all.' As it was now, on 16 August. Lyttelton recalled
of that shock conversation that the thought of the children was almost
too much for her. 'They do so bring me back to life!'

The older children had met death before. Meriel, at five, had been proud of her black gloves worn in mourning for her great-uncle, Earl Spencer. At eight years old she had understood more when her mother wrote, after a nursery maid died, 'you will have heard that poor Betsey is dead, after . . . having a good deal of pain. She is now I trust gone to heaven to be quite happy'.

> But we shall none of us go and live with God unless we have been good here. I am sure my dear child you will not forget that it is not long ago that Betsey was amongst us . . . Remember that it may please God also to remove from this world any one of us at any moment; and I hope you will feel very sorry that you were ever cross to her.[22]

In 1850 the children encountered two deaths close to the heart of the family. Their four-year-old cousin, Jessy Gladstone, died that spring of meningitis. Later, their father's sister, Lavinia (wife of Mary's brother, Henry Glynne, Rector of Hawarden), died in childbirth. 'Pray with all your heart', their mother wrote home, 'that you may be . . . so like her in her goodness that you may meet in Heaven. We watched her dying from eight o'clock; and at quarter past eleven the breathing ceased and we knew she was an Angel.'[23] Meriel (aged ten) read a suitable prayer to the Hagley household on this occasion and a few of the servants cried. The next close death – of their mother's mother, Lady Glynne – took place at Hagley. 'The blank of that great link with one's childish days', Mary Lyttelton confessed to Meriel, 'makes me turn more than ever to you all for comfort.'

She turned to them on 16 August and all twelve came into her bedroom: most in their night gowns, half awake. There was much jostling and confusion. 'But that she did not seem to mind', wrote Lucy. 'She wished to say goodbye to us all. So one by one we went up to her.' In ages, after Meriel and Lucy, came Charles (fourteen) and Albert (thirteen), Neville (eleven) and Spencer (ten); then Lavinia (known as Win) eight years old, and May who was seven; then the four little boys: Arthur (five), Bobbie (three), Edward (two) and Alfred, the baby, who was six months old by now. She did not say very much, it seems. 'I am going away from you. I did not think it would have been so soon.'

> She said to little Arthur to whom she had taught the first rudiments of religion, 'Arthur dear, I am going to Heaven, I hope'. He just understood and cried very much and said afterwards he should like to go with her.[24]

He also said, 'She gave me to Charles'. For Mary had asked her elder boys each to choose a small one as their special charge. Through it all she was quite composed – took the two youngest in her arms and made little cooing noises to the baby. Later, she asked to see the big boys again and spoke to them companionably.

> Well Charley dear, you see how everything seems to have gone wrong in little things. I was so anxious to see you play at cricket when I was at Eton and could not stay for the match. Then I thought it did not signify for I should have plenty of opportunities for seeing you at home, and now I shall never see you.[25]

You will make a friend of Papa, she told him, 'but remember that if ever you have anything in which Auntie Pussy can help you, always tell her as you would tell me. Don't be afraid. My dear boy, I thought I should have had to fork out a watch for you before this. Do you want one much?'[26]

Eleven-year-old Nevy's (Neville's) account was also included in the record made. She said she was very pleased with him and very glad to see that he had conquered his temper. This was something that had always worried her. On seaside holidays, playing on the beach, she used to fear that he would flare up suddenly and hit some other child with his spade. Now she asked if he still wanted to be a soldier and the future general answered, Yes.

She kept her children very much in mind in taking leave of Mrs Ellis, the housekeeper, and Grace Newman, the children's nurse. 'You have been very good to me. You'll do your best, Newman – you won't leave them?' 'You'll do your best for them, Mrs Ellis?' 'Miss Smith, you will do what you can for me, won't you?', she asked the governess, taking her hand. Miss Smith answered that she would indeed. And Mary said, 'it never struck me until yesterday that this . . . must end in – what it is going to'.

It was to her sister though, and Mrs Talbot, that she looked for her elder girls. 'You'll take Lucy to the Queen's Balls, Pussy dear?' (glancing across at Lucy and smiling). Her idea was that they should 'come out' together; Meriel could be kept back a year by which time Lucy would be old enough. 'I should not like them to be buried in the country but to go to London occasionally and make acquaintance with nice people, good people, people I like. There are some things they might go to with you,' she told Mrs Talbot, 'and it is such a way of getting to know girls' characters and feelings.'[27]

As to that, she felt there was a danger that Lucy, whose feelings were always on the brim, might be inclined to luxuriate in grief. Some such thought may even have prompted her gentle teasing of Lucy now. 'Well Locket, have you got over Mr Johnstone's farewell sermon?' Or when they spoke of the people waiting (often weeping) in the room next door, 'Dear, what a grim party!'

'Two more bits of her old fun!' wrote Lucy:

> She said, 'I can't imagine anything poorer than the Sundays at Hagley without me'. And as I wetted her lips with lemon and water . . . and washed her mouth with it she . . . sucked the brush. I told her she must not have too much lemon. 'Mrs Talbot was doing my mouth and left a great bit on my lips', she said. 'I ate it when she wasn't looking.'

But she was aware of the strain on them. 'You have both been so kind to Mammy, such comforts to me.' She was specially moved to learn that Meriel had known as long as anyone that she might die. 'I did not think you would shew such self control . . . dear old Meriel, you have behaved grandly.'[28]

This journey, like any ordinary one, was subject to unaccountable delays. There was a stage at which she seemed to feel like someone standing on a station platform, surrounded by friends, all farewells said, waiting for a train which never came. As she began to realise that death was not so close as she had expected she seemed puzzled what to do, wrote Mrs Talbot. To William Gladstone, Mary admitted: 'I cannot understand how this is to end. For you see the strength does not seem to give way.'

In a spiritual sense it never did; and here they recognised the hand of God, for none of them could doubt, wrote Lyttelton, that it was 'the direct, unmixed influence of the Eternal Comforter and Strengthener' which sustained her marvellous calm. Some of them saw a change in her after she had received the sacrament on the morning of 16 August. From that time to the end, said Lucy, all fear and reluctance were gone. Holy Communion had been administered in her room by the Rector of Hagley, the Honourable and Reverend William Lyttelton, the children's popular Uncle Billy. Mary sat up supported by pillows, 'white and thin, grave and altered, but looking grand and gentle,' wrote Sarah, 'like a Christian matron soon to leave us.'

> I spoke to her after she had communicated . . . her appearance and expression were most striking, full of a calm holy dignity as if her mind were raised above this world.

She had told Billy before the service, 'I don't pretend I am not sorry to go'. But afterwards she remarked to her sister that she did not now wish to turn back.[29] That at this point her pulse grew stronger was perhaps more surprising to the doctor than to anyone in this devout family.

'Oh peace of more than Angel's joy!' Lucy had written of her first Communion; and all that day, according to Catherine, Mary was more of heaven than of earth. Nothing agitated or distressed her, the weeping around caused no excitement. As William said, she was already half an angel. Yet the other half held up well. 'Now don't fash yourself about the children, you are too old for that' (to Sarah). 'Your province is to look after George and . . . comfort him'. To Meriel: 'Mind you are kind to the neighbours. I don't mean just now, but afterwards. The little civil things I used to do.' (As she had written through Meriel's childhood: mind and remember to tell Mrs Ellis; or, have this ordered; or, have that sent; or even – to her nine-year-old lieutenant – 'we shall not be back till the day before Xmas – dear love, you must get the hollies up!') The only time she lost her composure was when she suddenly seemed to realise that she was going to leave this child – not as in life; but soon, for ever. Sarah Lyttelton remembered that

> Rather suddenly she said, 'There is only one thing, except you dear (turning to George) 'my eldest child – Meriel, my eldest, I can't bear to think . . . I must leave her – not that I don't love the others as well. It is not that; but my first baby – how I remember her as I first saw her – little black thing!' . . . Then turning to Lucy, that she should not feel overlooked, 'My pretty Lucy!'[30]

'Her voice was raised and somewhat faltered and quivered', wrote Lyttelton.

They all feared to break down at one time or another. 'Poor Locket, it's hard on you', her mother had said when Lucy was reading out a hymn and reached a point where she could not go on. While Lyttelton wrote, 'With me, in particular, she was careful not to speak in any such way as she feared might be too overpowering'. For his own part, fear of giving way in her presence was one of the things which 'grievously obstructed my dwelling on last words and looks as I wish I had done'.[31]

Did he mean (for it was he who insisted that a record of her death should be made) that he wished he had written as others did – about her smile, her 'old fun', her kindness? Given more space to her as she was and less to a rather abstract analysis of what he conceived to be her spiritual state? Would he like to have written as Catherine did – in a way which evoked a lifetime's closeness? ('Often as I came in: "Is it you, my love?" Or, "How snug we are!" as I was lying by her on the bed. "I like to see your face." "Oh that is nice.")[32] 'It is so nice to see her with her sister', Mrs Talbot's son Johnny had written on first meeting the pair together, 'they are so fond of one another.'[33] And they had been – 'the two Pussies' – from their infancy a year apart: the beautiful daughters of Sir Stephen Glynne who had married such earnest and clever men. Through Mary's worries about lack of money and Catherine's worries about William's career, through eighteen years and twenty childbirths, they had been close and fond as ever. Well might Mary tell Catherine now 'that she found it almost impossible to fancy me alone on Earth without her'; and tell William, 'Take care of her, for it will make a great change to her, and after a time she will feel it more and more'.

Lyttelton's account of Mary's death is not generally much more intimate than the minutes of a Royal Commission.

> Two things in particular I wished to say. For one, I urged her to take comfort in the thought that if taken from us (as we word it) she and we might still believe that she would watch over . . . possibly even influence us, while unseen. And next I told her to be assured, as of the sure truth, that though no one ought to be told at such a time that they had nothing to repent of, yet in her behaviour to me and to the children . . . she had ever been as an Angel without spot.[34]

Just occasionally Lyttelton appears from behind the hedge of reported speech.

> She said to me, 'How you will miss me! We have always gone on so well together'. I reminded her of how little we had been separated for as long as a week; not more than once or twice for as much as a fortnight and never more. (I find that twice in 1843 and '49 we were separated for a fortnight: six or seven times for nine or ten days; never oftener for so much as a week.)[35]

In his presence she told Lucy, 'very cheerfully and fondly, as if she loved dwelling upon it', about her coming to Hagley as a bride.

> I remember Papa showing me this room and how lovely I thought the place! Dear! Quite beautiful. Papa was with her and she made him help her to sit up – making little jokes to make him laugh.[36]

She said to Catherine and to Mrs Talbot, 'We were so happy'. So happy she had prayed sometimes to be sent some kind of suffering 'to make me better . . . more spiritual – then I used to feel so frightened when I had done it'. But it occurred to her, talking to her sister, 'Perhaps this is the way He has answered my prayer'.[37]

Until the last day, 17 August, Mary experienced great discomfort rather than great pain, but she feared it. 'Oh if I could think that!' she said, when told she might not suffer much at the end. And to her husband, 'Oh if I may be helped!' 'I asked her how she meant? And found she was thinking of being helped, through the prayers of those around her, to pass safely through Death.'[38] Her thoughts would turn then to the radiant prospect beyond. 'Oh do think if I am permitted to see our Saviour!', she said to Sarah. To Catherine, 'the idea of seeing our Saviour . . . ought to make up for all one is leaving'. And, 'if I could but see our Saviour's face now, it would so help me!'

On the last day she was much as before: alert, even active from time to time (settling with Catherine that Meriel's allowance should be £100 a year); at other times waking from uneasy sleep ('When one is in this state of things going to sleep is very awful'). She complained of internal coldness and her lips were as cold as ice. Then she said to her sister: 'It would be so nice if you would sleep with me tonight in your arms, Pussy dear, to warm me'. And after a pause, 'Ah, the Everlasting Arms', as if her thoughts had passed on to that.

Again she was sleeping; when in her sleep all of a sudden she cried out, '"Pussy!" loud and clear, like a frightened child'.

'Here I am, darling', said Auntie Pussy, who had left off rubbing her arm for a moment. 'Did you think I was gone? I am always close to you.' Mamma answered in her natural voice, 'I thought you'd gone away', and shut her eyes again.[39]

The dreadful spasm of pain came later. She sat up, leaning in her sister's arms. Lucy heard her moaning from the room next door. 'She did not like us to see her in that great pain.' It seemed to last for about four minutes. 'I went in towards the end of this', Lyttelton wrote, 'I hardly looked but I held her . . . in my arms and recollect the violent shivering.' Then her face grew peaceful. She called Meriel to raise her and Lucy put a pillow behind her. 'You see, I'm quite helpless now.' And in a low voice, 'Let me go, let me go'. Her strength grew less and her voice weaker. She could only whisper to Meriel and Lucy, 'Goodbye dearies. You have been so good to me'. But it was her kiss that Lucy remembered – 'colder than I could have conceived possible . . . I could not get the feeling out of my cheek'. The doctor gave her some chloric ether. 'Your Ladyship will have this for this is what you like.' She died soon afterwards. The cause of death was certified as heart disease.

'All is over; last night at half past ten she left us', wrote Sarah.

Oh, I can't believe it or understand it . . . so peacefully . . . so bright her mind was to the last minute . . . her thought for others, her gentleness and even cheerfulness! The last thing of all was George saying as he knelt by her, 'My darling, you will smile upon me once more?' and she turned and did smile, and sank back. Today he is in a very terrible state of grief . . . but just now he has been down on my bed and has fallen asleep – thank God![40]

'What days, what a time it has been!' she went on. 'But never were greater mercies bestowed as supports to those who needed them.' One of these surely was George's sleep, for with him there was always the worry that sleeplessness might signal depression. 'I can, thank God, give a better account of him, my own darling! He was thoroughly tired out . . . slept six and a half hours in one sleep without a sedative.' As for the funeral, he had been quite peaceful and gentle in his sorrow and quite well. It had been touching to see the children's young faces round the open vault. However, now that the funeral was over things were settling back into their old routine. 'Cricket – and open blinds. Dinner bell. George gone riding. But oh! the change – already so great, and to be felt more and more – of no Mother!'

Public and private tributes flowed in but none were more to the mark than Gladstone's. Typically, in their last conversation Mary had disparaged her own abilities. He said, 'I told her that her gifts were remarkable'.[41]

# 3

# *Lord Lyttelton*

'Papa must not have vacancy next to him.'

Charlotte M. Yonge, *The Daisy Chain* (1856)

In later years Lucy's thoughts went back, as she told Meriel, to her sixteenth birthday – a week or two after their mother's death – 'and your wishing me many happy returns from the little bed foot and foot with mine . . . and how at the time I felt and said, there could be no more happy returns'.[1] The diary bears strong witness to that. 'Oh she has gone away! Oh the light of home and life gone never to come again! Oh my joyous childhood, Oh our bright years!'[2] Life had changed utterly and grief itself was quite different from what she had thought, 'when I pictured it with feelings of awe'. She went through 'monstrous dragging days' relieved only at the end by sleep. 'Then at least it is the same as in old days.'

Prayer had always been her first recourse and what she writes is often prayerful. 'O rest in the Lord, wait patiently on Him . . . and He shall wipe away all tears.' On All Saints Day she pictures her mother as another added to the multitude with white robes and palms in their hands, and on Advent Sunday reflects that Christmas has already begun, in Heaven. 'She has seen Him, it may be.' A brilliant star that hung over Hagley gave her pause for a moment or two. But she felt closest to her mother in church. And above all at the Holy Communion where the living combine in worship with angels and archangels, as the Prayer Book said, and with all the company of heaven.

In sharp contrast Meriel's diary is little more than a list of events. 'Of Meriel's thoughts I know so much less', their mother once said of these two girls.[3] And there is nothing to reveal them here – beyond the words 'God help us all', written on the day that Mary died. 'God help me!' she might well have written, at the thought of what lay ahead.

For although she had already developed the calm and rather middle-aged manner that led one of her brothers later to call her 'The Emblem of Repose', she was far from confident at heart. 'I keep fancying *she* will come back and make everything bright and happy again', she wrote to Mrs Talbot, the family friend.[4]

Mary in her last days, Gladstone recalled, 'spoke of Meriel as supplying her place'. She had in fact done so, after a fashion, in her parents' absence, since she was eight: earnestly transmitting her mother's wishes in regard to everything from prayers to puddings. More than that, in the final crisis it had been Meriel, of them all, who embodied for her mother the pain of parting. 'Meriel, my eldest . . . my first baby.' And it was Meriel who, through childhood, she had addressed as a special person ('dear little woman') in so many letters: ending one with a sweet valediction 'Goodbye, precious woman, kiss all six for me!'; another with a racy 'Goodbye, old girl!'

Meriel at fifteen had been ill with pleurisy, and on recovery had, as she put it, 'slipped out of regular schoolroom ways' and done 'a great many little things' for her mother,[5] whose health had noticeably gone downhill after the birth of the eleventh baby. Whether these little things – writing letters and helping to amuse the younger children – were an adequate preparation for running the household may be doubted. Running the *households*, her brother Edward might well have said, when he reflected later on the feudalism of Hagley then: marvelling at the servants' length of service, their pride in the family and the place – yet all consistent with 'the deepest gulf between the two groups of human beings'. Once, in childhood, he had glimpsed through the banisters the grand solemnity of servant rites as a procession of upper servants made its way from the servants' hall to the steward's room after dinner,

> headed by the white-haired seneschal, with the aged housekeeper on his arm, each carrying a half-consumed tumbler of table-beer, and behind them pairs duly arranged according to dignity of status.[6]

Possibly, to Edward's childish gaze, it seemed much grander than it really was, for Hagley's upper servants would not – alone – have made a very long procession: the steward and the housekeeper; Lyttelton's valet and the ladies' maid (whose services were shared by Meriel and Lucy); the cook (Mrs Shirtliffe) and the children's nurse (Grace Newman – 'Newmany', as they called her). Even with the footman and several maids, the total was only about a dozen – which was 'dowdy' by fashionable standards: especially as so few of them were men. As to outdoor servants, the coachman, groom, gardener and forester, listed at Hagley in the census of 1861, also represented a modest provision.

'We used to meet the maids on Sundays', Meriel wrote, in recollection; for on that day it was the children's task to carry up, to the stone-floored attics ('like prison cells'), the maids' plum pudding and glasses of beer. (All the household beer was brewed at home.) But with some of the upper servants they were on more intimate terms. Newmany had been their friend and comforter since she came as nurse when Meriel was born. John Daphne, the coachman, had started out as a little 'Tiger' [liveried groom] perched behind Lyttelton's cab in London. It was he who taught the children to ride; and he who Lucy had tried so hard to teach French to, on their rides together: this, like her attempts to worm from him the secret of the Oddfellows, came to nothing.[7] Then there was Elly, the housekeeper. 'You'll do what you can for them, Mrs Ellis?' Mary had begged, though it did not need saying. Mrs Ellis in her black silk dress and close white cap had been part of Hagley long before Mary came there, on marriage. She was sixty-six now; in full command of the general household staff and still in the habit of sitting up till everybody had gone to bed before going round, with the great Lyme mastiff, to check the house's security.

Meriel of course soon came up against problems which were beyond Mrs Ellis's remit. Almost as soon as she took charge, Newmany, vexed because a nursemaid was leaving, quarrelled with Miss Smith, the governess. And though she had managed to calm them down, 'the wretched feeling of a republic made me lose heart and miss Mamma so terribly', she confided to Mrs Talbot.[8] Up till now her only real authority had been with the girls in the Sunday School class which she had taken from the age of eleven, and at home with the little boys in the nursery and with Win and May who were in the schoolroom. She had long known her responsibility as the eldest girl in the family. 'God make you a blessing to all around you', Mary had written on her tenth birthday.

> As great a blessing as I . . . prayed you would be when I kissed your little brown ugly face just ten years ago. It seems very strange . . . to think that you have seven younger than yourself, seven little souls to look up to you for an example . . . especially the boys.[9]

The boys were only eight, six, four and three then, but boys were always to be worried about – though it is unlikely that Meriel, at ten, fully understood the reasons why. Or even now, when she was seventeen – by which time they had doubled in number. In these early days of bereavement the older boys were very subdued. 'The poor old boys went off today without being able to say a word', Meriel wrote to Mrs Talbot. Nevy, who was often the awkward one, had been so nice before he left for his last term at Geddington (the prep school which the older boys attended), begging her not to forget his birthday – as if he felt there was no one now who was sure to remember it. When Charles and Albert got back to Eton, 'I had *such* a letter from my darling old Charles . . . saying he never felt such desolation as when he remembered he had not to go up and wish her goodbye in bed; and then his first letter not being to her'.[10] As to the little nursery boys, 'I hear Bobbie and Edward their prayers at night . . . I cannot stop poor Bobbie's saying "Pray God bless Papa and Mamma".'[11]

It was not so much the boys as the thought of her father that she found so daunting. He had put her at the head of the household immediately and without reserve. Though his mother and his unmarried sister Caroline (known as Aunt Coque) were to come to Hagley during the boys' school holidays (and their help was invaluable), they never attempted to take the lead in the house or with the children. Her father discussed all plans with her, Meriel recalled in later years: education, money, everything.[12] But at this early stage at least he was not ready to discuss his feelings and her inability to comfort him seemed to project her uselessness. When they drove out together in the phaeton (which had always been her mother's great treat), she could not get over 'a feeling of stupidity and fear of not being companionable to him'.[13] Then there was breakfast. 'Dearest Aunty Pussy,' she wrote in November 1857, 'letters are the greatest break at breakfast for it is then that I feel as if Papa must hate the sight of me, sitting alone with him.'[14] 'You know what sort of things you can be useful to Papa in', her mother had told her in the final days, 'things like Mackie and the pines – what is to be done with them – and try to get things round him as he used to have'. The first injunction – to see that the gardener sent their gifts of pineapples to the right people – was easy; but Meriel felt much less certain how to get things comfortable for her father. In the evenings they had had some music, she told Mrs Talbot, 'and he says he likes it'. She tried to sit regularly in the gallery, which had been her mother's favourite spot. But 'Oh dear this gallery! the silence and stillness in the mornings are quite death-like . . . I think it is better to sit here though . . . Papa might want me'.[15] 'He is very very low.' When he was ill it seemed another failure. 'Poor Pappie in bed with influenza', wrote Lucy.

We have so dreaded the first illness – the missing of the loving nursing and care – making it a pleasant time to him . . . He always resigned himself to her management, always doing what she said. She sat with him and petted him and brought him his letters.[16]

It is unlikely that Mary Lyttelton, with her easy way of responding to people, could ever have feared that she was not wanted; a feeling which one of Meriel's daughters thought her mother never quite lost and which she certainly felt acutely in the autumn of 1857. The presence of the younger children helped; and her father took to having some of them to breakfast, for little children always amused him. 'You are a very good old cat for writing me such a famous letter', he had scrawled in his atrocious hand to Meriel herself when she was eight. 'I am afraid I cannot write so legibly as you do. Goodbye, old black skin, I hope to see you tomorrow.'[17] Now when they embarked on family walks he took even the little ones part of the way. 'He is so tender to all of us,' Meriel wrote to Mrs Talbot, 'kissing us before going out . . . holding Arthur's hand, and patting their heads.'[18]

Lyttelton's reserve did not prevent him from admitting to Catherine Gladstone his 'dragging, pining sense of a void, and the melancholy thought of the motherless children'.[19] Nights, he found, were the hardest time. Still he had returned to his public work. And there were personal things to get on with: selling the ponies of Mary's carriage (which they could hardly afford to keep and anyway could hardly bear to); changing the form of the children's prayers; ordering the lockets for Mary's hair (the little children's to be put aside and the schoolboys' not to be taken to school 'for a *small* thing . . . is never safe there'). But his major task was the Record. He was determined that everybody who had lived through those final days should contribute to a record of Mary's death. Catherine and his mother were against this at first; as was Mrs Talbot, who wrote to Catherine, 'I share your dread of its being shown to people. It makes one almost *shudder* to think how your sister herself would have shrunk from that'.[20] But they dare not oppose him and he pressed on, producing fifty-seven foolscap pages. On 21 September he wrote to Catherine, 'I have finished my Record of the last days. It did go through and through me so while doing it . . . but I am very glad it is done'.[21] Taking Lucy's work as a base on which to graft the other contributions, he had made a draft – which his mother copied; since, for all her seventy years, her handwriting was much the best. Once done, Lyttelton could hardly bear to let this treasure out of his hand and read it endlessly, in tears. In future years it was to be

copied out laboriously by Meriel and Lucy – and in due course by
Lavinia and May – for the boys and other family members. In spite of
the earlier doubts expressed, it seems to have been a great source of
comfort. And for Lyttelton its composition, though so painful, was
perhaps cathartic; for not long afterwards, when they went to stay with
the Gladstones at Hawarden Castle, he spoke to Meriel much more
freely.

In some ways Meriel had dreaded this trip – their first visit, in the
changed order, to her mother's childhood home: the scene of happy
gatherings since she could remember. In the past they had been thrilled
by journeys. The packing day beforehand was so exciting that as a child
she could hardly sleep and Lucy poured it all out in song:

> Packing-day! Sweet packing-day!
> The subject of my lay.
> Come, come! Thy pleasures bring,
> Thou sweet dear darling thing.[22]

Far from that now, they set out from Hagley 'clinging to every bit of
the place'. Meriel was hoping, as she told Mrs Talbot, that the change
would at least be good for her father, whose nights, she knew, were
still very poor; and admitted that she herself had recently come to feel
'such a strange yearning for Aunty Pussy's tenderness' as the nearest
thing to her own mother's love.

'I *understand* your letter far too well to be surprised at it', came the
response. 'To think of you all at *Hawarden* without her is almost worse
than anything.'[23] Five years earlier, Mrs Talbot – abruptly widowed
and far from home – had found in Catherine Gladstone a comfort she
had never anticipated; and in Hawarden, 'the only earthly thing that
it is *reposing* to me to think of'. It had been while they were staying at
Brighton for her husband's health that he had suddenly died and she
had so much need of the kindness shown to her by the Gladstones and
Lytteltons. From that moment the friendship grew.

But Hawarden for Meriel was not reposing. 'It is very desolate', she
wrote. 'I can't think why it should be more so than at Hagley, for
everyone is so very kind.'

> Still, there is the forlorn weary want of interest in things which I did
> not have at home . . . her pure bright presence seemed to haunt every
> place and hour there. And then, I have less to do, which is always worse
> for me.

Her aunt she had found 'so very low, more so than at Hagley'; and perhaps there had not been quite the comfort she had looked for in that direction. But there was one tremendous thing: her father had begun to confide in her.

> The Mondays, he told me yesterday, bring everything back very over-whelmingly. [It had been a Monday when Mary died.] It was such a pleasure his telling me that, after talking much as usual to the rest. It was as if he let me into his deep inner feelings which now he cannot talk about . . . before many people; and we have had many nice talks together.[24]

'You made Hawarden as pleasant as it could be made to me', Lyttelton wrote on return, to Catherine, 'but it would be strange if I knew the feeling of real pleasure now.'[25] It was in fact to be many years before he got over the painful memories evoked at Hawarden, where he and Mary, and William and Catherine, had celebrated their wedding in 1839.

At that time it might have appeared that their prospects were not so different. Gladstone had already made his mark in politics, but he was eight years older than Lyttelton (then twenty-two), for whom his Cambridge tutor prophesied a great political future. 'The sort of statesman I expect you to make', wrote Dr Blakesley in 1839, 'is a sort of mixture of Gladstone and Lord Stanley but with more caution and temper than the latter, and more courage (and I may possibly add, more genius) than the former.'[26] He was mistaken. His brilliant pupil may have had political dreams but seems from the first to have been more committed to the locality in which he lived, especially in regard to education. Lyttelton in 1845 was involved in the founding of Queen's College, Birmingham (designed for theological and medical studies); in 1853 he became first President of the the Birmingham and Midland Institute. He was President for many years of the Teacher Training College at Saltley, which he had also helped to found and where he personally examined the students. Such things meant more than lending his name, and the Headmaster of Bromsgrove School recalled how he would dash down by train from London – and post from Birmingham – to be in time to address the boys and give away the prizes. In contrast, Lyttelton's one experience of political office was a failure. In 1846 when Gladstone, then Colonial Secretary in Sir Robert Peel's government, offered him the Under Secretaryship, he struggled with conflicting emotions: nervous of being over-influenced by 'feelings of mere vanity and ambition', yet pleased, because he knew that Mary and Catherine liked the thought of their husbands working together; anxious lest he be 'a mere clog in the office' (even protesting that his 'whole education and habits' unfitted him for it), yet touched because the offer had been made 'to me, who have long since thought myself to be cast out on the political dunghill'.[27]

He took the post against his better judgement and held it for six months: until Peel lost office in the Corn Law débâcle. It was not easy. Later he told Gladstone that the job itself had no well-defined responsibilities. 'To be placed as a buffer in a railway train between two people, each of them competent to decide all the questions [Gladstone above him and James Stephen, the Permanent Secretary at the Colonial Office, below] can hardly', he said, 'have much effect in giving me real business habits.' On the other hand, his own tactlessness (for Lyttelton's candour often ran to that) had shown him up unfavourably here. Also he had suffered from a bout of depression which 'from real or imaginary causes' had 'partially disabled' him, he said.[28] The whole was an unrewarding experience for one whose career at Eton and Cambridge had been outstanding across the board. A cricket Blue, a daring horseman and a scholar of the first rank, 'he was the romance of life to us', his sister Caroline (Aunt Coque) said later, casting her mind back to a time which in other respects was sad enough, for their father was slowly dying. 'Those brilliant jewels, _his_ honours, were what we looked for.'[29] And they were many. He had won the Newcastle Scholarship at Eton, and the Craven at Cambridge – where he was also Chancellor's Medallist and joint Senior Classic with Henry Vaughan, later to become Headmaster of Harrow.

By 1857, of course, his spell in politics was ancient history. His mother perhaps had not quite lost her fear of some kind of depression returning – first, with his sister Lavinia's death and now with Mary's – but it had not done so; and as for Meriel, she had been a child at the time of her father's indisposition. They became very companionable. It was Lavinia's judgment later that he loved Meriel the best of his daughters. The brothers always spoke of her as close to their father and it was through her that they came to know how much self-discipline lay behind his incessant busyness for other people and care to occupy every moment. 'No one ever saw him sitting still doing nothing', Edward remembered. He seems to have felt the same need as Gladstone to satisfy God 'of the most effective possible use of time': dipping into Homer while watching cricket, reading Wellington's _Despatches_ while shaving; translating Milton into Greek iambics as he took fences on the hunting field. ('If there was a good deal of running he would get about fifteen lines done in a day.')[30] It is difficult to reconcile all this with his insisting, as Meriel recalled, that he envied the men who lay in the sun in St James's Park with their hats over their faces. But he was not joking. One of his admirers, Henry Solly, the pioneer of Working Men's Clubs, saw his labours for the working classes as the triumph of duty over a temperament which could easily have led him into 'a life of indolent self-indulgence'. This was Meriel's opinion later. 'Like all Spencers, he was naturally indolent';[31] and to be busy with work for others may have seemed unconsciously a shield against this, or against his tendency to nervous depression. At any rate, he resisted both.

> I *never* remember his saying he was tired, or 'What a bore', when some wearisome person wanted to speak to him, or delaying one single moment getting up to go to some meeting . . . After a long day at Worcester or Birmingham he would put on galoshes and go to evening service if there was one. When he gave up teaching in the Sunday School after thirty years, we found out for the first time that he had always hated it.[32]

'Sorrow is no exempter', he once said, 'but for a short time . . . from the duties of life.'[33] So the Stourbridge Working Men's Association, the Diocesan Board of Education at Worcester, the Kinver School Trust, the examination of trainee teachers at the Saltley college and other worthy purposes reclaimed him. And since no parish gathering ever took place without his being there if he was in the neighbourhood, and no society in the area was formed, whether to play chess or to dig allotments, without his being sought as president; and as his presence was of course required at the regular Poor Law Boards and sanitary meetings and Quarter Sessions as well as at any ad hoc gathering of magistrates nervous about trouble in the county, it all amounted to a heavy load of days and evenings away from home.

There was 'real *goodness*' in Lord Lyttelton's grief, wrote Mrs Talbot to Catherine Gladstone: meaning, presumably, the Christian goodness of resignation and true submission. For he tried to reconcile Mary's death with the sense, so deeply ingrained, that all God's mercies call for acceptance (all are ordered if not all are welcome) and found a Christian angle to the pagan saying: 'Whom the gods love die young'.

> Seventeen years of married life and the birth of eleven children were gone through by her with hardly a passing cloud . . . Such a life, to be continued to anything like the full term of existence, is not for man. The sure alternatives were, what has happened, or some real sorrow to her, if she lived.[34]

'I am inclined to believe', he wrote in the Record, 'that she was not physically fitted to struggle with suffering or adversity, bodily or mental. She would have borne it with entire meekness, and holy resignation, but her bloom and brightness and elasticity would have gone.'

But they had gone already! Or at least been sufficiently impaired after the birth of the eleventh baby to convince Dr Locock, the obstetrician, that she ought not to have another one. After that birth in 1855 Mary had suffered from congestion of the brain: 'a sort of wandering', wrote Lyttelton to Catherine. She could not say the names of the children and Dr Giles had ordered that she stop nursing. 'I did not know till a few days ago that there had been anything the matter with her.'[35] One cannot but think that he might have noticed, if he had been less intently absorbed in his numerous public duties.

Not that Mary seems to have complained of that. For all her rather racier style, she too believed in duty and goodness, and when they married it may well have been that she had counted his lack of grace, modest fortune and partial deafness very little against such things. Nor did she ever seem to doubt her choice. When his brother Billy, the Rector, got married in 1854 Mary told the couple she had often wished she could have her own wedding day over again. 'I now fear I did not think quite enough of George's future happiness on my wedding.'

> Well, I won't quarrel with my feelings then when after fifteen years I felt what I did for him yesterday during his glorious little speech with his deep voice getting that tone in it (which Billy knows) when he is feeling much; and then the words . . . come down to one's heart . . . with their solemnity and affection.[36]

She often longed, though, for more of his company, especially when she was feeling ill. 'Papa . . . away all day', she wrote to Meriel in October 1851, heavily pregnant with her ninth baby, 'but not much more than he is in the country'. In contrast, after the eleventh was born, 'Papa . . . nearly all day with me so nice'. As for the twelfth – that began badly, with rheumatism and dreadful sickness. 'I am so bad today I can hardly sit up', she told Mrs Talbot. And later, 'I cannot boast much of myself, have been giddy, headachy, sick . . . and so weak'. Through all this, George is 'home from Worcester' or 'off early to Birmingham'. 'This has been a very long day in my . . . bedroom as George is out from ten this morning to eleven at night.' She hopes Mrs Talbot will come for a visit. 'It would be such a help while George is away.' When he is at home her greatest pleasure is to go with him in the pony carriage, as she does on 5 June 1856, 'the first day he has not been at Birmingham or somewhere'. On another occasion it was Sarah, his mother, who insisted that they pay visits together. 'G. and I, so nice,' wrote Mary, 'and I hope no one will be at home.'

'Remember, God's gifts to us are but loans', Lyttelton was to say of other deaths, later. But there is no doubt that, inwardly, the calling in of this one overwhelmed him. Lord John Manners, he wrote to Catherine in November 1857, said that for six months after his wife died he never spent a day without tears. 'For one half of that time I can well say the same. Nor do I wish it otherwise.' It struck him painfully that even in her dying he had not talked to Mary as much as he might. 'I shrank from the misery of such a parting as I dreaded', he wrote in the Record. And to Catherine, 'I had . . . such an extreme and timid dread of seeing her suffer that it flurried me to have it over and I could not half dwell on all the last things'.[37] Even nine years later he was still oppressed by 'weary regrets, vain self-reproaches for faults and misused opportunities'; still constantly longing to see Mary again, 'if only for a minute, to tell her how I wish I had been more useful and more loving to her'.[38]

Husbands could be useful in different ways. Some, including his brother-in-law Gladstone, made very competent sickroom nurses; and a few (he would have blenched at the thought) stayed, as Gladstone had also done, to encourage their wives through childbirth. Such an eccentric crossing of the line between the spheres of husband and wife was not on the cards at Hagley, where nothing suggests that Lyttelton ever took more notice of the minutiae of procreation which dominated Mary's life than she did of Mechanics' Institutes. For all their informal quirkiness they were a conventional couple. Would she have admitted to him, for instance – as she did to Catherine – that pregnancy had come at last to be a yearly penance? Or said to him (as she did to Billy's wife, Emy) 'perhaps the ninth begins to give warning that I have had enough babies'? Her sister dreaded pregnancy for her and when Mary knew that a twelfth child was coming she was almost afraid to write the news. 'Poor dear Pussy,' she told Mrs Talbot, 'I *must* I think tell her about myself, it will be a greater blow if I delay.' And she went on, 'I hope it was not wicked hoping that the stomach attack would put an end to the poor little being'.[39]

From such essentially female matters Lyttelton seems – at best – detached. Always a lover of jokey nicknames, he had dubbed his wife 'the Mother of Millions' long before number twelve was born. And while undoubtedly anxious beforehand, after that birth he at once swung high: barging noisily into the bedroom ('George's *unearthly* sickroom manners' had become a family joke); and when calmer, as Lucy records, quite elated by his own situation as a patriarch of just under forty who could 'look round upon his multitudinous family without a noticeable grey hair'.[40] Early on in the Record he wrote, 'her strength was given to her twelve children. I remember saying that the twelfth baby was as the last gallant effort of the high mettled racer'. How many such efforts might be called for in an epoch when God sent babies, contraception did not exist and onanism was a sin, nobody could anticipate.

True, in Mary's case Dr Locock, evidently thinking of the strain on her heart, had said when Edward, the eleventh, was born that a twelfth would endanger her life. But this warning turned out to be useless. For although he was a plain-speaking man, apparently the doctor did not speak to Lyttelton. There is confusion about all this, but it seems that he probably spoke to Sarah. If so, Sarah (another plain speaker) did not pass it on to her son: for fear, perhaps, of provoking depression. 'I am so glad . . . you did not know the worst at the time', she wrote to him when the twelfth birth was 'safely' over. But he evidently knew it later, for Lavinia recalled that as a child she heard him ask Newmany if she thought 'the children' had had anything to do with Mary's death. Whether Newmany's loyal 'No, my Lord', gave him much comfort may be doubted.[41]

# 4

# *Meriel*

'Well, Mrs Tobbit, we must get on somehow.'
Meriel to Mrs Talbot, September 1857

Christmas passed, and in the spring came the reopening of Hagley church: a pledge of renewal badly needed and one which helped them to break away from the constraints of the previous year. The restoration (which the county paid for as a tribute to their Lord Lieutenant) had been carried out by Street the architect in his celebrated Gothic style. Gallery and old box pews were gone; obnoxious monuments (Lucy's phrase) were tucked away at the back of the church where they no longer obscured the altar. The blue east window was Mary's memorial and, at Mrs Talbot's suggestion, those who had known her personally subscribed for a porch to be built in her memory.

There were other changes. The third boy, Nevy, started at Eton that New Year – launched by his father, as his brothers had been. Lucy 'struck' seventeen in September, became a young lady and gave up lessons. Alfred the baby advanced with such force – laughing and walking and starting to talk – that everyone bowed in admiration before him. As for Meriel, it was never her style to quicken pace conspicuously; indeed her absolute refusal to do so led to her getting drenched that autumn walking on a breakwater in Cornwall. All the same, 1858 was the year when Meriel established her rule in the house.

With the youngest children it had not been hard. 'I think I am doing all I can to cultivate the little boys', she told Aunty Pussy, 'having them . . . for about three quarters of an hour in the dressing room before dinner.'[1] They were always delighted to come ('so glad to change from the nursery, poor dots') and she only allowed it when they were good. The big boys were a different proposition. Of the three who were now at Eton, Charles took to idling when he went back in January; but after she had written to him about it he was reported to be 'sapping like bricks'. And in the summer his reports were good, though she thought his gruff manner detracted greatly from his 'tall gentleman-like sixth form look'. Albert was just like himself, she said – evidently all that needed saying about this pleasant, self-contained boy. He had gone off without a word to anyone to fix himself up with organ lessons. But Nevy was often difficult to manage.

> He is too defiant and hard, certainly, and it is not easy to know how to soften him, for he wants a very tight hand, but I do my best by taking interest in all he does and only coming in with authority when it is quite necessary.[2]

This she admitted to Mrs Talbot, whose frequent letters helped her a lot, 'as what you write and say always does, perhaps more than what any one else does'.

Five years had passed since John Chetwynd Talbot's tragically early death at Brighton had thrown his wife upon the kindness of Gladstones and Lytteltons staying there, and turned what had been social acquaintance into honorary membership of a clan that rarely opened up to outsiders. Mrs Talbot, herself reserved, ('of concentrated rather than expansive affections', as her younger son wrote later) from that moment bestowed her heart on all who dwelt at Hagley and Hawarden, where rumbustious family life mingled with a religious devotion absolutely congenial to her. The Talbot couple had been early adherents to the ideals of the Oxford Movement. Not long married when Keble preached his 'National Apostasy' sermon, they were powerfully drawn to his vision of what the Anglican Church should be. Talbot, the son of the second Earl Talbot and a highly successful barrister, felt, like Lyttelton, the upper classes' obligation to improve society. Among other worthy commitments, he joined the Canterbury Association, formed in 1848 with a view to establishing an Anglican colony in the south island of New Zealand. Lyttelton had helped to found this body, 'out of a true desire to serve the cause of Christian colonization';[3] and chaired it heroically (through ups and downs far more testing, it would seem, than anything he met at the Colonial Office) before at length the Canterbury Colony and Bishopric of Christchurch came into being. John Talbot bought an estate in Kent, and began in 1850 to build the house which came to be known as Falconhurst, planning at the same time a church school in the nearby village of Markbeech. To his wife it was a special grief that this church conceived in the spirit of Keble had not been finished when her husband died. 'Completed by his widow' was the legend which Lucy read later, above the door.

Caroline Talbot, born Stuart-Wortley and only daughter of the first Baron Wharncliffe, had spent her formative years in circles where churchgoing had more than a touch of eighteenth-century worldliness about it, but came to find in the Oxford Movement all that her pious nature craved. She was a devout, clever woman, with a grasp of politics; a gifted artist in water colour; highly competent, highly disciplined. She took sole charge of the new estate with its building work not yet completed, and of the education of her two sons: Johnny seventeen, and Edward eight. In short, she accepted widowhood 'with the same thoroughness and devotion with which she had accepted the part of a wife, and set herself to complete the work which her husband left unfinished'.[4] For all that, and for all the authority she brought to the management of Falconhurst, where tenants and bailiff, it was said, 'felt themselves under a master's eye', the desolation of widowhood was felt by Mrs Talbot acutely. Her husband was only forty-six when he died and they had been a very close couple.

The distractions of Hagley were therefore precious, not only to herself but to her sons, to whom Lord Lyttelton over time came to be something of a father figure; and the Lyttelton children, friends – though neither of the Talbots was good at cricket. (Johnny anyway seems to have played rather in a spirit of social duty, finding it 'a satisfactory bond of union with rustics and dependants', when he was at home.)[5] Cricket apart, there were great attractions in that large and varied family circle. Long before he managed to visit Hagley seventeen-year-old Johnny was greatly taken with Mary Lyttelton's grace and charm. 'I like Lady Lyttelton very much, and feel as if I could get intimate with her', he wrote home, after strolling a little with her and Mrs Gladstone. He thought it nice to see the two Glynne sisters together. 'They are so fond of one another.' Johnny was also much amused by their conversation, which was variegated with highly idiosyncratic expressions thrown up by life in the Glynne family and current now among Gladstones and Lytteltons. Lyttelton, in his jocular vein, had recently amused himself by compiling a *Glossary of the Glynne Language*, where a hundred and twenty of its words and phrases were explained, and endowed with etymology so entertaining that Gladstone and others had subscribed to have the little book printed. 'Any one who reads it', Gladstone wrote later, 'will trace the easy hand and precision of a consummate scholar.'[6] What is harder to trace – at least, today, through the rather ponderous Victorian humour – is the raciness which Glynnese imparted to the talk

Johnny; till after Eas-
ter: the boys to begin
their holidays there!
Oh if this comes to pass,
... will indeed
... make us ...

Feb. 6, 7, 8, 9, 10, 11, 12.
Lent has begun — Other-
wise, all much the
same. The plan has been
well diges ted, & is to
be acted upon
Ash Wednesday on the 6th
hurrah —

Feb. 13, 14, 15, 16, 17, 18
Nothing particular till

Pages from Lucy's diary for 1856

of those who had grown up with it. It was this that diverted Johnny, who had no need of a glossary to learn that being bold in public was *blowing*; that *old shoe* meant a familiar friend, *maukins* were strangers, *moths* old women; and that if you said you took something *like pork* it meant that you took it as a matter of course.

During his mother's first visit to Hagley, in the summer of 1853, he let her know that he would like an invitation. 'If you propose to Lady L. please say that I am conscious of making her *old-shoe-issimus*', he declared (perhaps unaware of Mary's view that Glynnese sounded forced on the lips of outsiders), 'and hope that she will forgive the liberty.'[7] He did indeed visit Hagley that summer, between leaving Charterhouse (his father's school) and going up to Oxford as a member of his father's old college, Christ Church. Edward, nine years younger, was at Geddington, the Northamptonshire prep school used by the Lytteltons. He was destined for Charterhouse later – though his mother apparently met with objections that there he would have to mix with boys who were 'somewhat unaristocratic'. This, Mrs Talbot affirmed to Johnny, would actually be a great advantage.

> One of the things that I should deprecate in the results of Eton for Edward would be its starting him in London with a ready-made acquaintance . . . with all the idle young fashionables . . . It is always strongly my theory that it is the greatest mistake to consider the descendants in the *2nd* degree from the Peerage as being only rightly placed among the aristocracy – on the contrary, they should form the link with the *working-class* of gentry, carrying down with them into that class whatever is really good . . . in the aristocracy . . . And I consider it an advantage in a boy of Edward's position to be placed among boys . . . who are all looking forward to the same sort of working life which he *ought* to look forward to.[8]

In this declaration the Professor of Latin who many years later wrote her memorial would have seen Mrs Talbot's 'strong common sense' and 'entire absence of feminine weakness'. 'In her conversation there was no frivolity . . . no inability to see the point.' However they might speak to other ladies, 'men spoke directly to her understanding'. But her strength did not unsex her', the Professor insisted, treading a thin line between 'masculine attributes' and 'lack of ambition to thrust herself forward or . . . claim for her sex unusual functions'.[9]

It was the usual ones, no doubt, which inspired the intensity of maternal affection which Mrs Talbot felt for her sons. Her outward severity, the Professor wrote, hardly prepared a stranger for this. It certainly appears in her letters to Meriel; especially in regard to Edward, who was very much the baby of the family and the only child she now had at home. He went to Charterhouse (still then in London) as a day boy, setting out by cab from 10 Great George Street, the family house in Westminster, and returning by omnibus or penny steamer. 'I will begin by telling you how Edward has got on in that awful crisis of life, the debut at a Public School', she wrote fondly to Meriel in June 1856. At first, apparently, he had been so nervous that he could not eat his breakfast; but now the trouble was that he worked too hard. 'Even Johnny preached to him that he is over particular but he says he *cannot* bear to show up such papers as he sees others do, so he pores over every word till I can hardly get him to bed.'[10]

Mrs Talbot's habit of writing to Meriel seems to have dated from the year before, when the birth of the eleventh Lyttelton baby and Meriel's Confirmation looked set to clash. The upshot was that Mary Lyttelton went off to London to have the baby while Meriel was confirmed from Falconhurst, with Mrs Talbot *in loco parentis*. The birth had aroused much anxiety beforehand but in the event had passed off well, inspiring a little note from Mrs Talbot on the contrast between '*this* Saturday and last', with thankfulness 'that all that was *before* her then is now so happily over'. It did not prove so. Mary was unwell for a long time after – in fact never really returned to health; which led to many enquiries of Meriel as to the current state of things, and a kind of understanding between them. 'Your handwriting certainly does begin to have rather disagreeable associations', Mrs Talbot admitted, 'but on the other hand it is a great . . . comfort to feel that there you are, for one to hear from whenever your Mama *is* ill.'[11]

As Mary was often indisposed, Mrs Talbot took to giving Meriel advice of a kind she might otherwise have had from her mother: to be more indulgent to the governess, for instance; or a little less so to her cousin Agnes ('Don't lead her by your treatment of her to think herself as old as you and Lucy'). Though sympathetic she was always firm. 'I quite admit it is a *trial* to big girls to begin with a new governess.' All the same, 'I hope . . . that you and Lucy will do yourselves credit by getting on well with her'. Mary had consulted her over this governess as she had come to do on various things. For Mrs Talbot was quite decisive and had the confidence of a woman used to handling her own affairs. She had even ventured a little in public, having been one of a group of ladies who supported Miss Nightingale's work in the Crimea. She was also accustomed to manage money. All they had was what her husband earned, she once told Catherine. But he earned a great deal.

He had been a very successful QC – one who the volume of parliamentary business which came with the railway boom made rich. The
building undertaken at Falconhurst must have cost a lot but Caroline
Talbot remained a very generous friend. It is not clear what arrangements were made when the two families went on holiday together, as
they did at St Leonard's in 1856; or exactly what lay behind Mary's
saying, 'all things considered : . . and all the help you have given us,
I think it but right to pay for Amelia and the girls'; but clearly at times
the help was substantial. 'We do not want the money till Michaelmas',
Mary wrote in June 1856.

> All we wanted was to let the Agent know that we could answer for £2000
> when the land had to be paid for. I hope it is not hard on you asking
> you to lend us, for we are quite aware that without a Mortgage we ought
> to pay better interest, so we do not take it like pork.[12]

Mary worried a great deal about money. They both did, though
perhaps not to good purpose. Where she fastened on the price of
muslin or the cost of sugar in the children's milk, Lyttelton would deny
himself the pleasure of buying a new walking stick. He would joke about
it. It amused him greatly when a four-year-old called him 'Lord Little-
tin' ('very correctly', as he said), but he knew that it was serious. He
was diligent about the estate and cut down his hunting (it was always
a treat to be mounted when they went to the Spencers at Althorp); but
he could never set his mind to investment, and had eight sons to put
through Eton, and was an exceptionally liberal giver to churches,
schools and all good causes. There was 'a sort of freedom and generosity
and *grand Monsieur* about him', Lavinia once recalled: thinking perhaps
of his having provided the headstone for a poor governess's grave; and
having been so good to old Rowe, his valet, who had to be sacked when
he took to drink. It goes with all this that money matters very easily
slipped his mind. 'George so shocked about the £50', Mary reported
to Mrs Talbot in July 1856.

> He now remembers my telling him to pay it, he looked quite ashamed,
> but I own I am not happy about his forgetting always every thing
> connected with money, poor old darling, it makes me so dread being
> away from him.[13]

She was deeply touched by her friend's kindness and the warmth of
the many letters that enlivened her days in bed. Mrs Talbot was always
ready to set aside her own affairs when help was needed. 'I can only
say that I pray God to make me sufficiently thankful', Mary wrote;

looking back to the previous year and her illness after Edward's birth, 'and so helping me onwards and the children too'.[14]

Knowing Mrs Talbot's interest in the children, she passed on anything that might amuse her, especially about her godson Bobbie. ('Bobbie said to me, "Don't drop the whip, darling!"') But this same Bobbie – now aged three – may well have found his godmother rather austere. On one occasion, as she struggled to write in a room that was crowded with children, Mary bewailed her own lack of firmness. 'You would have sent them away had you been here!' And they would have gone, undoubtedly. Their cousin, Mary Gladstone, many years later, said she thought her diffidence had its roots at a point in childhood when Mrs Talbot made her feel that she was stupid. Even May Lyttelton (six years old, but far less easily overborne) seemed to feel that there was deference due. Reproved by her nurse for calling something 'swell', she came back with, 'Mama calls things swell, Mrs Talbot never would. She is too much of a lady'.[15]

Possibly few, outside her family, had ever got close enough to Caroline Talbot to sense her vulnerability as Mary did.

> I fancy you all through the day sometimes . . . muzzing over the papers with no one to cheer you . . . then your accounts and letters and then I hope some nice interesting book and then dear little Edward, but it must be sadly solitary.[16]

Frequent letters from Hagley arrived, anticipating her friend's next visit. 'Your coming is . . . something enchanting to look forward to.'

> They are cutting the grass and the smell and the sounds of the scythe sharpening and the birds (though not nightingales) is ravishing. George has been sitting on the lawn . . . reading . . . but in spite of all this I do miss you uncommonly.[17]

It was the appeal of a younger sister. Mrs Talbot had none, but under the influence 'of the fascination of your Mama's society', as she described it once to Meriel, she may have allowed herself to feel that she had.

The end when it came was not, for her, as it was for Catherine, the death of childhood, but it was the death of summer, perhaps; a summer she had never expected – composed of Mary's warmth and smile and the faith ('peculiarly simple and entire') that Lyttelton had described in the Record. She read and reread all her letters. ('Only, when one gets up from reading, it is like fresh parting with her.') She meant to put them open in a portfolio, 'but have not the heart to throw away the envelopes directed in her hand'.[18] 'I find myself thinking I shall tell her something', she wrote to Meriel, 'and then comes the feeling of intense loneliness.' 'Darling Mrs Tobbit', Meriel answered gently, borrowing something of the children's style, 'how I can fancy you thinking of things to tell her.' She went on to explain her own trouble over wanting to see her mother again. 'Don't you find, no, perhaps you're too good, but I do, that the thought of seeing her again comes first? Though of course it ought not to.'[19] Mrs Talbot's reply showed that she found this frequently. So they went on, supporting each other, though Meriel seems to have been the stronger.

Edward Talbot, who was now thirteen and showing great promise at Charterhouse, had been terribly upset at the death but wrote to Meriel composedly, telling her the locket with Mary's hair had been added to the chain his mother wore and that he had dreamt that Lady Lyttelton told him to be very careful about his prayers.

> I don't know how far we may carry such things . . . but I certainly think that it is not impossible that she and all the departed may have some connection with us in these ways – and that has made a great impression upon me. I am sure that in some ways her death, though it seems odd to say it, has been very good for me. It has given me a fresh impulse in the path of righteousness. God grant that I may not fall back again.[20]

Meriel the stoic (who Johnny alleged was never excited by anything) uncurled a little and found some comfort in this kind of freemasonry of grief. Not that she was starved of any other source. She took consolation increasingly from her father's companionableness; and warmed herself in the love and kindness which poured down on her from Aunty Pussy. But these were both persons whose right to grieve she placed without question above her own. She was protective at times towards her aunt – conscious of what a sister must feel, even in addressing a letter to Hagley: 'I can't help thinking too of the . . . blank it must be to you not having Mama to tell everything to'.[21] She gave her detailed accounts of the family, often sought advice on practical things and sometimes asked her to do commissions. In March 1858 Meriel wrote, 'You come nearer to making up for her than any one else ever can'. Yet her letters to Hawarden were not so free as those she was writing to Falconhurst. Perhaps the fear of adding to her aunt's distress stopped her from exposing the depths of her own – that 'dreadful craving desolation' which she confessed to Mrs Talbot. 'Oh, don't you know? Yes, that's what's so nice, I feel so sure you *do* know and *feel* yourself all these ins and outs of the great all-pervading sorrow. I never knew sorrow would be like this.'[22] 'Well, Mrs Tobbit, we must get on some-how.'[23]

Getting on with Lucy she foresaw as a problem. Of course they were intimate – could hardly not be, so close in age and, as Lucy once said, 'catching the eye of each other's noses' whenever they woke in the shared bedroom. For all that, Meriel told Mrs Talbot, 'I despair of our ever amalgamating well'. Which was not strange, for their temperamental differences were heightened by the fact that she now had the duties and standing that went with running the household, whereas Lucy was still in the schoolroom, under the eye of Miss Norton Smith ('Monday and Thursday for Italian, Tuesday and Friday for French, Wednesday and Saturday for English, with a half-holiday on the latter day').[24]

Some of the children called Meriel 'the Old One' but Lucy they found tremendous fun, game for anything in any weather; a fearless rider – and who else would have thought of calling the new mare The Maid (of All Work) because of the duties it would have to perform? 'I rode till six with Arthur . . . Delightful! The child asking all manner of questions about macadamised roads, poor law guardians, fire insurances etc.' On another day, 'we went, eight strong, excluding that most pin-toed Meriel up Sparry's and Obelisks Hill'.[25] 'Pintoed', the Glynnese term for someone who never attempted anything strenuous, was only too justly applied to Meriel, whose participation in the outdoor world that so delighted her younger sister is represented by such diary entries as 'Sat under the trees'; 'sat on the lawn'; 'sat in the hayfield reading aloud'.[26] She and Bobbie were the only ones, out of the twelve, who did not like riding. However, she had other occupations.

'I find my days very well filled up now, and can pretty well fancy what the life here will be', she had told Mrs Talbot early on.[27] Apart from the routine household chores of ordering meals and checking accounts, and paying wages and issuing tickets for the clothing club which they ran each month, it was to her that Mrs Ellis presented the urgent need for a stillroom maid and Newmany the lack of stuff for frocks for when the little girls came out of mourning. Print for frocks could be got in Stourbridge – or Birmingham, a short train ride away, where a more comprehensive shopping trip might be combined with a visit to the dentist. But important shopping was done in London; and it was to Shoolbred, the London draper, that Meriel wrote now for chintz patterns. A regular part of every day went of necessity in letter-writing, particularly of the social kind – though left to herself, she would have done the minimum. For Meriel had never felt the urge – common

enough in girls of her class, and brought to virtuosity by Lucy – to put
every thought and experience on paper. She wrote of course to the
boys at school; and copied out the papers her father wrote; and began
at once on the lengthy task of making a copy of the Record. She visited
the village school, sometimes taught there, and spent a morning in
1858 hearing the inspector examine the children. She visited the poor,
as she had always done since she was old enough to go with Newmany
into the village with pudding or soup – or sometimes vegetables from
the Hall garden. Taking her mother's place beside her father to visit
the gentry was something new, and not always interesting, but yet a
part of 'trying to do the work she left me'.

For herself, as she told Mrs Talbot, she had liked the great quiet of
those first days. Yet in another way she was glad when people came to
dinner again, for she felt her father enjoyed the distraction; and remembered what her mother had said about doing 'the little civil things'
for neighbours – sure that she could never now find them boring.
Certainly, when the house was full she could not easily shake off the
sense 'that something or somebody wants looking after'. Yet at quieter
times, with the elders absent, it felt like a house without a head. 'It is
very nice having them all again', she noted once when her father,
grandmother and Aunt Coque had just returned: 'gives one a feeling
of repose and headship'.[28]

'Sarah Lyttelton, the General Granny', as she signed herself on one
occasion, was a great tackler of Meriel's problems, whether they had
to do with buying carpets, the etiquette of visits or a new hair wash.
And having once been 'Governess of England', as her son put it, she
was more than able to take a hand with the little boys' lessons or talk
French to Winny and May. Her very successful eight years at Court as
Governess to the royal children (after four as a Lady of the Bedchamber,
a post she had been offered when her husband died) had come to an
end in 1850: by her own choice, for she wished to be free to help the
young family of her daughter Lavinia who had tragically died that year.
She lived now in London with her unmarried daughter (Aunt Coque)
and a niece, but they were often at Hagley: where she was always happy
to be, for it had been her own home before she was widowed and was
now the home of her favourite child. Sarah's first thought was always
for him. If he dropped in on her in Stratton Street when he came to
London, her cup was full. 'Your Father is always in my mind', she wrote.
'*You*, dear children, have the . . . buoyancy of youth.'[29] Yet she herself
was a demonstration that buoyancy is not confined to the young. Her
letters are full of it. Her thoughts take off in buoyant flight at the least

provocation. So in her eye an ugly blot becomes 'an arctic lunar phenomenon'; her son, rigged out for the Volunteers, reminds her of a parish beadle; and Meriel, for whom she made great efforts to find Mrs Ellis a stillroom maid, is told 'we must go on and be patient, in search of the singing tree, and the flying carpet and the magic lamp: for I look upon a stillroom maid to be quite as *unfindable* . . . as these items'.[30] She took the greatest possible interest in every one of the twelve children, though in 1858, for obvious reasons, she was most involved with 'my dearest of Meriels' and with 'Lucy the Young Lady'.

Meriel had reflected with mixed feelings on Lucy's coming young ladyhood and Mrs Talbot said she hoped that Lucy would not get intoxicated with her liberty. Lucy, of course, could hardly wait. 'Can you imagine me writing in the gallery, having breakfasted with the "grown-ups", with my time in my own hands?' she asked Aunty Pussy on 6 September, the day after her seventeenth birthday. Her diary is full of grave thoughts, ending: 'Oh the deep sadness of the flying years!' But she had plans.

> I mean to read a good deal – such a number of books that one ought to know, and in this way I hope to learn more than I could in the schoolroom with those perpetual repeated lessons . . . Then it will be nice being more *au fait* of everything, from hearing the talk at breakfast &c. Altogether, I look forward greatly to my *out* life.[31]

She was revelling in it, Meriel confided in a letter to Falconhurst; adding that she had persuaded Lucy to study in the dressing room an hour each day. 'I am sure Mama would not have liked her to "play at young lady" all the morning.'

Probably not – in the sense of idling. But she had certainly meant her to acquire the usual young ladies' accomplishments. 'I want Meriel and Lucy to be polished up with dancing and singing and Italian lessons.'[32] They became fluent in French and Italian, good at dancing, bad at sums. 'Please to tell my dear Locket with my kind love', wrote Sarah in Lucy's last year of lessons, 'that Dr Johnson was right when he said, "a woman cannot know too much arithmetic" and I advise her to consider the subject.'[33] However that might be, in later years one of her brothers wrote a skit entitled 'Problems in Arithmetic: New and Startling Results by Lady Frederick Cavendish'. Lucy was in fact like her mother, who, after looking in on the clothing club, admitted that she had done the sums wrong, 'but I love seeing the poor people'. Lucy's education proceeded now by undirected, voracious reading. 'She is a girl that sits opposite the looking glass while her hair is dressing and *reads* !!!!', Sarah's maid remarked in dismay. Macaulay, Clarendon, Carlyle, Guizot, Shakespeare (bowdlerised), Racine, Dante and any number of works on religion were to hand on her father's shelves.

'How it makes me gnash my teeth at not knowing Greek!' she told him once, piqued to find that she could not follow a flattering review of his *Comus*. But she was never to be Ethel May, the bluestocking in Miss Yonge's best-seller, *The Daisy Chain* (which she loved to read), poring over Greek in her private hours. Nor does it seem to have struck her father that he could have opened this door for her. 'Dear dad,' she teased him in later years, when he was active among reformers trying to establish high schools for girls, 'your daughters' bringing up was as slip-sloppy and feminine as if you had never cared a rap for girls' education!'[34] And he probably had not; his mind being fixed on their coming out: the next step for them, as Cambridge was to be for Charles.

Lyttelton took it seriously. 'Meriel and Lucy begin to see something of the world', he told Catherine, in the summer of 1858.[35] 'I am pleased with the impression they seem to have made on those who have taken notice of them.' In the autumn he arranged country house visits: to his friend from the Canterbury Association, Sir Charles Adderley, at Hams; to their cousins the Wenlocks in Yorkshire; then by train to Cornwall to see other relations – the Robartes at Lanhydrock and the Pole Carews at Antony. 'Oh, there is something forlorn in us two alone with poor Papa!' wrote Lucy; moved by the sight of her father coming to take them down to dinner.[36] 'Meriel and Lucy have got gorgeous gowns', he wrote proudly to William Gladstone, 'and cut a great figure in an evening.'[37] The Adderley visit was dull, however. 'I am amused at everything, dulness and all', Lucy claimed, but she was glad to get home. She had looked pretty and very grown-up, Meriel reported to Mrs Talbot, but her manner was not quite right. 'There is a want of repose about it which I think comes from over-effort.' Things were far more lively in Yorkshire, where Lucy's diary was given its head as to rides and the cousins' fun and a trip to Rievaulx, four-in-hand, her father driving, herself on top and 'the aged Meriel within'. The aged Meriel's verdict now was that Lucy's manner was much improved, 'quite natural and nice'. So by easy stages they approached the Season of 1859.

'London, June 20th, 1859 – Nearly a quarter to four and daylight. Three mortal hours and a half have we been at Mme de Persigny's ball and sorrow a bit have I danced', wrote Lucy.

> Till two o'clock no chance of it; then Ld Sudley engaged me for a quadrille, which he performed with another lady . . . One or two other hopes were dashed . . . It was a brilliant ball, for them as danced . . . there being hardly any but beauties present, on principle, for Count Persigny asked U[ncle] W[illiam] if we were pretty enough before inviting us.[38]

Mme de Persigny's eventless ball could not detract from the splendid world into which Auntie Pussy had launched her nieces, and her own eldest daughter Agnes, from No. 11, Carlton House Terrace. 'Anything more scrambling, casual and unarranged can hardly be imagined', Meriel recalled, for Catherine Gladstone rarely bothered with the minutiae of preparation.[39] But Lucy does not seem to have minded that, nor the restrictions that had been laid down. 'Two balls a week Papa has fixed . . . while some people go to two a night!' she informed Uncle Billy's wife, Aunt Emy (a distinctly unfrivolous woman).[40] And it was understood that they did not waltz (though the Princess Royal and the Prince of Wales, who were exactly their ages, did). They were coming out as their mother had wished – as she herself and Auntie Pussy had done ('never waltzing', Mary once recalled, 'and never dancing with Officers'). So Lucy found that her first home ball was a simple thing with piano and harp. But the next morning, 'what did I do but go to the Opening of Parliament!!! I must take up space!' she says, dashing off into an account of red-robed peers ('Papa looked very comical'), the Commons pouring in like a herd of bullocks, the royal voice, and of course the Speech; though that was not at all interesting. 'The peace of Europe has been broken etc. – things that are talked of every day.'[41]

The diary had to be written now ill or well by the light of dawn for they were seldom home much sooner, even from the opera (to which they went only when it did not include a ballet). For both of them, beyond all question, royalty was the heart of it all. Brought up on Granny's life at Court, with some embellishment from Lucy's memories of going to a children's ball at the Palace, they were in London to meet the Queen. They were presented at two o'clock: a moment of great happiness, Lucy wrote, 'after all the frightful bathing-feel' (which was Glynnese for apprehension of the sort experienced in childhood by those about to be dipped in the sea).

The look of interest and kindliness in the dear little Queen's face . . .
filled me with pleasure . . . She said to Aunty Pussy: 'You have brought
your nieces to me', with great feeling . . . so touching of her! for no
doubt she was thinking of our having no Mamma to bring us. And to
Aunt Coque, 'I am so glad to see them; tell your Mother how nice they
looked'.[42]

A few weeks later came their first Queen's Ball; and that same day
another brush with royalty: an introduction to the 'King of France'.
'God bless him!' added Lucy, for her loyal warmth towards any member
of the Bourbon family was in proportion to her disapproval of the
'fidgety' nation which had driven them out. A good deal of diary is
now given over to various occasions when she failed to achieve her aim
of dancing with the Comte de Paris, as this royal young man was called.
The uncertain element at every ball, where cups overflowing could be
dashed by anything from failure to get *vis-à-vis* for a quadrille to an
untimely fireworks display, seemed to operate in full force. It did not
check her hopes, however. And she did manage to converse with the
hero in ready French – while up in arms that such a charming man
should have been banished from his own country 'with that upstart
Napoleon on the throne in his eye!'

Early in July her hopes were crowned at Ashridge in Hertfordshire,
at a 'breakfast' – that oddly-named style of entertainment between a
dance and a garden party – for which, with many others, they arrived
in the evening (having been met off the London train) to stroll and
chat and eat cold viands and dance, when dusk came, to the Grenadier
band. Afterwards, 'we sat in the beautiful darkness . . . looking at the
pretty illuminations and who should I shoot but the Comte de Paris!!'
How they danced the Lancers and what was said – up to the time when
a beautiful bow and a curtsey closed that 'delightful transaction', is
recorded at length in her diary. They did not get home till two in the
morning: 'everyone hideously tired except me'.[43]

'Well, dear auntie [to the anxious Emy], I quite agree with what you
say about society . . . only I do hope very earnestly that it may do me
good in many ways – teaching one carefulness in talk, giving one
opportunities to avoid silliness . . . and then the perpetual need of
self-control.'[44] Such admissions would have reassured Mary, who had
found Lucy quite a handful when she came to London at the age of
fourteen. ('She has such brilliance that people make much of her and
alas! there is so much want of stability.')[45] But even then, for all her
tomboyish ways (Aunty Pussy had called on them once to find her

rolling the grass in St James's Square), Lucy had a deep sense of sin, and a great need to seek support in the religion that served her still.

In London they tried out different churches – she and her father walking sometimes as far as Vauxhall – and were hard to please. At St Martin-in-the-Fields the singing was brisk, but they faced 'the inconceivable bore' of a fifty-two minute inaudible sermon. At Westminster Abbey it often seemed that things were got through in a slovenly manner; at St Mary's, Munster Square, to which they walked through rain, they had nothing but the Litany, 'gabbled so bewilderingly that, without my book, it might have been the Alphabet for aught I heard. Disgracefully irreverent and distressing'. Not that their services at home were perfect, but the Psalms were beautiful 'and helping [helpful] to remember in London whirl. I hope I shall keep such things in mind'.[46]

There was no fear of her forgetting them, or anything else connected with Hagley. Along with balls and royalties she noted the birth of the sixth of the ten babies expected in the village while they were absent; and the death of the blind man. 'My poor old Preece . . . I shall never read to him again! But please God, I shall see him again; and he me, with opened eyes there, in the Light that sorrow can never dim.' God was everywhere, but especially at Hagley, and at the end of July they returned. 'Thank Heaven,' she wrote, 'we came safely home to the dear bright snug quietness of green summer Hagley . . . and I went in the twilight to see our *own* Church.'[47]

'Come back, Papa, come back Lucy, come back Meriel', Alfred had written, with whatever help from Newmany this required at the age of two. Lyttelton had made haste to reply, 'What a clever little pig you must be to write such a funny letter. I want to see you very much'. Back at Hagley, the usual round of committees and local business claimed him. He was working too on a Greek translation of Tennyson's poem *The Lotus Eaters*. For all that, one of his keenest pleasures was to be with the children again – even although the sight of them made him painfully aware of his loss. In that quarter there was little change. He would sit gazing at Mary's picture, placed on an easel in his study, which from a certain angle seemed to look across the room at his own. He could not whistle, he confessed to Catherine. 'I feel a sort of repugnance to it. The only thing, besides . . . sleeping well, which I feel the same pleasure in is . . . chess.' And there were the usual money troubles. 'It is difficult to see how we can go on living here. But I suppose we shall hobble on somehow.'[48] He sold the Rubens and yet considered buying pictures to replace it; he contemplated selling the deer, but then, 'the children are so fond of them'. 'Mind and tell me anything facetious the children do', he wrote to Meriel.[49]

His letters to her give an impression of warm and easy companionship. The best of life had gone, it might be, as he once insisted to Catherine. Yet there was Meriel, like a waiting wife, ready to be told who he had dined with and how the Mission Committee dragged on; how he had played at chess, but badly; at billiards – badly; and the weather was bad. He sketched for her the eccentricities of fellow worshippers in Westminster Abbey; and of the little boys at Brighton (where they had gone for the sea air) – greatly tickled that three-year-old Edward addressed his four-year-old elder, Bobbie, as 'my dear boy' continually. He kept in touch on his trips to Eton, with prompt reporting of Charles's cricket, Albert's Confirmation, Nevy's scrapes ('I fear Nevy is in disgrace and shall try and get him out of it'). All three boys were weak in mathematics. 'Nevy must mend his or he will die a pauper.' But no report on any of them suggested less than upstanding morality. Meriel rejoiced that Charles's tutor praised his influence for good in the school, and she found him 'quite as nice as ever' in the summer of 1858, 'full of interest in everything, quite open with Papa'. Miss Smith, the governess, thought the boys were much better than the previous year, and Meriel agreed. She told Mrs Talbot, 'There is so much more principle and steadiness in doing right, surely one may believe it is partly the effect of those precious last days and words'. On the anniversary of Mary's death she hoped to get them to read the Record:

> One would not like the day to go by for them quite like other days, and yet they are so reserved about the subject that merely talking would not do. Dear old boys.[50]

From top to bottom, Lyttelton took pride in his children. 'There is none of them in which I could wish any change, nor have I any fear of the reverse in you and Lucy.' Yet his was always 'rejoicing with trembling', as Lucy put it later on. A dread of giving so many hostages to fortune seemed to follow from Mary's death. 'You might not think it', he admitted to Meriel, 'but I shall be more pleased that you and Lucy should get married than I should have been if dear Mamma had lived, for it is an imperfect home now.' To which he added less seriously:

> I do not commonly approve of young ladies marrying at eighteen but I think you would make an average sort of wife even now; so if you are

struck by any young Welshman at the Archery Meeting in the uniform of the British Bowmen I beg you will let me know.[51]

None appeared. Nor did any romantic attachment weightier than Lucy's for the Comte de Paris mark the Season of 1859. Lyttelton remained secure in his daughters. And boys, he joked, one could never be sure of till they had passed the years of *indiscretion*.

'Maximus, major, minor and minimus', had been Lucy's admiring little note when no less than *four* Etonians – Charles, Albert, Nevy and Spencer – went back in January 1859. 'One more dear than another', she added. It had been a first term for Spencer: not yet twelve and the only rich Lyttelton, for his godfather and great-uncle, Earl Spencer, had endowed him in 1857 with landed property in New Zealand, from which an income was already accruing. 'I imagine he looks on Eton as a place of entertainment', his father said. Hagley, which set its pace these days much according to the Eton calendar, was tediously quiet when they had gone. But in a month or two they were back and another tutor's report was read, prophesying great things for Charles from his gravity and thoughtfulness and praising the rest, while not concealing that Albert giggled, Nevy was rough and Spencer's work was not very good apart from parsing and Bible history. Present or absent, the Eton phalanx seemed to generate a kind of momentum which had not existed in Mary's day but now engrossed the entire family in 'trials' and 'sapping' and football injuries and unusually distinguished cricket. Charles had been noticed by the *Morning Post* for his grace and skill as a batsman. He was turning out to be the best cricketer, football and fives player Eton had, and was already over six feet tall. Lyttelton, himself a cricket blue, took every chance to watch him play; and one match above all consumed them. 'I trust cricket will look up under Charles's captaincy and not be everlastingly beaten by Harrow', Lucy had written when they went to Eton for the Fourth of June in the recent Season. Yet when the Harrow match at Lord's came up, unhappy Charles was dismissed for nine, as she recorded, on the opening day. On the second, they drove from Lord's in a fury after seeing him out third ball.

'Cricket', wrote Sarah to Mrs Talbot, 'is certainly a great part of human life. What would become of us all without it is not to be imagined.'[52] For Eton v. Harrow was followed close in the eternal scheme by Stourbridge v. Bromsgrove, the battle fought on the cricket field behind the house, with Charles and Albert on the Stourbridge side and Nevy and Spencer soon to join them, and even in the nursery a sense of approaching 'the annual climax of the history of mankind'.[53] So who should wonder at their amazement in 1860 when this was trumped by Johnny Talbot's proposing to Meriel and Meriel's accepting him and getting married?

# 5

## *Lucy*

'We (meaning henceforward Lucy and me) went to Hagley.'
Lord Lyttelton, diary 19 July 1860, the day of Meriel's wedding

'Dear Lord Lyttelton, I feel in such a state of excitement . . . I hardly know what to write.' Miss Smith, the governess, strove to express the feelings aroused by Meriel's engagement. What a loss she would be! 'I know how you will miss her.' But 'happiness, for dear Meriel's sake is the first and strongest feeling, with such a longing for her now to have her blessed mother to tell it to'.[1] She thought Johnny Talbot a lucky man, though foolish not to have abandoned sooner his very childish fancy for Agnes Gladstone. Miss Smith had always thought he would turn to Meriel if Agnes refused him, but of course it was best that he had come to his senses of his own accord.

Johnny had known both girls for years. And in 1860, at the start of the Season, when he had asked his mother to guess the name of the person he hoped to marry, the usually shrewd Mrs Talbot guessed Agnes. She had inherited her mother's beauty and Johnny was keenly aware of *that*. As to Meriel, he had lost his heart to Mary Lyttelton while still a boy and it seems to have been to please her that he began to write to Meriel (then thirteen) when he went up to Oxford. They got on well enough for Mary to tease them, later on, as 'the two prosaics'; but strict propriety was observed. 'I like nothing better than that he should be quite at ease with you and tell you his real sentiments', Mrs Talbot remarked in a letter to Meriel, then sixteen. But she added, 'no doubt any boy's doing so imposes some degree of responsibility upon you to treat them rightly'.[2] While Meriel, at seventeen, closed a letter with 'It isn't proper now, I suppose, to send my love to Johnny so I won't'.

Through the terrible summer in which Mary died, no outsider (apart from his mother) 'lived' her dying as much as Johnny. 'I wish I could suddenly be transported to Hagley', he had written once before when Mary was ill. Now he was distraught. 'I rashly said I would write to Lady Lyttelton but I don't know what to say', he confessed to Meriel. 'I cannot bear to give you the pain of writing . . . what must be so distressing.' Yet he had to know. His thoughts, he said, were always at Hagley, 'when the life over which you are watching is one in which my own happiness is so much involved'.[3] He hoped, on every little upward turn. But then a commonplace word like *spoonfuls* from Meriel's pen would at once evoke the dying woman's pitiful weakness. And finally: 'I shall never forget the sight of Hagley darkened by the loss'. In the midst of these fearful distractions he was trying to work for his degree exams and wrote to Meriel that November:

> Sometimes I find that I have forgotten for some days . . . what it is which is less bright in the world than six months ago and then the recollection comes back like the thought of something dreadful when one wakes.[4]

He was anxious about the exam results; felt the loss of Mary's encouragement and hoped her smile 'may perhaps come back to me in success *or* disappointment'. It turned out to be crushing disappointment. He had hoped for a Second and got a Fourth – the lowest class of honours degree. Lyttelton wrote of it to William Gladstone, 'I am infinitely grieved about Johnny'. It might not matter very much in the end, but for the present 'there is no getting over the mortification of such a thing'.[5]

'Bear it one may and bear it I hope I shall; but the bruise remains', wrote Johnny to Meriel, in a letter which largely dwells on their common experience of greater sorrow. She must, he knew, be suffering still as he had suffered when his father died. 'I don't think I dreamt of what the change would be in my home, before May 1852. But now I think that neither of us can be quite unprepared for sorrow . . . we shall never forget this 1857.'[6] Yet in 1858, instead of drawing them closer, Johnny's gloom seemed to set them apart – in that he was less keen to visit Hagley. And on one occasion stayed instead with Uncle Billy and Aunt Emy at the Rectory.

> Not that I mean to cut the Hall; but you can understand . . . why the actual gap and feeling that things are not as they should be are more forced upon one in your home than elsewhere. One feels as if one has no *right* to be happy there.[7]

His happiness suffered another blow not long after this when Edward succumbed to a severe attack of periostitis (inflammation of the membrane surrounding bones) and Johnny, who helped to nurse his much-loved brother and strove to assuage his mother's distress, found it difficult to make any plans. 'I have been very little in the gay world lately', he wrote to Meriel that July, 'but when I have been in London I have often found myself in Carlton Terrace [where the Gladstones lived]. I may perhaps be mistaken but it occurs to me that the dearth of beauty does not extend there.'[8] Mrs Gladstone herself, he said, still put most modern beauties to shame; but it was not her he was thinking of.

In April 1860 it was plainly Agnes that his mother expected as a daughter-in-law. 'You have guessed *wrong*!' Johnny wrote, amazed. Agnes, true, had been his first idea.

> But for the last few months I have come to the conclusion that I should not be perfectly satisfied with that, whilst there is one other person . . . (I believe only one) whom I could with the utmost confidence receive as the wife whom God has sent me.[9]

There is no saying what changed his mind. But its being changed marks the start of what turned out to be a three week courtship in which the main problem seems to have been getting a chance to talk to Meriel alone. He managed it at length as they walked to the station (followed by Mrs Talbot, Edward and Lucy) after a concert at the Crystal Palace. Meriel's diary passes this over (except that she underlines the date) but Lucy naturally records it in style.

> I had a strange feeling that something was happening . . . and when my old darling, in a state of agitation so unlike any I had ever seen over her quiet face – clutched me, saying, 'Oh Lucy, he's done it!' my breath was taken away . . . We stood at a rail, clinging to it, and I don't know who trembled the most.[10]

It was odd then to have to try and look normal 'for fear of maukins seeing us' and Mrs Talbot did not quite succeed, seizing her arm and saying 'O Lucy, I couldn't have believed I could be so happy!'

Other people's happiness bowled them along through the seven or eight weeks before the wedding. The Eton brothers said they went into corners and laughed for half an hour when they heard. Granny expressed her joy and wonder that '*the* happiest thing should have been dispensed to us!' And her father wrote to Meriel from Hagley, 'It is little to say that you will be much missed here. I do not know how any daughter could have been more than you have been to me'.[11]

Meriel's feelings are hard to get at; compared with Lucy, she wrote so little, and so little of what she wrote survives. Johnny himself, on the brink of courtship, had told his mother he had no idea what feelings there would be on Meriel's side, and as things turned out, she had a very short time to decide whether to accept as a husband a man she had known as a kind of brother. Still, Lucy gives us a glimpse of her sister returning from some dull dinner on the night of the engagement so radiantly happy that 'she looked quite pretty in her blue silk'.

They were married in Westminster Abbey on 19 July,1860. 'I don't think darling old Meriel and I slept very calmly on . . . our last night together, after all these happy years of sisterhood', wrote Lucy.[12] But in the event she found herself quieted by the grandeur of the Abbey itself; and doubtless also, though she does not say it, by a feeling of immense relief that her father was able to give Meriel away. For only a month before she had written,

> A great care and heaviness is sent us in poor Papa's unwellness – miserable depression, sleeplessness and loss of appetite, and we are puzzled as to which of these is *cause* and which effect. It's natural enough that Meriel's engagement should bring back to him overwhelming memories of his own past happiness . . . but he is unwell in himself besides.[13]

'Miserable with a sort of nervous attack', Lyttelton noted in his own diary. He had been lodging alone at the time at the Chancellor's residence in Downing Street (which Gladstone only used as an office), and solitude may have led him to brood on the consequences of the great change coming, a change which on all reasonable grounds he approved of most heartily. Granny, who was greatly alarmed, told Emy that no mental explanation had been given, 'except that the marriage preparations reminded him of his own – and that he felt how sad it was for a bride to be motherless'.[14] The illness lasted about two weeks and cleared up well before the wedding day, but by then it had been decided to avoid the stress of an occasion at Hagley. The Abbey was the Talbots' 'parish church' in London and through the influence of the Sub-Dean, Lord John Thynne, as Meriel wrote later, a centuries-old tradition was broken to allow them to be married there. Afterwards, Abbey weddings became quite common.[15]

From Ingestre – seat of Johnny's uncle, Lord Shrewsbury – where the first part of the honeymoon was spent, Meriel wrote to her mother-in-law of great and ever-increasing happiness. 'I feel so guarded and cared for and blessed because I belong to Johnny', she said. A week or so later, from Alton Towers (which she found fusty, but where they had gone 'to please Uncle Shrewsbury who had just succeeded to it') Meriel wrote, 'it begins to feel natural to be left alone with Johnny, and not so decidedly improper as at first'.[16] Every post bag set Hagley around her. Her father had written:

> You will probably find it rather a strange existence at first, and its blessings will develop gradually. You can realise them . . . better when your marriage is founded on affection growing up through the . . . years, and a full assurance of your husband's depth of goodness and piety than if it stood on a little fancy or flirtation, as is often the case.[17]

'I slept fairly and feel much as usual', he added, as he might have done over breakfast, 'but all these things make one old, and conscious of "life's ebbing stream".' As to that though, and by the same post, Granny wrote joyously 'I can't help repeating . . . that your dear Father is *perfectly* well'.

> Every hour since his arrival at home has done good . . . no trace of morbid spirits left – and the dear old groove fitting and suiting and supporting him just as we could wish. He is alway talking of you, and so cheerfully and naturally, as if you had been married a year.[18]

Lucy was not quite happy, perhaps, but that could hardly be expected yet.

Lucy's letters to Meriel were frequent and often poked fun at her own desolation. 'Dearest Old Creature', the first began,

> I am writing, as you will know, in the Gallery where I am painfully conscious that the furniture is not put rightly but in what respect I don't quite know and you aren't here to whisk everything into its proper place.

Along with a great deal of joy and excitement she had been stalked by suppressed desolation ever since that day at the Crystal Palace, but it was nothing to what she felt now. How mournful seemed the green depths of Hagley! What pain to go into the room they had shared! How she had stared at 'Meriel Talbot' at the end of the first letter! Though Meriel's blessing went to her heart.

> Which is an expression, old thing, whereat you have often cavilled in bygone days of fancy freedom; now I imagine you know what it is to have something go to your heart . . . Oh, dear old soul, when shall I get on without you?[19]

She begged for an adequate number of letters ('we don't expect them

every day from Mooners in Honey') and awaited with intense excitement
the couple's visit to Hagley in August preparatory to their tour abroad.
'I know it will be very different to old times . . . but I pant for your
old phiz so.'

The longed for visit went off in style, with crowds and cheering and
triumphal arches and villagers taking hold of the shafts to draw the
carriage up from the station, but Lucy in fact felt much like Bobbie
who burst out crying when Meriel appeared. Having longed passionately
to see her again ('were it with seven rings on your finger') after it was
over she had to admit, 'my second wrench out of your short old arms
is considerably worse than the first'. And as for the 'poor sisterless
birthday' – her nineteenth, on 5 September – it was, she said, the first
'when your old button nose didn't catch my eye from the opposite bed'.
'I don't know why I get facetious, old thing: I suppose it's hiding my
feelings under a sickly mask of mirth.'

'Though I never had a sister', wrote Aunt Yaddy (the young widow
of the fourth Earl Spencer), 'I can well believe how one-handed you
feel without dear Meriel.'

> It is so difficult to forget oneself and to be able to rejoice in other
> people's joy when that joy has brought pain to oneself; but the horrid
> wrench is over and you will find such comfort in dear Meriel's happiness
> and in feeling that you are doing your best to fill up her place in your
> own dear home.[20]

So Lucy buckled down to her new duties. 'Except the Duke of Wellington', Granny wrote, 'who once held . . . the seals of all the Cabinet
offices . . . there never was such a responsible Minister!'[21] But Johnny
Talbot had left Hagley thinking that this second attempt to fill Mary's
place made it somehow less filled than ever. 'Lucy holds up brave', had
been her father's verdict, 'but it will be rather a struggle in her new
position for a time.' Meanwhile, he had promised to 'hook' the guests
at the first big dinner they gave, 'and not leave me to stammer forth
"Aunt Marryat, will you take Mr Emy?" with other similar requests',
wrote Lucy.[22] Though she was older than Meriel had been on assuming
her present role, Lyttelton thought that her mother's death had forced
upon her 'a life for which she is naturally somewhat too young, viz. at
the head of a household'. Not that the *result* showed that, he told Meriel,
'for she seems to me to do perfectly well here'.[23]

By her own account, till the boys went back, she had been busy with
colloquial French and helping Nevy with *Les Fourberies de Scapin* and
Albert with Shakespeare and organ playing. Then in October came the

excitement of launching Charles on his Cambridge career and seeing and furnishing the rooms he had in his father's old college, Trinity. Despite all efforts they had spent a lot (on furniture, plate, glass, linen, china). 'But I think Papa is enjoying this visit extremely', she reported to Meriel. He had taken her to see his own old rooms and was very sentimental about them 'and the rooms where his friends congratulated him on the Craven and the Something Medal and what not'. Love and pride in him swell within her. 'Ah, that *was* a college career! madly I make a castle in the air of Charles being just the same; anyhow, dear old fellow, I do believe and think he will keep straight.'[24]

It is hard to know how much awareness lay behind this kind of remark. Her father had not concealed his feeling, when her mother died, that no worse could befall him, 'except one of the boys going to the bad'. Indeed, she and Meriel had been encouraged to pass this on to the older brothers. Yet Lucy had grown up, like any upper-class girl, to a much-chaperoned and sheltered existence. Lyttelton's expressed ideal for young women was standard for his day: that they should be protected from knowledge of the seamy side of masculine life. 'Ignorance is bliss', was the phrase he once used to describe their condition in the 'favoured classes': 'the ignorance of innocence and purity'.[25] It seems most likely that Lucy was ignorant of what her brother Edward once described as the 'rottenness' at Eton, for instance. Yet her lack of any real knowledge of vice did not affect her faith in their power to resist it; and clearly she played an important part in creating an atmosphere from which they set out with 'a really vital feeling for the honour of the family name, and the deep concern it was to our father and elder sisters that nothing should be done to tarnish it'.[26]

Lyttelton's own problem with the boys was shyness. Though wishing to be accessible to them, he was too reserved to bring himself even to utter a word of praise for their cricket, let alone talk about intimate matters. However, his solution was to write a letter. He began in 1858, with Charles. 'There is a subject on which I think it necessary to write you a letter, at the age which you have now reached [sixteen], as I mean to do to all your brothers.'

> At your age you must expect to be tempted to the sin of fornication. I do not mean to go into a general lecture on this subject. You cannot doubt the great sinfulness of it; you also know the great safeguards against all sin: and in your case need only mention the memory and thought of your blessed mother – what happiness it would have been,

perhaps may even now be, to her, to see you leading a pure and virtuous life.

Vicious and profligate men, he said, would deny that fornication was a sin, saying it was simply unavoidable. This was false – a delusion of the Devil. There were greater and lesser temptations in life; but this could be resisted, like any other.

> I should not say this if I did not know this by my own experience. I daresay I had as strong passions as any one else; but I never fell into vice, not once, nor did it even occur to me as a question of *possibility* at all.[27]

'I do not wish you to acknowledge this letter, or even to say anything to me about having received it; though on this and on any other subject', he concluded, 'you know you can always speak to me when you wish.' Many years later he in fact told Lucy about sending this letter to all the boys (except his ascetic second son, Albert). But by then, of course, she was older, and married. Whereas, in the autumn of 1860, though nineteen and in charge of Hagley, she seems to have been still in pupillage; for she did not participate fully in the anxious family discussions of a problem which had sexual undertones.

The problem concerned not Charles but Miss Smith. From her arrival, in 1856, everyone had liked the governess. Very ungovernessy, Mary had called her: pleasant, straightforward, with a sense of fun which went down specially well with Lucy, who had very soon become her friend. Strong through the dreadful year that followed, Miss Smith was the only one apart from the family (and Mrs Talbot) who had been asked to contribute to the record of Mary's death. So things went on, it seems, pleasantly (though there were signs of her losing patience oftener than she should have done with Winny and May) until the summer of 1860 when, as Lucy explained to Meriel in the midst of her honeymoon tour, they were faced with the prodigious blow-up of Miss Smith over Penmaenmawr.

She had been furious, evidently, when informed of the date arranged for the children's holiday there. Lyttelton played this down, to Meriel, saying, 'Miss Smith was extremely foolish but is in good humour now'. As for the visit to Penmaenmawr, he did not expect any trouble there, though Auntie Pussy had said 'mysteriously' that the governess would have to go. Mysterious indeed are the anxious letters written by Granny and Mrs Talbot and Meriel herself upon this subject. All that can be gathered is that Penmaenmawr seemed to strike them less as a problem than as a way out of another problem. In short, Miss Smith had done something worse than lose her temper so heedlessly, but losing it was to provide the basis of a civilised way to get rid of her.

Lucy was not kept abreast of this. She realised that something was up but not 'the real horrid truth', said Meriel. Her comments therefore are sad and confused, for she had once been close to Miss Smith. 'The secret must be a most blackguardly one to prevent my great compassion for her,' she told Meriel as the end drew near. 'I don't want to know till she is out of the house for I wish to be nothing but kindness to her.' [28]

Miss Smith left Hagley for another post early in 1861, feeling she had been unfairly treated but with no outward signs of rupture. There were leaving presents from the family and she kept in touch with her former pupils. Lucy learned the secret then, no doubt: which was that Miff (as the children called her) through contrived encounters and embroidered slippers had shown that she had designs on their father.[29] Lyttelton seems to have been quite unaware. But then, he had designs of his own.

Time had gone slowly, with Meriel abroad. 'How much I could say,' wrote Granny, 'if I were not a model of unselfishness . . . about the gap and blank and reverse . . . caused by the absence of the one among all whom we do think of and miss . . . every minute.' She reported on a Hagley breakfast:

| | |
|---|---|
| *Lucy* | I shall write to the old cat today. |
| *Edward* | Meriel is *not* old; and she is not a cat. She is young. |
| *Papa to Alfred* | How old is Meriel? |
| *Alfred* | Why, four! |

'I am sorry to add that Papa having said, "oh you little owl!" was answered by the irreverent remark, "oh you *great* owl!" which reduced us all to a vain attempt to be grave.'[30]

No one missed Meriel more than he did. 'Papa is looking out for a letter from you more than ever I saw him', Lucy told her, 'why do you write to Aunt Coque, Aunt Pussy and Aunt Emy before him?'[31] He had much to do; and the younger children were a great amusement. But this first break was keenly felt. 'These domestic events, like your engagement and Arthur's going (the first of the *little* boys to go to prep school) seems to affect me some time afterwards. I have not been quite at my best.'[32]

It was apparently about this time that he began to think of remarriage. This is the theme of a letter to Gladstone written in November

1860 on the subject of 'Mrs M'. It starts defensively. Whatever
they thought of Mrs M. in the place of Mary, the Gladstones had
evidently been taken aback to learn that he had discussed the matter
with Meriel, with his mother and sister and even Mrs Talbot at this
stage. 'I must say, my consulting one or two people seems to me as
unlike an "appeal to public opinion" as it well could be', Lyttelton
retorted. 'About Mrs Talbot's being included, I can only say that,
considering all things . . . if I may not look on her as "an old shoe" I
hardly know whom I could.'[33] He had in any case only consulted her
about the boys, he said. And at this moment the boys were patently his
main concern.

For 'Mrs M.' had attractive daughters. What if relationships developed
there? Apart from actual falling in love, there would be 'perpetual
*squiggles* as to proper and safe things to be allowed etc., which would
make it all uncomfortable. And an *unreturned* attachment, or an objection on the mother's side, would surely be a most inconvenient thing'.
He agreed with Gladstone that attraction was unlikely in the case of
children brought up together, but this would be different – a case of
young people *first* thrown together in their late teens.

> I cannot indeed but be a little amused at your thinking yourself a good
> judge of the susceptibilities of young gentlemen. I fear that men of
> a very different life and character from yours [are] more likely to
> be so.

As Gladstone had fought unceasingly, in his own youth, against strong
passions – often possessed, as his diary shows, by a sense of irredeemable
sinfulness – it seems surprising that he should have been casual (if
indeed he was) about this problem. Lyttelton, of whom his sister records
the 'beautiful example and spotless course' that gladdened the family
in his Cambridge days, did not leave behind a comparable account of
the running battle against lust. But he spoke to young men on the sin
of impurity, broadly along the lines of the letter he had composed for
his own sons. To both he urged the benefits of 'constant occupation of
mind or body'; and the *possibility* of early marriage. 'When you grow
older', ran his letter to Charles, 'I may give you more advice on this
point.'

> At present I need only say that while I shall leave you quite free to
> marry or not as you please, I shall be always ready to give you all
> possible facilities in marrying; and that, though there are, in a worldly
> point of view, some marriages better than others, I shall never refuse

my consent to your marrying anyone whom you have real affection for, and who is of good character and not wholly unsuitable in rank.[94]

For himself, as regards remarriage, he would weigh one thing with another, he told Gladstone. 'But . . . I cannot balance anything about myself with the *risk* even of misleading . . . my sons.' Meriel, whose views he always sought, was no longer at hand these days and his letters to her often have a melancholy note. All eleven children were there at dinner, he wrote that Christmas, and so uproarious as to bewilder the young Curate. But even this lively, happy scene inspired reflection on the risks ahead. How could anyone ('even those who have none of the spirit of sad foreboding which I have always been liable to') hope that this mass of intense young life could burst upon the world, as it was about to, 'without sometimes overflowing its permitted channels'? 'What I most wish to see,' he told her, 'is one after another of my children, as I see you, safe in some still and holy anchorage' (i.e. marriage), which he considered 'the best for all of us, but a few'.[35]

While immorality threatened the future, the accidents of childhood were already a threat. That same autumn five-year-old Edward had tipped a heavy table on top of his head. 'It terrifies me to write it', wrote Granny as she relayed the tale to Meriel (the child inert – the doctor sent for); and 'Your Father! Oh how he suffered!': tormented by the thought that he had been in the room yet had not stopped the table falling, and assuredly expecting death. Through the very anxious night that followed he had hung over Edward's bed murmuring 'I shall lose him . . . I must look at him once more!'[36] In January 1861 his concern was directed to sixteen year-old Albert who had developed a lumbar abscess and instead of returning to Eton was ordered indefinite weeks in bed. This the exemplary boy accepted with the calm they had come to expect of him; while his father was writing to Gladstone that it was the sort of thing he had most dreaded. He admitted, too, to being always afraid of having another fit of depression, 'which gives me a morbid horror of the inevitable troubles . . . of life'.

Nor had he shaken off remorse. Thanking Meriel for her birthday letter in April 1861 (he was forty-four) he spoke of vanished happiness, adding, 'would that I had used it better and had no feelings of regret'. Such feelings seemed to intensify his search for the 'holy anchorage' of marriage. 'Best for all of us', he had said; and he certainly thought it best for him. In the fear expressed for his sons one feels the strain of his own position. He found celibacy a trial; and was lonely. 'It is hard', he admitted to his brother, Billy, in the summer of 1861, 'to look forward to perhaps thirty or forty years without some real hope in prospect.' This seems by now to have become an obsession, for the previous month he had despatched a proposal which was completely wide of anything on which a real hope could have been based. Incorporated in a twelve-page letter, it might as well have been a classified advertisement: 'Widower, poor, twelve children, needs wife'. The letter was written to Lady Canning (whom he knew slightly) and ventured to ask if she thought her widowed sister, the Marchioness of Waterford (whom he scarcely knew) would entertain his suit. Little is said of Lady Waterford but he is blunt about himself:

> Looking at my very inadequate means compared with my position it would not be unnatural to suppose I was thinking less of her than of her wealth. Now such a point *must* have some weight. I *could* not marry any one without a fortune. But I may perhaps trust that my character is decent enough to protect me from the idea that I formed such a notion without being determined by other motives.

As to incentive on the lady's side: she had a great property to look after and help with that might not come amiss; she too might be lonely; and she might love children (she had none of her own). While such a large family might seem a drawback, 'I do believe there is no family of children equally numerous who give less trouble [or] are much pleasanter, than mine'.[37] So the extraordinary appeal ran on. Not surprisingly it came to nothing. 'I feel as if I might as well think of wooing the goddess Juno', he told Billy. As to that at least, he was right.

One would never guess from some of Lyttelton's effusions that there was more to his personal life between autumn 1860 and the following summer than the lonely widower, the anxious father and the failed suitor. Yet from the start he had been overjoyed at the thought of Meriel's expecting a baby. 'Whether your Dad will be able to keep the secret is I fear very doubtful', wrote Granny, as an addendum to good advice about fresh air and not breaking stay laces in a vain attempt to appear slender. 'I can hardly think of anything else, it is such an astonishing fact', wrote Lucy. Lyttelton wrote that she must be careful, 'for it really seems to me that these first attempts fail oftener than they succeed'.

Meriel was the only one not pleased. In the first instance she had felt too shy to write about it to Aunty Pussy, 'for which feeling I think you will honour rather than blame her', wrote Mrs Talbot, who made the announcement on her behalf.

> I do not quite know what your feelings will be . . . Such events bring too many and mixed feelings for one to treat them lightly, but I think on the whole you will be pleased, as, I believe, I am. It is after all the natural *completion* of the happiness of married life – whatever sacrifices or trials it may bring, and after a few years I think nobody's happiness is quite complete without it.[38]

To her own family in later life Meriel recalled that in her childhood she had wished for a husband and no children and Lucy for children at any price. Lucy rallied her gently now on her defective maternal sense, recalling Aunt Emy's situation. 'I suppose she would give anything in the world, poor little aunt, if she could hope for what you do.'[39] Years earlier, Mary had written, sitting in the lovely Rectory garden, 'Poor Emy, I do pity her not having a child here'. Emy had been only twenty-two and only a year married when she underwent some sort of remedial operation (probably dilating and curettage, but in the 1850s without anaesthetic) on the advice of Dr Locock. 'It has made me unhappy to think of you having gone through so much suffering', Mary had written; though somewhat comforted by the idea that she had gone through it for Billy's sake. 'Nothing remains but to trust the having children or not in His hands, who will do what is best for you.'[40]

'My New Year's wish for you', wrote Lucy to Meriel, 'is a magnificent little boy, who I'm sure you won't really treat like pork.' And Meriel, once the ice was broken, had written to reassure Auntie Pussy, 'you see I'm not quite unnatural about it, though I don't suppose I have the sort of thrill which many have when thinking of a baby'.[41] Seeing Johnny's pleasure, she tried to focus on the joy of a little child belonging to them both. But, the fact was, she had been happy as they were.

Their continental honeymoon tour – her first trip abroad – had opened her eyes and inspired her with something like Lucy's elation. 'Oh Mrs Talbot, it is so very nice, such perfect enjoyment all day long', she had written from Austria, 'I had no idea how amusing the commonest things would be . . . one can be [happy] merely looking about one.' Back again in England, life at Falconhurst ('your real home life,' as Granny reminded her, 'your husband's pursuits . . . your dear mother-in-law') seemed like another stage of the holiday. They all got on so well together. Meriel was fond of her young brother-in-law, Edward, and he had always looked up to her. 'I should like very much if you would tell me privately', he had written in 1858, then fourteen, 'if there is any particular fault which you see in me or any . . . bad habit to be got rid of, for I think that *that* is the only true Preparation for Confirmation.'[42] Things had been very difficult for him. The periostitis had not been cured: had led, in fact, to his leaving Charterhouse that same year to carry on his schooling at home with a tutor. He was, though, an optimistic boy and his semi-invalid existence was lightened by its being shared with Albert Lyttelton, who was the same age and away from Eton for health reasons. Sixteen when Johnny and Meriel married, Edward was 'sentimental to the last degree' after the wedding, Mrs Talbot revealed. 'I begin to think that Johnny was right in looking upon him as a lover to be jealous of.' However, it seems that he had soon cheered up.

In February 1861 Johnny and Meriel were installed in the Talbot house in Great George Street, Westminster; while Mrs Talbot went on living in Kent. How generously she set them up is apparent from the memorandum she prepared at the time of the move: a lengthy piece but clearly drafted, as one might expect of the only person to write in the Record, 'The exact words were'. Now her subject was house furnishing: a servant's bed, a carpet, curtains – soon to be replaced (at her expense), and inventories of wine and linen. 'I think I make over the Cellar fairly stocked, except with port wine . . . I shall add about six doz. of that to it shortly.

> I hope you will look over the lists of linen and that J. will *himself* look over the cellar to see that every bottle is accounted for and show that he knows and means to know what is [there]. Of course you should have a duplicate list of plate, wine, linen etc. besides the one the servants keep.[43]

The cook was willing to share the maids' bedroom – 'and *make her do so*'. For unless they did, it would limit the accommodation. She also thought new carpet was needed on the landing by the drawing room door. In short, authority and assurance penetrated to the cupboards here; just as at Falconhurst, where, they said, the estate did not suffer from a female owner; on the contrary, tenants and bailiff 'felt themselves under a master's eye'.

'My Blessing to you in taking possession of the house which has been so happy a home to us.' It was like sunshine to think of them, she had told Catherine after the wedding. To Meriel she had also spoken of evening sunshine brought into her life and of the joy that it was to see the *morning* light shining upon those she loved. From her husband's death her deepest affections had been centred upon her sons. It was as if he lived again in her children, wrote her memorialist, 'and she shared once more, with congenial minds, interests in literature and politics and religion which women of feebler understanding . . . leave for the most part to the other sex'.[44]

All this produced an unusual closeness. Hardly two days had ever passed without a line from Johnny when he was away, and all great questions were a shared concern: his career (for though he had chosen to follow his father's profession, the law, he had thought first of ordination); his courting (for after her initial blunder Mrs Talbot was kept in touch and 'the absolute certainty' that his choice would please her had undoubtedly weighed with him). In the early days of the honeymoon he wrote, 'I liked your simple words of blessing . . . And your letter to my own darling . . . touched me very much'. As to former days: nothing, he assured her, that was happy then need be less happy now.

> Does that seem too strong to say? I don't think it is in this particular case tho' I can well imagine what a mother's loving jealousy must be in most cases. But now you have got a real addition to those you love most dearly; and though the first place in my heart is now hers, yet it is not yours she has taken (that can never be filled by any other) but one never occupied before.[45]

Obviously the settling of these new relationships was greatly aided by the affection – quite spontaneous from the start and specially warm since Mary's death – between Meriel and her mother-in-law. 'The sociable quartette we called ourselves,' wrote Meriel of her early Talbot days, 'and a very happy one it was.'[46] They were *old shoes* in the Glynnese sense ('just ourselves and Mrs T. and Edward') and her situation had none of the strangeness which would normally confront a bride. Meriel at twenty was not, however, the girl of seventeen who had thought, fainthearted, of the prospect of ruling Hagley. The challenge of these past three years – and her father's firm if little-expressed conviction that she was up to it – had greatly improved her confidence. Whether to a point where it would transplant to Talbot soil is another matter. For who was ever equal to Mrs Talbot?

'My old darling', Lucy wrote, 'I do think so much of you as the time draws nearer. I know your quietness of mind and trustfulness *will* keep you from over-frightening yourself.'[47] Meriel noted in her diary for 19 June 1861, 'Our first little boy was born at six minutes to five p.m.

after I had been ill more or less all day. Johnny was with me all the time.'

Her own people were not far off: her father much involved in promoting a Subdivision of Dioceses Bill to provide more Bishops to meet the needs of an expanding population; Lucy taken up with the Season – though her pleasures were curtailed this year by her having contracted typhoid fever, from which she had only just recovered. No happier end, though, to her convalescence could have been conceived than the birth of this boy who bore his grandfather's first name, George, and for whose sake she was now invited to take on herself the solemn trust (so much longed for at Alfred's birth) of becoming a godmother. She went home thrilled at the end of July.

'It feels wonderfully nice to be writing *Hagley* at the top of one's pages again.' Rediscovering its summer glory and enchanted with everything, she told Meriel that Miss Window, the governess (Miss Smith's successor), was a dear; that Aunt Emy *raved* about Win and May's niceness; that Mrs Ellis was in strapping health, 'Newmany radiant . . . the new footman a paragon, Bobbie brilliant, Edward beautiful, Alfred Perfection!' At which high point she drew a sun with a smile on its face. 'The peerless Alfred!' she had written once, after quoting something funny he said, 'he must be lived with, not quoted from!' He had been four that February. 'Four years!' proclaims the diary, incredulous. 'He would rejoice Mamma's heart, with his bright generous temper . . . winsomeness . . . quickness and noble looks.' And it really does seem as if Alfred Lyttelton ('King Alfred', as they called him) had all those gifts. The Bible lessons of the youngest children, Bobbie, Edward and Alfred, had been in Lucy's hands from the start ; and many other lessons she inculcated. 'Today there was a bit [in their story book] about not giving in charity what costs us nothing', she noted at the stage when Alfred was seven.

> They soon understood what was meant and thereupon we went into luncheon. I put some broth into a can and told Alfred I should like him and Newmany to take it into the village. 'O', says Alfred, 'but I want to go and slide!' 'Now then', said I; no more; to remind him of what we had been reading'. 'O, I forgot!' said the little fellow in a moment, getting quite red; and he went as willingly as possible.[48]

She was always very patient with the little boys and her father cannot have been thinking of them when he advised her to guard against 'a certain pepperiness which I fear you have inherited from Uncle Ignatius and Aunt Kitty'. He also spoke of the need to treat children 'with a little wholesome neglect', but certainly neglect was not her line. 'You know I never am quite happy about Nevy', she told Meriel in August 1861.

> He is to be Confirmed this winter and I can't help being afraid that he has no right thoughts about it . . . If he alludes to it, it is with his usual lightness and want of reverence. And why is he the only one of the boys who sneers?

Nevy's school report had not been good. His tutor spoke of defiant idleness, neglect of duties and disrespect. 'It's rather horrid altogether', said Lucy. Though she thought that there were grounds for hope, for he was much more civil at home. 'He is generally the one to give Granny her candle . . . and they all get up now when she comes in . . . And he minds me pretty well and is a dear old fellow in doing Tasso and La Fontaine with me.'[49]

Nevy was confirmed the next year, at Eton, and Lucy wrote to him at length beforehand.

> I can't help writing a *Sunday* letter, for you know, dear old fellow, a time like Confirmation is an immensely important one; it never comes again and I can't but believe that what a man determines to be *then*, he will be to his life's end, very likely. If one makes it a time of steadfast resolution to be God's faithful soldier and servant then one sets out on the path of the just.

She felt sure he must be thinking about his mother.

> Perhaps she is close to you. We *know* she is with us in the Holy Communion, because it is a part of the Communion of Saints. Perhaps she is praying for you. God grant that every one of us may see her face again.

'My darling, you won't be angry with me for preaching?'[50]

Nevy kept her letter, along with others written to him at special times; and Meriel (to whom perhaps he spoke more freely) evidently offered Lucy proof of his having 'such right and earnest feeling' as to fill her with joy.

> Oh I never imagined anything so good would happen, for think how impossible it has hitherto been to see outward indications of the good which one could only guess at in him. Papa is *so pleased*![51]

Yet Lord Lyttelton's piety often seems a touch more tolerant than Lucy's. He asked her to copy out the Record for Nevy, but there is no sign that he was seriously worried. Writing to Gladstone, who was Nevy's godfather, he described him as a boy of 'very strong sense' who he considered was also right-minded, 'but not naturally of much reverence or sentiment'. In such matters, as in most things, he kept his sons on an easy rein: insisting in a letter to Meriel that churchgoing should not be *pressed* upon them on weekdays during the Easter holidays.

> I hope you did not say too much to Charles for I have a strong objection to anything like influence being put upon them on that subject. Knowing as I do what boys are, I am rather afraid of the constant talk which in these days [Lent] they have all around them giving them a distaste for the whole thing.[52]

In fact, as Lucy was pleased to tell Meriel, they went to church frequently in Holy Week.

> Of course it was a blow that (except Albert) they only went on the evenings of Wednesday and Thursday; but on the whole they have been very good. Albert and Spencer have listened every day to the *Thoughts for the Holy Week* and really liked them, and yesterday Charles and Nevy came in and remained in the room, at all events.[53]

Luckily her responsibility for the family's spiritual wellbeing was much simpler with the little children. When Edward's answer on being asked who Rebecca married was 'Mesopotamia!' what could one possibly do but smile? Winny and May were less amusing. In fact there were times when she had found Win's manner distinctly pert and superior, said Lucy, but they were very much nicer now. And they were terribly keen on church.

'I shall be thirteen in three hours', wrote Win in January 1862 on the opening page of the journal Lucy had given her as a birthday present. 'From her old journal-keeping sister', it said; and though she never had her sister's wit, the way she embarked on what turned out to be seventy-odd years of journal-keeping showed her quite worthy of the gift. At first there was the problem of privacy. For if Lucy was critical of her, she was herself sometimes critical of Lucy. 'That is the worst of having a journal, she *will* read it and . . . tell everyone. Horrid.' So, with the squares and angles and dots composing the code (still popular with children) which is often known as the Pig Pen Cipher, Win felt freer to make such comments as, 'May has begun *that*, unfortunate girl'; or 'Uncle Billy is not always so affectionate to Aunty Emy, who is so nice'.[54]

Though she had so far been 'Win' or 'Winny', the summer after her thirteenth birthday people started to call her Lavinia, 'my own proper name': as if a curtain lifted for her to come forward and make her bow. But there had been at least one other occasion, since Mary's death, when she claimed attention. In 1858 at the age of nine she had reported a wonderful dream. 'It is easy to believe it is something divine', her father had written to Mrs Talbot, describing how she dreamt she had stood on the perron with Lucy and Meriel and Miss Smith, all singing a psalm, when the sky opened and her mother appeared.

Lavinia had shed bitter tears for her mother, as she recalled in later years. And she encoded in the new diary, 'I wonder what makes one so unhappy sometimes. Oh Mamma!' But she was usually happy: played the piano (for which she was gifted), acted in plays (for which she was not), skated and taught Charles the quadrille, 'toodled' round the park, enjoyed stick races, and rode ('Glendower went like a dead sheep'). It was a great thing to ride with Lucy, whose skill on horseback evoked respect, and perhaps they were closest then. For Lavinia – like Meriel – was reserved at heart and not always able or willing to produce the eager response which Lucy craved. By now she accepted this trait in Meriel – found it rather endearing perhaps; but in her younger sisters it was irritating. 'I have never seen them [Winny and May] really carried off their legs with excitement, or anything like it', she put in her diary, at a time when she felt they should seem more thrilled about an impending visit to Cornwall.

> They enjoy things (especially Lava) as grown-up people do, to whom life has a little outgrown its freshness. Take events and pleasures, I mean, with sedateness . . . And this is a little sad at their age.[55]

It is not a picture which seems to fit with the glimpse we get in Lavinia's diary of her flying through the shallows on the Cornish sands in the ecstasy of a three-mile gallop which she called 'the most blissful I have ever had'. From the diary one might judge her almost as likely as Lucy to feel 'cracked' (Lavinia's word) over almost every new experience: from hearing her father's poetry lecture ('Papa read in a way to make one burst!') to the Handel concert where her thrill began 'on listening to the tuning of the mighty orchestra'. Thinking about Lucy, many years later, Lavinia reflected that her very gifts produced a defect in her dealings with others.

> She was so animated, so full of ideas cherished and thought out, and she was so good a talker, that she was not equally perceptive and discerning in 'taking in' or understanding the real nature . . . of others.[56]

However, she recalled how Lucy had brightened their rather monotonous schoolroom life by coming to tea, 'and telling us with much vivacity and many jokes of any visit she had been on with my father'.

A very grand one indeed occurred in November 1862 when Lucy, as Lavinia recorded, came back from Chatsworth with *such* accounts. She had never been to Chatsworth before and had felt very shy about going. 'Dearest daddy,' she had written to London, where Lyttelton was busy on a government commission,

> I could not well confess to the Duke or his daughter that lack of clothes, or a preference for Sunday at home, was my objection! So I suppose I am *in for it*; and if they are shocked at my dirty gowns, it's their fault and they must put up with them![57]

As her father was not free to go with her, she had gone under the wing of Aunt Yaddy, whose presence sustained her, especially at the start; for the house, she said, seemed immeasurable, and even when she left she had done no more than glimpse some part of its prodigious splendour. The Duke, a silent man whose engrossing interest was the application of science to industry (he was the donor of the Cavendish Laboratory to Cambridge), was out shooting most of her first full day, with all the other men except Lord Frederick Cavendish, his second son, who was recovering from 'intermittent fever'. The ladies had a little tramp in the grounds, admiring Paxton's conservatory and the marvellous Emperor Fountain. ('Oh dear, I have an oppressed feeling, which is my form of shyness I suppose.') The next day, Saturday, seemed more pleasant ('but be at my ease I cannot', she wrote). Then Sunday. Sunday was an experience such as she had never had before. 'Oh my dear, the Church!' she wrote to Meriel.

> The *whole* of the E. wall is occupied by a gigantic and purely heathen monument to the 1st Earl of Devonshire, who is represented lying side by side with a skeleton, supported on one hand by Mars and a suit of armour; on the other by Minerva and a peer's robes, while on top a bloated angel (or cupid?) is trumpeting. We sat in worse than Smithfield pews, and the care necessary to avoid falling foul of everyone's eye, kicking everyone's hat, and sitting on everyone's lap, was most oppressive.[58]

'How can people', she wrote in her diary, 'go Sunday after Sunday to such a place, and think they are worshipping God in the beauty of holiness?'

What were other beauties compared with that? Lucy had begun to feel more at ease by Monday, when it was time to go, but it was still a relief to escape from 'the terrific grandeur of the place and people'. Everybody indeed was very kind and she was given a parting kiss by Lady Louisa, the Duke's daughter; but 'I have not often done a more blowing thing than marching into the breakfast room this morning . . . and bidding a round of good-byes to all the august guests there assembled!'[59] Had she known then that the silent Duke was to become her father-in-law, and Lord Frederick her husband, and *that* church her church – she would more likely have fled in panic.

# 6

## *Coming of Age*

'We must now think of everything as brightening and brightening.'

Lucy to Lavinia, 8 June 1864

'I heard Papa whistle (softly and half to himself)', wrote Lucy, 'for the first time since '57.' That was in November 1862. Taking them all in all, the 1860s lived up to this early hint of brightness, for they were prosperous years at Hagley. Not of course in the financial sense. On money matters Lyttelton as usual was both despondent and Micawberish. 'It is very difficult to get on', he told Catherine, 'but somehow I expect to manage.' And one or two good things did turn up. Lucy, for instance, was offered a post (at £400 a year, no less – with the prospect of a £1000 dowry) as one of the royal Maids of Honour. And she married a wealthy man. Spencer, turning twenty-one in 1868, was then entitled to draw on his New Zealand inheritance. Lyttelton himself, at the end of the decade, was appointed chief Endowed Schools Commissioner, at a salary of £1500 a year – the first pay he had ever received for any of his work on government commissions. But of course there were heavy expenses: the huge outlay when Charles came of age and the cost of the old-style tour abroad which he hoped to make when he had his degree; the steady paying out of fees to Eton (round about £200 a head per year); and the even greater expense of Cambridge where Albert and Spencer succeeded Charles. None of which he grudged, for he felt, like his father the third Baron, that one should never cheesepare on boys' education.

How he found the money, unless by mortgaging his relatively modest estate, is a question. But if money was in short supply, health, success and satisfaction were not. Death did not touch them in the 1860s, though at moments it pressed them close – as when Nevy's pony bolted and knocked him off beneath a low-hung tree or Albert ran against a fence in the dark and was impaled upon its iron spikes. Lavinia described how the traces broke as they were ascending a hill in Devon and the vehicle with herself and May, her father, Charles and Uncle Stephen Glynne ran down backwards 'in a frightful manner'; also how on another occasion a drunken postboy tipped all twelve of them – plus two horses – into a ditch. Apart from accidents there was illness: Eton epidemics, May's scarlet fever. But the ranks of the children were not thinned and it was, as Lucy said, a pretty sight to see them capering about to greet her at the sound of the carriage wheels. Meanwhile the family circle grew, with Meriel's babies (five that decade), Lucy's marriage, Lavinia's engagement and Lyttelton's finding a second wife.

Cambridge bestowed on him an honorary doctorate in the summer of 1862. 'Papa is always a lion', wrote Lucy, who saw him cheered in the Senate House 'enough to make me nearly burst with pride'.[1] His verse translation of Milton's *Comus* was published in 1864 and, though unable to follow the Greek, she took delight in a learned reviewer's appreciation of its scholarly power and lively absence of pedantry. As to public work, the 1860s were his Royal Commission years. Commissions were great bores, he once told Gladstone, 'and unpaid bores; but such as they are, the only quasi-official work I shall ever do'.[2] Which by no means meant that he thought it a kind of work not worth doing. Commissions were instruments of change. And if he generally took as given the world of the cultivated ruling class – so congenially linked, in his case, with the cultures of Greece and Rome – Lyttelton's was not a stiff mind here, any more than in verse translation. He did not shrink from the need to modify ancient things in a changing world and had in fact given early support to that forum for reformers great and small, the Social Science Association. His fellow members on its general committee included giants in public health, education and the protection of child labour: Chadwick, Kay-Shuttleworth and Shaftesbury. Lyttelton was hardly of that stature but he was responsive to the need for change. 'I am a great *hodiest*, as Sydney Smith said', he once told Gladstone: meaning, concerned with what was best, given the conditions of the present day.[3] Thus he had promoted vaccination; sought to divide those teeming dioceses where 'the clergy could be counted by thousands and the laity by millions', as he said;[4] and welcomed reform of the public schools.

A Royal Commission, called after Lord Clarendon, had been appointed in 1861 to look into the revenues, management and teaching of Eton and other leading schools. Lyttelton was on it. To have an excuse to poke round Eton was no penance. He was often there. There

1. George, fourth Lord Lyttelton, 1869. *(Charles Talbot)*

2. Sarah, Dowager Lady Lyttelton, 1863. *(Charles Talbot)*

3. Caroline Talbot, 1867. *(Charles Talbot)*

4. Mary, Lady Lyttelton, portrait. Hagley Hall. *(Viscount Cobham)*

5. Sybella, Lady Lyttelton, 1871. *(Charles Talbot)*

6. Meriel Lyttelton, 1861. *(Charles Talbot)*

7. Johnny Talbot, 1860. *(Charles Talbot)*

8. Lucy Lyttelton, 1863. *(Charles Talbot)*

9. Lavinia and May Lyttelton, 1864. *(Charles Talbot)*

10. Hagley Hall, Worcestershire, from the south. *(A.F. Kersting)*

11. Hagley Hall, the gallery. *(A.F. Kersting)*

12. 'The Old Dozen'. The children of the fourth Lord Lyttelton by his first marriage. Back row, left to right: Lucy, Neville, Charles, May, Spencer, Albert. Front row, left to right: Alfred, Arthur, Meriel (sitting), Edward, Lavinia (sitting), Bob. *(By Gracious Permission of Her Majesty the Queen)*

13. Falconhurst, 1877. *(Charles Talbot)*

14. Lord and Lady Frederick Cavendish, 1864. *(Charles Talbot)*

15. Edward and Lavinia Talbot, *c.* 1871. *(Charles Talbot)*

16. May Lyttelton, 1873. *(Charles Talbot)*

was always a tutor to be consulted about the progress of one of his boys, a game to watch or a problem to settle. Besides, the Clarendon Commission's inquiry threw up questions of exactly the kind he liked to mull over in letters to Gladstone.

> Is the *object* of instruction in boyhood to get into the boy's head as much knowledge and information as it will bear *or* to make his mind as good an instrument as it can be made for . . . self development?[5]

It was of course irksome that the Commission, meeting three days a week in London, took him so much away from home. But even this had the compensation that he quite often stayed with Meriel (paying to her his expenses allowance). 'If *anything* can be said to give me real happiness *now*', he told his mother, 'it is Meriel's marriage [and] those little children.'[6] He was a besotted grandfather. 'I want to hear what all the children say about the bab', he wrote home to Lucy when Meriel's little girl was born, a year after George. And later, 'I saw its eyes quite open but the colour is not known yet. Little George at first would not notice it, but I believe now thinks it some kind of calf, for he says moo to it. She is to be called Mary'.[7]

Lucy, at Hagley, became accustomed to managing a good deal without her father, though letters passed almost daily between them. 'Poor Mrs Shilrock is so dismally weak, though it is nine weeks since her confinement, that I thought you wouldn't mind allowing her meat and ale . . . till she is stronger, so I have written to that effect.' Or again, 'Can nothing be done at the Board for the poor Harrises at Stakenbridge? The man [has been] disabled from work for seven weeks with a bad leg which gets no better and they have only had three shillings relief.' Matters like this were easily settled but there were some she would have liked to discuss. It troubled her, for instance, that so few of the servants took Holy Communion, though all were confirmed. 'I am rather making up my mind to talking to little Jane Tandy about [it]. I would take your little tract and go through it with her. Do you think it would be right for me?'[8]

The tract in question was one he had published twenty years before: *A Master's Address to his Domestic Servants on the Subject of the Holy Communion.* In it, though acknowledging that humble people were often put off by a false impression that Communion was meant for their betters, or the very good or for great occasions, he did not hesitate to tell them plainly, 'No Christian who . . . neglects this holy office has any right to hope for salvation'.[9] Of that, like Lucy, he remained quite sure. Yet as to action less sure, perhaps, than he had been in the 1840s.

'You might very properly talk to Jane Tandy and indeed to any of the others', he wrote. 'I am not at all pleased that so few of them come, but my talking to them could be too much of a pressure brought to bear.'[10]

He was equally reluctant to bring pressure to bear when it came to Lavinia's Confirmation. She was to be confirmed on Palm Sunday – with Spencer, two cousins and some of the village – and the sense of reverence and inner quiet with which she approached this was very striking. Here, at least, she and Lucy were one. For Lavinia was transparently 'right-minded'; loved, as Lucy did, 'a Hagley Sunday', and the coming home, after a visit, to their own church in all its *rightness*. She had been preparing for her Confirmation 'quietly and gravely', Lucy told Meriel, 'without excitement, but with her whole heart; and there certainly is a simplicity and peacefulness about her religious feeling, like Mamma's'.[11] She told her father, 'I do cling to the thought that Mamma does look down upon her dear little girl'. As did he also. Writing to Lavinia, he had assured her that 'there is none of her twelve children on whom . . . your blessed mother looks down with more fondness . . . on such an occasion than on you'.[12]

Mary's looking down was surely envisaged (if at all) in the church at Hagley. And even though Lucy could hardly claim that she could not look down in any other, it was a horrid shock to learn that the Confirmation was to be at Belbroughton, a village five or six miles away. As to preferring *their own church*, the church so lovingly recreated and so close to them in every way, she could not pretend to be impartial. 'I am going . . . to drag Uncle Billy to Belbroughton in the pony carriage', she told her father, 'that he may prevail on Mr Woodgate to let the Confirmation be here. The Bishop is quite willing, so really!' But Lyttelton answered that he could not meddle in such a purely clerical matter. And even, next day, 'I do not see that we have any right to be preferred to Belbroughton'.[13] The appeal to Mr Woodgate proved to be useless. 'Nothing would move him.' On the contrary, he may even have moved Lucy a little by pointing out that he had eighty candidates, compared with the much smaller group at Hagley. 'One must resign oneself', she said. 'Good bye, my own dear dad. It seems ages since I saw you.'

However, after Easter she too came to London, for the beginning of the new Season: a very bright one in 1863, for people were ready to escape from the mourning that had followed the death of the Prince Consort and fête the marriage of the Prince of Wales to Princess Alexandra of Denmark. Captivated, like the Poet Laureate and most of the nation by the Princess's beauty, Lucy set down a full account of their wedding (which she attended) and turned now to other brilliant occasions to which the presence of the golden couple gave a special *frisson*, a sense of spring. There was brilliance nearer home, as well; for here was Arthur, only eleven – little pig Arthur, as his father called him – all decked out as a royal page in attendance at the Prince's Levée. He had come up for it from Eton and she went with her father to to see him dressed.

> I must say he looked bewitching, in his red George II coat faced with gold, his white silk tights and stockings, his red-heeled, buckled shoes, his cocked hat, shoulder-knot of satin ribbon, lace ruffles and rapier! He stepped into the pompous Royal coach which came for him with amazing dignity.[14]

And not long after that, Granny told her of soundings from the Palace in regard to whether, if it were offered, Lucy herself would accept a post as a Maid of Honour. Which of course she did. 'Was there ever, will there ever be such an honour for the lucky creature?' Lavinia wrote. 'I am nearly cracked with it myself.'

> She is to be in waiting about three months, have £400 a year!!!!! and £1000 when she married!!!!!!!! Oh dear dear dear me! – She will, of course, miss a little of Hagley, but fancy being so near the Queen! Oh the most fortunate of mortals, the luckiest of womankind![15]

Lucy's feelings at the time were mixed. 'The very anticipation is so overpowering that I have had a headache all the afternoon and I certainly dread the prospect, viewing my perpetual blunders, and the probable cuts into Hagley holidays and Papa. But! £400 a year! I shall be *more than* off his hands.'[16]

She was not expected to begin till Christmas. But then, with the muddle and change of minds which she came to know only too well at Court, she was summoned abruptly in September – having, naturally, nothing to wear and only two days to get things made. 'My bathing feel *va crescendo*', she wrote, in an awkward mixture of Glynnese and Italian. But she was almost too rushed to think. In some ways, arriving at Windsor ('my bonnet hot from the shop on my head') seems to have been homelier than arriving at Chatsworth. She was shown up to snug little rooms and taken charge of by Lady Ely, a very kindly Lady-in-Waiting who, when the awful moment came of being presented, explained that she was nervous. 'Nervous! O no,' the Queen said, smiling, 'she will soon get over that ' 'Her sweet . . . smile went to my heart', wrote Lucy. 'She asked after Granny, Papa, Aunt Coque and Meriel, saying of the latter, "She has two children, has she not?" Said more than once that I was like Mamma.'[17]

'I think I must have met the pick of the Court for pleasantness and kindness', she concluded, as this first short stay came to an end. Yet by then she had also felt the muffled quality of life in the shade of royalty and widowhood. 'The sotto-voce conversation on very Courtly and regal subjects'; the solemn drawing room, the noiseless servants. And was she not a kind of servant herself – asking leave to go to church on Saturday? ('Pleas'm, may I go out for an hour?') 'Oh dear, I shall sympathise for the rest of my life with poor peggies [maids] launched at their first place!'[18]

Windsor, she found, confirmed her view – formed the previous year at Chatsworth and reinforced on a visit to Cliveden – that the most magnificent houses had inferior church arrangements. St George's Chapel itself was glorious. But there were bad tunes to indifferent hymns; and Morning Service was divided in two – which had no merit for a healthy person 'whom the longest service cannot tire'. 'One wishes (I fear vainly)', she reflected,

> that something could lead the Queen to find comfort in that most consoling and peace-giving thing – our Church's Liturgy – that she might . . . be strengthened on her desolate way. How the words of the Psalm went to one's heart – 'He is the Father of the fatherless and defendeth the cause of the widows'.[19]

But very soon royalty slipped behind her and she was back at home again, finding the first rumbustious evening a funny contrast to the previous four. In agreeable September weather the regular Hagley life went on.

> Played at billiards with Aunt Emy and afterwards walked parochially with her. Took a partridge to Mrs Stringer, who held up her hands in speechless bliss before bursting into gratitude, poor old body. Met sweet Mary and Annie Herbert in their little white sun-bonnets, out of which they look at one with shining open eyes of a kind peculiar, I think, to tiny maidens under five. Also took pudding to Mrs Meredith with twins, which have both lived after all.[20]

But she precedes this rural idyll with a reference to 'dread October'. For only five weeks ahead of them loomed the climax of the year – or strictly speaking, of twenty-one years: Charles's Coming of Age. A ball for the county (about 500); forty in the house (apart from servants);

and when every bedroom was counted, and those at the Lyttelton Arms reserved, it still meant relying a lot on neighbours. Granny and Aunt Emy had already visited all the big houses round about, collecting offers of accommodation.

Meriel could just recall the fireworks which had been let off for Charles's christening – and the patter of her own small feet as she ran the length of the long table which was laid for the tenants' dinner to celebrate the birth of an heir.[21] Over the intervening years Charles had acquired many heir-like qualities. An heir should be a prince, and Charles looked princely. He was tall and handsome ('such a splendid creature among other young men', as Lucy thought) and with such striking grace in athletics. He was not, alas, a prince among scholars: unlike his father. Lucy had to face that when he was placed last in the Second Class. But there were other important things. He was modest and kind and not extravagant: impressing Mrs Talbot in his schoolboy days by travelling Second, and not taking cabs when he came to London to visit the dentist. Most important of all, so far as anyone knew, he had, as his father and elder sisters so earnestly prayed and hoped, kept straight.

'I know we may be quite deceived in the real life of our sons', wrote Lyttelton to Catherine.[21] Yet he felt it a providential compensation of his 'heavy and weary loss' that his own, 'in the most important respects', seemed to live up to expectations. This he attributed in part to Charles, whose 'sort of *loftiness* of character and horror of anything low', he said, gave him influence over his brothers, 'and probably kept him from vicious habits as much from natural instinct as from deliberate princi-ple'. Lyttelton gave credit to Eton too. Rating moral development higher than intellectual or athletic prowess, he thought Eton generally favourable to the moral character of boys 'well-disposed' (a rather surprising judgement, perhaps, in such a very high-minded parent). He meant to place no bets for the future. 'I know too well the incessant worry of temptation to feel any confidence in this so continuing.' But the fact is that he was pleased with his sons, though quite unlikely to tell them so. Those of them who attempted, later, to convey their father's moral influence dwelt on their sense of his expectations rather than on anything ever said, whether in praise or blame, by him.

Much more freely flowed the admiration of Lucy, with her taste for heroes, and Meriel, whom her father teased for trying to make out that Charles's poor showing in the exam was a kind of success. 'To be actually the last', he said, 'is dowdy.' 'It is all some horrid history questions that were not the right sort', wrote Lavinia – who as a child used to screen this brother from the heat of the fire till her own face scorched. Now, in the whirl of preparations, she had a private rub at the gallery floor which was being polished for the ball in his honour.

'You did not know me in the character of getting up a ball', wrote Lyttelton to Catherine, 'but I expect it will be pretty good.'[22] He for the most part was pinned to London where the Clarendon Commissioners were busy with the final stages of their report. If anyone was getting up a ball it was Lucy: she, who had once quailed at the notion of having to 'hook' the dinner guests, was now the author of amazing changes. The doors between the drawing room and gallery at Hagley were to be removed to give space for dancing; the billiard room to be used for receiving and the drawing room furniture moved in there – always supposing that the billiard table could be got out by some means or other. The library was to serve as a kind of sitting room (with some of its furniture put in the hall) and the ante-room cleared (from which the collection of rubbish and dirt was terrific, wrote Lavinia). Various rooms were to be repapered – including those in the fourth tower which had been shut up since Uncle Billy had scarlet fever there twenty years before. While this went on she was fielding queries, comments and directions from her father in London: had not the wallpaper cost too much? ('I am glad to say that *Uncle William* thought a *good* bedroom paper ought to be the price I hit upon', said Lucy); why did they need to repaper the tower? ('It was filthy and musty in the extreme'); and what about cloak rooms? ('Why daddy, we have *two* cloak rooms: the gentlemen shall put . . . their . . . coats in your bedroom; the ladies go through to your study', she wrote; adding, after further explanation, 'I do long for you to be back, dear dad').

He thought the band should be hired near home, for a London band would cost far too much. Gunter's, the well-known London caterers, were doing the supper and would have to know what perishable items such as cream and milk could be provided locally. 'The great Gunter, or some myrmidon of his, will be at Hagley on Monday next . . . and I very particularly [wish]', said Lyttelton, 'that you, and Herbert and Mrs Ellis and A[unt] Henrietta [his brother Spencer's wife] will go with him . . . into the whole matter.' The nub of it was seating – a complex question on which he and Lucy were quite opposed. 'I am bent on a sit-down supper', he said, positing the hire of a myriad chairs from some local upholsterer. The guests of honour were to be French 'royals': the Duc and Duchesse d'Aumale and their son, the Prince de Condé. D'Aumale, a son of King Louis Philippe, was one of those 'descendants of the hundred kings of France ousted by this scrubby Napoleon' for whom Lucy felt such admiring compassion. If the royal party had its own small table, and if all the *ladies* at least could sit, Lyttelton argued, 'the rest may be a scramble which will not matter'. Lucy thought that it would matter greatly and was glad to tell him that the man from Gunter's ('an exceedingly affable gentleman with an elegant lisp and courtly bow') had condemned the sit-down supper outright. *He* suggested a horse-shoe table, and a little round table in the middle for 'the royalties'; which would mean more people could get into the room to hear the speeches and drink the health than if it was filled with seated women. 'I think it will do very well,' she said, 'and the man seemed to have no doubt of it.'[23]

> Dear Lucy, We here are by no means struck with the excellence of the supper arrangements. We understand that the royalties will squat while the rest stand, which seems very awkward. Moreover Auntie Pussy said that the *chief* people ought to be at table with the Duc which is inconsistent with a very small *table*. Moreover I am certain it is much better for a speaker to have an audience sitting. Moreover I think there must be plenty of chairs in all the rooms, not only the ballroom.[24]

'Thank goodness you will soon be at home,' she replied, 'so I need not go very fully into the Great Squat or No Squat question.'

> Aunt Henrietta and I are not shaken by your letter; first and foremost, because I do believe there is no choice. One is in Gunter's hands, you know; and the man was so positively against a sit-down thing that it would certainly come to smash. Consider, daddy, that the result of all the women sitting down would be, in fact, an enormous *double dinner*; the wretched 'scramble' being unable to have bit or sup till the ladies had got up (which they couldn't do till the speeches were over, and sitting down they would eat twice as much as standing) . . . It would take hundreds of waiters and thousands of plates! Gunter would have to cut down and alter his tables regardless of expense and we should have to order another army of chairs.

'Well, I daresay I haven't convinced you, but soon we shall be able to talk . . . Oh, and as to great folks sitting with royalties, Aunt Henrietta thinks, and so do I, that it might lead to affronts . . . But we can talk over that.'[25]

Nothing came to smash. It was a red-letter day from four o'clock on the birthday morning (when guns were fired) till four on the next, when the last guests left 'and the happy, successful end of everything rubbed out all the previous anxieties'. To her, it was not a day of unmixed

enjoyment. 'On the contrary,' she records, 'I don't think I began . . .
to enjoy myself (such was one's anxiety) till after midnight! But it was
a day of deep thankfulness, and awakened bright hopes for the future.'
She had never before heard Charles make a speech; but from his
opening words that morning, when the procession from the school
arrived, saw he could do it. And what was more: that this most reserved
of all her brothers *did* feel strongly and was not too shy to speak of
what he owed to his father. 'Not that I can hope to emulate him, for
who could?' he remarked, to cheers. Some twelve hours later, with
dinners eaten and quadrilles danced ('our first grown-up ball', wrote
Lavinia), they ceremoniously went to supper and in due course the Duc
stood up and proposed Charles's health with a strong French accent.

> Charles . . . stood for some minutes while everybody cheered him. He
> did look grand . . . his face softened by feeling, and a little paler than
> usual. He spoke slowly, especially when what he said moved them, and
> there was a manly modesty about his manner that went straight to one's
> heart. He thanked them all most heartily and [dwelt] on how he felt
> that he owed their kindness entirely to their love for Papa, reserving
> nothing for himself.

This reaffirmation before the County of all that his father's example
meant: the public putting into words by Charles of thoughts so close
to her own heart 'was an overpowering joy to me'. Then, unluckily, she
left the room and did not hear her father's speech in reply to an
unexpected toast; but 'it was beautiful, all say who heard it'.[26]
The celebrations took some days yet – with a labourers' dinner, a
poor women's tea, a tenants' dinner held at the Lyttelton Arms, a
gentlemen's dinner at Halesowen and, to wind up, a servants' ball –
perhaps the most spirited thing of all, where she was charmed at the
sight of Charles lifting up Alfred during 'Sir Roger', 'that the couples
might duck under his little arm'. Nor was her mother forgotten in the
speeches. 'The longing for her presence . . . to smile upon her boy
whom she would have been so proud of . . . was the one thing wanting.'
Then it was over. The last guest gone. 'Here we are, Lucy and us,'
wrote Lavinia, 'for Papa goes away for a whole month on Friday for
his last commission work.' So he and Lucy were back to letters, though
she had little to report, apart from callers who came to enquire if they
had recovered from their exertions, 'just as if we were the English army
the day after the battle of Waterloo'.[27]

'Don't you remember', she asked Lavinia, when things had taken a

different turn, 'the end of that long quiet bit at Hagley?' They had
played casino and read in the evenings and had high tea and walks
and talks. And then the invitation from Chatsworth came. 'And I was
quite lazy and cabbage-like and didn't quite want to go', she recalled;
passing over the uncertain thoughts which had already crossed her
mind regarding the intentions of Lord Frederick Cavendish, one of
her partners in the recent season.

'You will feel as I do', Granny had written to Meriel before the
birthday ball, 'that the poor darling is not *fancying*. Your father's words
were strong for him to use: "I shall certainly think ill of him if he has
meant nothing".' However, she was pleased to say, Lucy looked well
and was working hard on Nevy's *Tasso*. 'I am keeping a furnace of rage
and contempt ready for Lord F. if I find he deserves it. If not – bless
me! I shall have to buy a grey gown again.'[28]

The Chatsworth visit, in early December, did not get off to a propi-
tious start, for there was a great hurricane blowing which dislocated
the trains and telegraph so that Lucy, with her maid, Gielen, and Rowe,
the valet, got to Derby too late to meet her father at the time arranged;
while *his* wire that she go on to Chesterfield came too late for them to
catch that train, so that in the end the night was spent not at Chatsworth
but Derby, in the Railway Inn. Furthermore, for long stretches, her
maid regaled her with all the squabbles of herself and Ellen (who was
maid to the younger girls and had in fact given notice that morning
because she could not stand Gielen's moods). This outpouring at last
was checked, Lucy told Meriel, by her own suggestion that a little
Christianity might have helped.

> And it is *this* consideration which makes me doubtful what I ought to
> do . . . Surely it is a terrible thing that two women should be unable
> to work together in peace and kindly feeling, and that the only way to
> prevent quarrels is to chain them like dogs in separate kennels. Besides,
> my dear, it could not be feasible for the girls' maid to be independent
> of G. . . . she must have G.'s help and teaching . . . I had thought of
> letting them sit in different rooms but that would be giving way to G.'s
> bad feeling

And there was another important aspect.

> It does so *press* upon me that I ought to try and put it all before G. on
> the right high motive. She is a Church goer and Communicant and yet
> how can one think of her state of mind with any comfort if she has not
> the beginning of Christian charity? It must be my duty, as her mistress,
> to try to open her eyes to this.[29]

But she then got on to Chatsworth and the '*wonderful* difference it did make going there with Papa'. Lord Frederick had taken her in to dinner and they got into an argument on the Church. 'I don't think I was wrong,' she notes in her diary, 'as I did not introduce the topic on purpose; but I wish I had been somebody who could have convinced him!'[30] Sunday churchgoing was much as before. Yet again the crush in the family pew, placed as if for worship of a ducal forbear with accompanying Mars and Minerva, 'and Lord Frederick's legs to kneel down amongst'. But it was in high spirits on the Monday morning that she set out from 'beautiful Chatsworth and all its nice kind people' for Hawarden.

'What a quiz it would have been', she wrote to her father, 'if Lord Frederick and I had travelled here together!' He came the next day; and a good crowd followed, in readiness for the Gladstone ball, including his sister, Lady Louisa, whom Lucy had taken to at Chatsworth. As for the ball ('the most enjoyable ever'), 'I danced till I got rheumatism in my right leg'. To Meriel she confessed that her head was turned by Lord Frederick's obvious interest in her. 'He is so very pleasant . . . I know this may be stupid and that it may all come to an end; but oh dear!'[31]

> I am going to try and keep quiet about it and trust it all to God, knowing that whatever it is, it has not come about through my own legislation. Do write me a dear bit of comfortableness. If I could only be with you! Papa and Granny know; nobody else. Bless you darling old thing, I can't help telling you everything about me.

And Meriel, it seems, could not help making some comment which provoked a defensive response. 'I *think* I am sure . . . I have done nothing wrong', wrote Lucy.

> Chatsworth began it, but at Hawarden he always seemed to be talking to me and I was continually *feeling* that he was looking at me; and at the ball he danced with me, asked to take me to supper and came up to talk again and again; and I know these are things that are for ever happening to some girls. But they never did happen to me before.[32]

It had been wrong, perhaps, of Auntie Pussy to tell her that he had asked for her photograph, but she had meant well.

> You will think, old darling, that I have let myself go very wrongly; for all this I know doesn't amount to much, but I have so tried to do right. For the life of me I couldn't help the overpowering excitement; but I can't believe I showed it one bit. My comfort is that I did not seek it

out; and I can rest in the certain feeling that God will guide and settle all for me

'One thing makes me sanguine,' wrote Granny to Meriel, 'I do believe dear Mrs Talbot would be pleased – and . . . marriages do seem to fall out to please her! at least one has.'[33] But it was Mrs Talbot who drew attention to the fly in the ointment. Exactly what line she took is not clear, but what it came to was a great doubt raised about Lord Frederick's religious opinions: had he, in fact, caught some of the thinking of the notorious *Essays and Reviews*? This, from its appearance in 1860, was to many Anglicans nothing less than a second serpent in the Garden of Eden: in some ways more shattering in its impact than Darwin's *Origin of Species*, which had come out the previous year. *Essays and Reviews* exposed the widening gap between fundamental Christian doctrine and the beliefs of many educated people. Was the Bible *literally* the word of God? And how could a clergyman square such doubts with his having affirmed at ordination that he unfeignedly believed the Scriptures? Two of the clerical essayists, Rowland Williams and H.B. Wilson, were prosecuted for heretical teaching. Could a more corrupting fruit have been offered (and by clergy, for only one of the seven essayists was a layman) than these slurs upon the word of God? Parables, prophecy, miracles doubted: open statements by men of faith that faith did not depend on giving literal credence to every word that appeared in the Bible. Though with no special interest then, Lucy had encountered one of the authors – 'the too-famous Mr Jowett' – in Oxford that summer. And from his mild intellectual face no one, she thought, would ever have guessed that the distinguished Master of Balliol was a tamperer with the Faith: 'as, however, he must be called'.[34] Though the next year she thought it 'spiteful and blind' that, on account of this, the university should vote down an increase in the salary he received as Professor of Greek.

Over Christmas and into the New Year nagging doubts about Frederick Cavendish were never far below the surface at Hagley. To Lyttelton, as to Mrs Talbot, religion had to be grounded in dogma. Christianity could not be reduced to 'a mere guide book to . . . moral virtues', as he said on another occasion. 'I must assume a definite Creed.'[35] In fact Lord Frederick, in the family context, posed a problem which was all too familiar to Lyttelton, as one concerned with education in the public sphere. He was not himself an embattled Anglican who was ready to go to the stake to keep Dissenters out of Oxford colleges; he allowed himself to be persuaded of the need for a conscience clause in schools to enable parents to withdraw their children, if they wished, from religious teaching. He urged fellow churchmen in 1870, when undenominational Board Schools were launched, not to indulge in factious opposition. But there were limits: and Board School religion – teaching Christianity without dogma – was to him a contradiction in terms.

He wrote now to Lord Richard Cavendish – Lord Frederick's uncle – about his concern; and the reply, he reported to Gladstone, though highly satisfactory as to personal conduct, was not altogether what one could wish on the point of personal belief. It struck him that his eminent brother-in-law, leader of the Liberal political connection to which Lord Frederick Cavendish belonged, might put in a judicious word. 'It would be well if you could even dwell (should the occasion present itself) on the importance of fixed dogmatic belief and profession. R.C. seems to think him rather . . . weak on this.'[36] And a few days later, 'With regard to F.C. . . . I suppose any word about fixed belief should only come in incidentally, so as not to appear to have any personal significance'.

If Gladstone took up this ingenuous notion it does not seem to have helped them much. 'I almost wish we had never heard anything of his *perhaps* faulty opinions', wrote Granny to her usual confidante, Meriel.

> Before the *Essays and Reviews* appeared, one should hardly have minded the degree of liberalism which is so likely to go off again and which, accompanied as it is by high moral character, is hardly to be feared. *But* considering the time we live in, I do rather fear . . . People do slide downhill so awfully, when once they have begun to doubt or cavil! . . . The long and the short of the matter is, that I terribly wish for the event, with one half of my foolish old mind – and terribly dread it with the other.[37]

It would, she thought, require more tact and liberality than Lucy could be expected to possess to enable her to rectify a husband's error without distressing herself and him. Lyttelton took a similar view. 'I should not condemn . . . a marriage undertaken in the hope of influence to be exerted', he wrote to Lucy on 10 January, as she resumed her duties at Court, 'but neither would I *recommend* such a venture.' They might, of course, be making too much of it all. 'I think anything like *scepticism* . . . inconsistent with what we have heard, especially his words to you about believing the whole Bible.' And as he seemed to be a practical man, 'not (as I suppose) fond of abstract speculation', there was no great risk of his drifting further. Still, it could happen, and 'I think Mrs Talbot did right in talking to you as she did'. For himself, he had told Gladstone, he was never hard on those who were habitually reverent yet held rather imprecise opinions; and to Lucy he wrote that Lord Frederick could have 'any amount of *liberal* notions as to the condition of others. He may think what he pleases about Romanists and Unitarians; the only question is his own belief and practice.' There were such advantages in the connection that it was not easy to be quite unbiased, and that was why it was right to be cautious. But he left no doubt as to his private feelings.

> I can never again look for acute enjoyment . . . But of such as remains to me, I have not known any greater than in Meriel's marriage, though I have by no means seen as much as I had hoped of her and her children; and I should fully expect the same from yours.[38]

'I am always fearing', wrote Granny to Meriel, 'that the immense earthly advantage of the event . . . may be making me wish it.' As the daughter of an Earl, and herself related – if at some remove – to the Duke of Devonshire, she could not fail to respect the eminence of rank and fortune which they now confronted. Yet it was also a little alien to those who were accustomed to live economically. The *size* of Chatsworth! ('I feel I should not like to live always here . . . though admiring it greatly', she wrote on a visit). And the *scale* of wealth which could defy calamity! When 67,000 panes of glass at Chatsworth were smashed in a hailstorm in 1858 she had commented that it would make a pin-hole even in His Grace's pocket. Wealth like that was remote from Hagley (where a few years later it was an event to put plate glass into the *front* windows; they could not afford to replace them all). It may well be that their lack of funds gave a sense of moral superiority. 'That white and gold palace!' they would say of Witley, a house created on the Chatsworth scale by their wealthiest neighbour, Lord Dudley; infinitely larger, more elaborate, better heated and lit than Hagley. Wealth was not held against a Duke, however. 'A Duke is a Duke and should be treated as such', Lyttelton told Lucy when urging promptness in answering one of the Duke's invitations. Granny, swithering from one view to another, begged that Meriel should give her assurance that Lucy was not being put under pressure to enter into an ambitious marriage. So far as Lyttelton was concerned there is no sign whatever of that. On the contrary, he took the line which he generally took with his children: that there was no need for him to interfere.

> Now if you had been seventeen, or even at your age if you had been less called on to decide and act a good deal for yourself, we might have

taken the matter more into our own hands but as it is I think it must
be left almost entirely to you.[39]

It was especially for her to decide on the thorny question of religious
opinion, though she might well have no chance to do so until the
moment Lord Frederick proposed: '*then* . . . you will have to inform
yourself'.

So Lucy began her next spell of 'waiting' in a very unsettled state of
mind. She had seen Meriel on the way to Osborne – snug on her sofa,
convalescing after the birth of her third baby. 'Old Meriel has a calm
good judgment and serenity about her that infect me.' This benign
influence seems to have waned by the time she had crossed to the Isle
of Wight. Miss Bowater, the other young lady there, noted: 'Miss
Lyttelton and I started some squabbles and shall, I forsee, differ in
most subjects.' She summed up Lucy as deeply religious, with an or-
thodox bias 'and some prejudices, lots of good sense and a dash of
intolerance'.[40] The restrictions of Court life began to be irksome. 'Princess Louise put her foot in it on Monday by taking both Miss B. and
me riding with her', wrote Lucy to Meriel, 'whereas the rule is for only
*one* young lady, and a govey to go.' Then Miss Bowater departed
suddenly when news came of a family death, and Lucy was left the only
young lady 'among a knot of moths and dowagers'. It was, as ever, a
fidgetty business waiting and waiting on the Queen's intentions. 'The
Queen's presence has an unquiet effect upon me, lest I should be sent
for or trotted out in some way or other', she admitted.[41] And in her
diary a few days later:

> Poured all the morning. After many vacillations of the royal will, the
> upshot was that the Household went to church on its own account, Lady
> C[hurchill] and I being diddled out of half the service by the Queen's
> keeping us to go with her for the latter half. And she did not go.[42]

But Lucy's impatience was mostly checked by her sense of the Queen's
deep sadness. On leaving Osborne she wrote in her diary, 'I could not
help pressing her hand as I kissed it; for what wouldn't I do for her?'

She spent the last days of January in London – pleasantly enough,
and yet confronted now and then by those troubling opinions which it
seemed one could not escape from. She had been reading one of Dean
Stanley's sermons, she told her father.

> Uncle William gave it to me and I couldn't bear the tone of it. In spite
> of all its eloquence it seemed to me to put before one something not
> definitely *Christian*; a sort of refined philosophy.[43]

Stanley, Dean of Westminster, and strong supporter of liberal theology, was too much for her. 'Where are the old paths?' the diary asks. 'These "dangerous days" are full of teaching that . . . bewilders one with false liberality . . . God keep us to the strait and narrow Way!' But it was no longer clearly marked. A few days later she dined at Lord Russell's where the most striking talk she had was not with Dickens or Sir Edwin Landseer but young Lord Amberley, Russell's heir, who 'like so many men nowadays takes one's breath away by unchurchlike, not to say unbiblical opinions'.[44]

Back to Hagley and her usual duties, Lucy read to the little boys, rode with the bigger ones sent home from Eton because of an outbreak of scarlet fever, took broth and pudding to Stakenbridge (where there was a strike) and earned much praise for being quite unchanged, said Granny, 'by Court life or anything else'. There was another governess crisis through February and into March. Poor Miss Window, who succeeded Miss Smith, had died in 1863; her successor, Miss West, had not stayed long – to be followed by Miss Merlet who was now to leave. 'Not unwelcome news', wrote Lavinia, 'considering the last six months.' In April Lucy went back to London where she stood on the steps of the throne at the first Drawing Room of the season and watched other girls make clumsy curtseys. She was to go to Windsor later but before that enjoyed a spell staying with the Gladstones, where the usual parties (in which Lord Frederick was included) were but a prelude to a greater event, 'for Garibaldi is in England, which fact makes everyone stand on their heads'. Red shirts had suddenly come into fashion and London was preparing a tremendous welcome for the peasant-patriot who had freed Italy from French and Austrian domination. On 11 April, with Auntie Pussy and Lord Frederick and her cousin Agnes and Mr Francis Palgrave, the poet, she spent long hours at an upper window waiting to see the hero pass, while down below them the people gathered and the banners of Working Men's Clubs processed. 'I suppose such a scene as greeted him has never before been known,' she wrote proudly, 'and never could be but in England.'

All the working people, of their own free will turned out in his honour; nobody directed or controlled them (very few policemen) it is grand to feel the perfect trust that may be placed in the mighty free action of Englishmen and their sympathy with what is high-minded and disinterested. They poured round the carriage, shaking hands, waving hats and handkerchiefs, and he was accompanied all up the street by unbroken cheers.[45]

Auntie Pussy got her an invitation to a luncheon in Garibaldi's honour, 'so I saw the great man close', and on the evening of 13 April the Duchess of Sutherland at Stafford House gave a dinner for him which the Gladstones attended.

Lucy went to the reception later, and at this fête to freedom and courage Lord Frederick Cavendish proposed. Rather diffidently, it seems: saying she was not to answer at once but must give herself time to think. 'My own darling daddy, I am in a dream, but it is a *very* happy one.'[46] The following day was still more dreamlike for she was back at Windsor again. 'Such fits of bathing feel . . . kept coming over me all through the pompous dinner and evening!' To Meriel she wrote that she was troubled and doubtful about the strength of her own feelings. 'Nevertheless, I have a *knowledge* at the bottom of my heart of what my answer will be; and I do believe and hope that God has put it there.'[47] In a little bid for home reassurance she had her Eton brothers to tea, begging unlimited eggs and muffins from Sir Thomas Biddulph, who had charge of such things. 'I longed to tell them something of my wonderful secret but I could only hug them', she said. She eagerly awaited her father's letter which arrived a day or two later saying that Lord Frederick had been to see him.

> He was naturally rather nervous, and moreover had a snuffly cold but he was very amiable and rightminded. I took care not to commit you in any way, and said you acted quite independently; but I said I thought he had nothing to reproach himself with [and] advised him to take any opportunity of seeing you that might occur.[48]

When the suitor expressed concern at the loss that Lucy's marriage would be to her father, 'I told him not to mind about me, for I was not as some persons are on that matter. He said he thought what it would be for the Duke if Lady Louisa [his only daughter and the joy of his long widowhood] married.' 'I said that I thought the Duke ought to wish for it.'[50]

'You have been a great blessing to those around you', Lyttelton told Lucy, 'and I have no fear but you will be so to a husband . . . I am not quite sure why you should say no, unless you have taken a vow of celibacy.' They became engaged on 21 April. 'My doubts and fears have been all absorbed in the wonderful happiness and peace . . . I wrote to all my darling boys: even to my little fellows at Hagley.' And the next day, the diary goes on, 'I had a long talk, a *Sunday* one, with him; and he told me all his opinions that he thought I should not agree with him about. I don't – but he has built his house on the Rock, and I can't but trust him!'[49] He gave her a locket with his hair in it and she wore it on a chain that had been her mother's. 'It felt to me as if I was telling her about it.' Then all too soon she was back at Court. But now its tedium was enlivened by congratulations and the Queen's warm interest and the kindness shown her on every side. 'His photographs sit opposite me,' she wrote to Meriel from Osborne, 'but they are very unsatisfying. His letters are the joy of my whole day but . . . they don't tell me half enough about himself.' Much better was his turning up at Osborne in his capacity as private secretary to Lord Granville, Lord President of the Council. The Queen was very considerate then and exempted Lucy from some of her duties so that they had time for real talk together.

'Your novel is certainly not "love in a cottage". All your dramatis personae', wrote Granny,

> are Dukes, Princes, Presidents of the Council, Maids of Honour – and your bowers and arbours are Palaces and Courts! Well, as long as the flower is real and the *personae* good – never mind![50]

A week or so later a family dinner was held for them at Devonshire House, which was so far from being a cottage as to be most intimidating. 'It will make an immense difference to me going under my dad's wing', Lucy told him; adding assurance that 'Fred will manage to come up the Marble Stairs with us'. There followed Lord Frederick's visit to Hagley, which he got through with flying colours. Lavinia thought her future brother-in-law delightful and the little boys were so pleased with him that they immediately called him Fred. So Fred – whose own experience of home included Chatsworth, Bolton, Holker, Hardwick, Lismore and Devonshire House – was introduced to the one and only Hagley, rode its hills and admired its vistas. 'And he *is* worthy of it,' Lucy told Meriel, 'much more than he expresses.' He may not have had a chance to express very much for she herself was over the moon.

> Fred and I have just come in from *such* a ride about Clent Hill . . . ending with a mighty gallop down Ashmore's approach. Oh my old dear! it is altogether the Garden of Eden! . . . Golden days! and my cup runs over.[51]

There were quiet times too: 'sweet converse', often; 'Communion together in my own dear church'; and reading to each other – when Lord Frederick's choice sometimes lit upon radical things like Uncle William's recent speech in favour of universal suffrage, for which he had been hissed in one of the clubs. Gladstone often made radical speeches but did not like to be called a Radical. That Fred was a Radical,

and proud of it, seems to have caused no stir with Lyttelton, who
certainly attached much less importance to a man's political allegiance
than to the fundamentals of his Christian belief. His son-in-law Johnny
Talbot was a Tory. The Lytteltons by tradition were Whigs and Lyttelton's father had played some part in promoting the Reform Act of
1832; but he himself as a young man was Tory – as, of course, had
been William Gladstone. Lucy's diary, as she grows up, reveals some
implacably Tory feelings and at the time of her engagement she was
far more likely than her father to be shocked by some of the views of
the man she loved to call 'Wicked Radical Fred'. For Lyttelton in the
1860s was drifting gently in the Whig or (as it soon came to be) the
Liberal direction. 'I should always wish to support one of your tail', he
had told Gladstone in 1863.[52] Two years later, though he insisted he
meant to keep his place on the cross-benches, he asked Gladstone to
convey to Lord John Russell the (Whig) Prime Minister, where his
sympathies lay.[53] By then he was beginning to look ahead to the time
when Charles might enter Parliament. 'He has considerable Conservative tendencies . . . which I cannot thwart and I do not think I ought
to thwart if I could', he told Gladstone. But, 'I certainly should not like
to see him in the H. of C. as an opponent of your Government'.[54]

The Gladstones naturally were delighted at the union of their favourite niece with a scion of one of the great Whig houses – also a most
congenial man. 'My *dear dear* Locket', Auntie Pussy had written, 'her
child but become from events like my own!' Having early gained Lord
Frederick's confidence, she had done her best to help things along
(sometimes unwisely, it was thought at Hagley) and the outcome thrilled
her romantic soul. 'Dear Locket and Fred', she wrote from Brighton,

> You will both like in the midst of your own happiness to know we are
> the better for sea breezes, bathing and walking by *soft moonlight*. Last
> night we started (past eleven) for the beech [*sic*] together. I cannot wish
> you both to be happier please God twenty-four years hence than we
> were in sweet communion that evening! We sat upon the beech watching
> the tide by moonlight whilst golden stars in showers came dancing in
> the moonbeams with the coming tide and rippling gentle waves.[55]

But Lucy now was suffering the pangs of having had to tear herself
away from Hagley. 'I can't write about my last day at home. The last
time I shall sleep in this little room!' The servants' presents had reduced
her to tears and Evening Service brought further anguish – 'O when
shall I be in my dear dear little church again!' London was given over
to fittings, and occasions at Devonshire House where it was Lord

Frederick's elder brother, the Marquis of Hartington, who overawed her.

'You are so right about the Londonums blunting the pain of separation', she wrote to Aunt Emy on 3 June (using the Glynnese *ums* to convey her state of being utterly preoccupied with London). 'The last night at old Hagley was, I believe, greater pain than any I shall feel now.'[56] Yet her happiness was overlaid by 'fears and shrinkings' as the time drew near.

> The blessed thought to me is of all the sunshine which is in my heart breaking out bye and bye, and scattering all these indefinable clouds. He is so gentle and tender with me and when he is with me they do a little scatter!

'Last Sunday with Lucy', Lavinia wrote, 'in spite of everything these days are very mournful.'

They were married in Westminster Abbey on 7 June by Uncle Billy, with Lavinia and May among the five bridesmaids. They spent their first days at Chiswick House, perhaps the smallest of the Cavendish mansions, and as they walked about the lovely garden the stillness and brightness calmed her, says Lucy in the first letter she wrote to Meriel. 'The sunshine is beginning to scatter the clouds. That sounds melancholy for a honeymoon letter, but you know exactly what I mean by it . . . I can't tell you how dear and loving Fred is.' 'If our whole lives may only be like yours and Mamma's!' she wrote to her father.

'Dear Lord Lyttelton', Lord Frederick wrote, 'how can I thank you for your letter, it made me feel that you think of me as belonging to you. May I be enabled to be both to Lucy and to yourself what She of whom I have just been reading in the "Record", would have wished me to be.' And Lucy added, 'Your letter overpowered me. I won't stop to say again how little I deserve it. But one thing I will say, that not this great new joy nor any other, can ever alter my love to you.'[57]

# *Lavinia*

'It is not all so difficult as I once thought.'
Lavinia to her sister Meriel, 2 January 1865

'Ah me . . . when shall we get used to Lucy as Lady Frederick Cavendish?' wrote Lavinia:[1] dashed – as Lucy herself had been when Meriel departed – by the awful loss, yet without Lucy's propensity for anguish, and far too busy at the time to brood. For after the wedding she embarked, with Uncle Billy and Aunt Emy, on a journey to Ems – to try its famous medicinal waters. Lavinia had suffered bad headaches from childhood. From time to time there appear in her diary weary little appeals in code: 'Oh that my head would get better!' and so on. Doctors had prescribed, but to no avail. However, after Ems, there was an improvement, 'which makes everything brighter to me'. The trip, besides, had been a huge success: taking in Brussels and Cologne, Heidelberg, Strasbourg, even Paris. And in the midst of it a letter from Newmany, addressed to 'Miss Lyttelton', marked her new status.

Though only fifteen, to Meriel's seventeen and Lucy's eighteen when they took charge, Lavinia was not ill-qualified to do so. A confident and sanguine child who had cured her stammer at the age of nine, and at ten had led the schoolroom in pinching tarts, her diary shows a taste for positive achievement. 'I am top at last' (in the examination her father set for them every year); or, 'I jumped with great success . . . with three pummels: next time I shall do it with two'. Her first experience of a choppy sea convinced her that she would be a good sailor, and her first lesson on the concertina provoked the comment, 'I think I get on'.[2] Lavinia was not easily flustered. When Lord Lichfield called and her father was out, she was quite up to giving him luncheon and introducing the governess. True, when Lucy went away to Court, Lavinia had said that she hoped the house wouldn't go 'head over heels' in her absence. But a few months after taking charge herself she concluded, in a letter to Meriel, 'It is not all so difficult as I once thought and I have . . . many helps; pray God I may keep humble'.[3]

The crisis of her mother's death was seven years old now: always remembered in their prayers. But this third daughter, only nine when it happened, could hardly have felt she was succeeding her mother in the sense that her elder sisters had. For her it was a matter of succeeding Lucy. She was pleased when some of the maids came up to her with mission money, 'just as if I was Lucy'. 'Which I am not', she wrote: well aware of the eight years' difference between them and their different positions in the family. When Lucy had taken charge at Hagley, the four elder brothers had all been schoolboys. Now Charles, at twenty-two, was beginning to size up his prospects of a parliamentary seat; Albert, near the end of his time at Cambridge, expected to go on and train for the priesthood, as they had always felt he would; Nevy, who had an equally firm but quite different vocation, had now left school and come out high in the army exams; and even Spencer, who was still at Eton, was two years older than his housekeeping sister. In no way then could Lavinia be said to be in charge of the elder brothers. There were still the young ones. But even here the time to move away was approaching. Arthur (twelve), the most gifted academically of all the boys, had made a good start at Eton; Bobbie – ten and the least gifted – was still at prep school, where Edward and Alfred (now eight and seven) were due to join him the following year. It was all very different from the state of emergency in which Meriel had had to take over; and things were more in train than in Lucy's day. Lavinia had no real problems at Hagley till towards the end of her five-year reign.

Her situation was strange at first: mistress of the household, yet not quite. It was she who spoke to Mackie about the garden and to Newmany or Miss Smith about the little boys; who, on occasion, helped with their lessons; went to see the village school inspected and continued with her 'district' of the poor, as ever. But, 'Was it intended for me to dine except when Papa is nearly alone?' Young enough to be still in the schoolroom yet old enough to be taken out of it if there were household things to see to: 'Yesterday I was interrupted by Papa telling me to give the servants' wages, rather awful', she told Meriel, 'but I got through with no mistakes.'[4] Lucy came home, with Fred beside her, straight from their honeymoon trip abroad; drawn through Hagley's triumphal arches in the britzka by men from the village. Fred made a speech with a lump in his throat, but full of feeling, Lavinia reported. Lucy was trembly, 'but got all right and so was received Lady Frederick

Cavendish. What a stupid account but it all feels so mad I am not quite *compos*.' It felt less mad on the Sunday evening when Lucy made tea as she always had ('I rather wonder she doesn't give orders and all the rest of it').[5] And less mad still when she rode with her brother-in-law and found him 'more worthy of the view than I should have expected, after Switzerland'. But for all that, a few days later, 'the F. Cavendishes went away'. It was a shock. 'I did indeed realise she is no longer Lucy Lyttelton.' As Lucy, bereft, had said to Meriel when she left Hagley on Johnny's arm: 'Tell John with my love this is the tug-of-war!'

It was not the tug-of-war to Lavinia; for while she missed Lucy she was soon caught up in the boys' being home and the summer holidays and riding the hunter and reading Scott. 'I am perfectly miserable at the end of *Kenilworth*, I had no idea any book could make one regularly unhappy', she wrote. Apart from her enjoyment of life at home, she was pleased at the grand new prospect of visits opened up by her sister's connection. So the pangs were rather on Lucy's side; as appears in her account of their arrival at Holker, which was to be their northern home but was not quite 'home' yet, as she admitted – being for one thing deathly quiet, with nobody there in early August but themselves, the Duke and Lady Louisa.

At Hagley summer was loud and tribal, with boys in the ascendant; enough deep voices to unbalance the singing and the place given over to rowdy games. 'What extraordinary beings the boys are!' Lavinia had observed the previous year. 'Spencer took it into his head with another boy to play fighting with *open* knives. The natural consequence was that Spencer had a most frightful gash on his hand.'[6] There is no mention of knives at Hagley but the boys struck her as 'somewhat wild' in the summer of 1864; and her brother Edward, in later years, came round to thinking how rough they had been, blaming it on an education devoid of any aesthetic content unconnected with the beauty of cricket. That they played cricket in the gallery on wet days, without regard to its Rococo mirrors or Grinling Gibbons carving, seems to bear this out. 'Of course if our mother had lived on', wrote Edward, 'the whole atmosphere would have been different.'[7] Certainly Lavinia could not have changed it; and indeed she took such things for granted, for her father himself was the initiator of the celebrated napkin fights, which even Edward recalled with joy. These were liable to break out on any occasion when Uncle Billy, the Rector, dined. After the ladies had retired and the conversation had gone on for a while, 'the Peer' with a roar would hurl his napkin, rolled to a ball, at the nearest son – to be answered by a bellow from all the boys as they joined battle against their elders. The shouting, stamping and hurling of napkins would continue until Peer and Rector escaped to the library, took up their books, and settled down as if nothing had happened.[8]

That other ritual, the Expedition, went off with its usual éclat in September 1864. They were thirteen (including Meriel, with Johnny and Edward) and went to Kenilworth, where they inspected 'everywhere mentioned by W. Scott', before a great dinner at the King's Arms, 'with such a row as never was'. A day or two later came the Bromsgrove cricket match; then the Birmingham Handel Festival for a performance of the *Messiah*; but then, 'the whole tribe of Talbots went'. 'I feel somewhat sisterless', complained Lavinia: rather misleadingly, for she had May.

May at fourteen was very likely as busy a diarist as her sister, but unluckily only those diaries relating to her early twenties survive. Which means that there is little to set against the often unfavourable comments on her made at this time by other people. She had been ten in 1860 when Lucy began her reign at Hagley and found her 'as good and sweet-tempered a child as I would wish to see'. But two years later the verdict had declined to 'May seems behaving more like a Christian'; while Lavinia smugly encoded, 'May is not so nice now she is with the boys, so bold'. In 1863 May's thirteenth birthday drew from Lucy an earnest letter about the milestone of entering one's teens; and the pleasure it gave her to feel that May was 'working more in earnest in doing right'. But she went on,

> I have been grieved about you; afraid that you were not learning to listen to conscience, or to take your faults to heart; but you have been so much better lately that I hope and believe the Great Realities are becoming indeed real to you.[9]

Though active and lively, May had never been strong. Like Lavinia she had frequent headaches; and later that summer caught scarlet fever and was nursed for weeks by Newmany in an almost empty house. The other children were sent to the Rectory till all was well – her linen burnt and rooms repapered and the place washed down with chloride of lime. The next year Granny summed up May (then fourteen), as very clever, 'but not captivating – *yet*': a fault she thought remediable by 'really good training'. But a more preoccupying question that autumn was the impending departure of Nevy.

He, having passed the army examination with flying colours the previous spring, was now filling in time while waiting to be commissioned in the Rifle Brigade. 'Nevy's turn comes the very next for actually joining', Lavinia wrote in December 1864. 'It gives one a gaunt feeling being so near.'[10] Would he even be there at Christmas? Spoken or unspoken the thought was with them, that here was the first boy leaving home. However, on the bright side, Lucy informed them, 'There is every reasons for 'agley 'all to higspect fred and Me for Xmas . . . Tell Aunt Emy that sich is the case' – and similar nonsense before concluding that this sort of thing was 'grievous rubbish for a Married Woman to write'. She was sometimes homesick. A family letter, with 'a nice odour as of a Hagley Sunday about it' was the sort of thing that could make her pine; but she was evidently very happy. 'A month of ever-deepening happiness', she had written on the honeymoon tour.

> A sort of rocking on bright waves before launching out upon new seas – which I know is never to come again; but as long as this wonderful sunshine is poured round me – I mean the great new sunshine of our love for each other – all the coming waves must look bright to me.[11]

'You suppose, I daresay,' Granny wrote for her birthday, 'that your present happiness is the greatest possible – but I trust you may find that it will still increase.'[12] Back at Holker the diary tracks it through the interstices of daily life. A Sunday reading and talking together; a dance with Fred at a local ball; the days they spent alone at Hardwick, loveliest of all the Cavendish houses – a second honeymoon, once they were clear of the special train and twenty-two servants, six horse boxes and two carriages which ducal circumstance required. Then Chatsworth. 'Coming to this stately place as my Fred's wife' was a different thing from the two shy visits she had made before.[13] Though it was here that sorrow struck: the first separation, with Fred off to London for a meeting of the Furness Railway Company (which owned the steel town, Barrow-in-Furness, source of the Duke's industrial fortune). 'He has only been gone six hours and yet I miss him grievously!' ('I hope', wrote Lyttelton, 'you will have no more of these deplorable days of widowhood.') Yet worse followed.

> 16 November: A sad day for me and a very long one. My Fred went away for three nights, and though that isn't really endless, yet it feels like a great separation, as except for one night, we have not yet been away from each other.

> 17 November: The time crawls . . . I dated a letter the 18th today, thinking two nights must have passed![14]

They went to Hagley in mid December – straight from the excitement of going over the brand-new house in Carlton House Terrace which was to be their London home. With the help of Meriel, Mrs Talbot and the builder's man they agreed the painting, chose the papers and the principal grates. With equal energy Lucy then turned to a work she had done at home since childhood: helping with the Christmas church decorations; and to talk. 'I never ran from tête-à-tête to tête-à-tête to such a degree', she wrote to Meriel. To her she admitted (for the two of them saw themselves still as guardians of the dear old home) that she had given May a sermon on showing respect to the governess and had found the little boys rather spoilt, 'by nobody looking very much after them', though she did not think they would be really the worse.[15]

Counting Fred, they were twelve at dinner. 'A regular jolly Christmas dinner with . . . snap-dragon, games and all sorts of songs', Lavinia wrote. While Lucy declared euphorically to Meriel that she had never enjoyed Christmas so much 'since the days of singing at doors and putting . . . shoes in the corner'. And the great thing was not feeling responsible, 'even as to the decorations!' Then, Christmas was above all a time for the joy of having no blanks in one's heart. 'Fred filled them all up; you know in what sense I mean.'[16] She admitted to having been anxious till she saw how well he got on with everyone, especially the boys. Unlike them, he had had a sheltered childhood, for the Duke did not care for public schools and preferred to educate his sons at home. This, and life with a reclusive father – widowed now for twenty-four years – no doubt had its effect on him. For though he had gone to Cambridge later, served in a regiment, travelled in America and shot two buffalo, Fred was quiet. 'Wonderfully quiet', Lavinia wrote in an after-Christmas account to Meriel. 'Sits . . . in a corner of the sofa reading the *Globe* or the *Leeds Mercury*.' She felt she was getting to know him better though he did not seem quite like a brother yet. As for Lucy, she was just the same, 'and tells everyone that she wants a baby!'[17]

The New Year of 1865 began very well for Lavinia and May with a visit to Holker, Lucy's favourite Cavendish house, on its lofty site above Morecambe Bay. May arrived tired out with the journey, but soon proved equal to three or four miles of good hilly walking, Lucy said. And their both being 'simple and ungrown-up' made a very favourable impression. Lavinia had looked extremely pretty; May's looks had improved, she conceded. 'I think May can look very nice in the evening.'[18]

Lavinia came home armed with a plan for reorganising the garden at Hagley, worked out with the help of Lady Louisa; and a memory of the Duke being much like her father and snoring audibly in the evening. 'Awoke to a Hagley Sunday', she wrote: with some relief, for the church near Holker had been unrestored and cluttered with galleries. May had been despatched to Brighton to stay with her great-aunt, Lady Wenlock. 'She had a bad bout of headache', Granny told Lucy, 'I try to be sanguine. At any rate, her general health will gain by Brighton and I think the *visit* will be of great use.'

> A little peep into new ways and people – a little necessity to be *very* civil, *very* grateful, *very* humble, and a little demonstrative. She will soon find that all that is necessary and I gave her a few hints.[19]

But the sad thing now was that Nevy at last had been gazetted to the Rifle Brigade. 'I need not say how *many-coloured* the news feels and is', she wrote. 'The very first step out of home duties, and into public responsibility of one of the dear eight!'[20] And a far-reaching step; for the fourth battalion was under orders for Canada later; and the prospect of that hung over them all at the first parting, when Nevy went off with his father in March to report for duty at Winchester barracks. 'Lucy may be very glad she is married and has not been here for this day', wrote Lavinia, for even Nevy had broken down; and as time drew near for his actual sailing Newmany cried whenever he was mentioned.[21]

May was confirmed on Palm Sunday. 'How one hopes that in some way Mamma may know of her eight children's Easter Communion', Lucy wrote at the end of a solemn letter. 'At all events, we must be brought nearer to her in the Communion as we are to all Saints, and to Christ their Head . . . I have just written down what has come into my head; for you see I did not mean to preach you a sermon.'[22] After Easter, the youngest boys, Edward and Alfred, went off to join Bob at the Brighton prep school, which had replaced Geddington some time ago. 'There's something very horrid', Lavinia wrote, 'seeing the very youngest leave home, and they each had a lump in their throats, poor little monkeys.' She had been having great fun with these two, now that they could ride without leading reins. 'The house feels unnatural without them.'[23] Three weeks later, a family party – her father, herself with May and Lucy – went down by train from London to see them and found them thriving and full of it all. But then the going back next term was bad. 'Alfred . . . very red eyes. Bob niobe [a personification in Glynnese terms of the weeping Niobe of Greek legend]. Edward the calmest. Poor little fellows.'

Nevy said his last goodbyes in August and went off after what Lavinia

called 'the longest morning I ever remember'. His father had gone
with him to Portsmouth to see him on board the *Himalaya*; and she
wrote sadly, 'not one of the twelve could leave a greater blank and
hole'. It was bound to be worst for Lavinia and May, 'the only *home*
sisters', Lucy acknowledged in a prompt and consoling letter. 'Dearest
pussy cats, This is for both of you . . . to do as much as may be in
cheering you up under what I know must be a real great trial.' But
how glad they should be to see Nevy launched to do his duty in a noble
profession! She recalled the special fitness of the words of the Baptism
service, where a cross is signed on the child's forehead:

> In token that he shall not be ashamed to confess the faith of Christ
> crucified, and manfully to fight under His banner against sin, the world
> and the devil; and to continue Christ's faithful soldier . . . until his life's
> end.[24]

So Nevy was absent from the Expedition that set off for Church
Stretton a few weeks later; and from the Bromsgrove Cricket Match. 'I
hope it will not take grievously out of Papa', wrote Lucy to Meriel,
admitting she was rather afraid for him. However there were no unto-
ward signs, though it may well have been by way of distraction that
Lyttelton organised a West Country holiday that autumn for Charles,
Lavinia, May, himself and his brother-in-law Sir Stephen Glynne. Off
they went, as Lavinia describes, from train to stagecoach and open fly;
often rained on; soaked in spray and mesmerised by the surf breaking;
finding inns and visiting churches; and, in true Lytteltonic style, making
up doggerel all the way across the moors from Dunster to Lynton.

> Hinx, spinx
> The butter stinks
> The cash begins to fly
> At breakfast hour
> The bread was sour
> The peggy stiff and dry
> We vainly regret
> The small store that we set
> On the words of the patriarch Punster
> Ah! trust not to Porlock
> Take time by the forelock
> And lay in your luncheon at Dunster.[25]

Their racketty progress through wild scenes was the keenest delight to
Lavinia – ready, like Lucy, to be drenched or dry, scramble on boulders,

walk to the limit or ride on the box and feel the wind. From Bude, Clovelly and Tintagel ('I can't imagine anything more glorious than the sea breaking under and against the rocks') they left with salt on their lips for London; where they took in the Lord Mayor's Show, a conjurer, a theatre and 'a quantity of shopping' before returning at length to Hagley. Christmas preparations were under way. But of this Christmas, Lavinia said, 'One misses Nevy dreadfully'.

'I cannot write on those things as Lucy can', Meriel put in a letter to Nevy which she had hoped to send before he went, but had delayed in order to get a little prayer book bound in such a way 'that you may have it always with you, and that it may not look remarkable if others happen to see it'.

> I like sending it to you, dear old boy, because every day I become more and more sure that the great safeguard, the great comfort, the great help in our way through life . . . with all its dangers, sorrows, joys and difficulties, is prayer.

She went on, 'I often think that our family is perhaps too much tempted to be self-reliant, and satisfied with having attained what is no doubt in many ways a high standard'. But if they dwelt on Christ and His Apostles, how could anyone be satisfied with their achievements? 'All this has been on my mind to say for a long time and I don't think you will mind my saying it now.' Since he left, she said, four-year-old George had been 'perfectly insane on military matters, is perpetually talking about going to Canada to be in Uncle Neville's regiment, unceasingly scribbles letters to his "Colonel"etc'.[26]

Meriel had four children now and George, the eldest, took pride of place in the little book where she jotted down details of their development.[27] He was very clever, but she worried at signs of an ungenerous nature; and also about his religious training, which she had embarked on diffidently. 'Don't have the cares too much about the teaching him, my precious old thing', Lucy had written, 'one can't but trust so much for yours and Johnny's little boy.'[28] Theirs was indeed a pious home. Johnny prepared and read a sermon to his household every Sunday, and George was but the first of their many children to be catechised at his mother's knee.

The grosser aspects of infant life were in the hands of Fuller, the nurse, who had been trained by Newmany at Hagley (and had even been taught to write by Charles) and had become attached to Mary Lyttelton before moving on to grander things. Turning her back on

Belvoir Castle to come to Meriel when George was born, she was already
a major figure with the Talbot children, and known as 'Toody'.[29]

The other important person was 'Ganma'. Mrs Talbot's home now
was Falconhurst but a bedroom and sitting room were kept for her at
10 Great George Street, and she used them often. Not just for the
pleasure of a family visit. In 1860 she had been a prime mover in
founding the Parochial Mission Women's Association: an Anglican initiative aimed at reaching the poor in London by means of the poor;
for its guiding rule was that the mission women should be *'bona fide* of
the lower class'.[30] This work brought Mrs Talbot to London, where
Meriel's dining room was called in aid for PMWA committee meetings.
Granny, whose respect for Mrs Talbot's energy and powers of organi-
sation was boundless, told Meriel that she ought to be divided in
portions, 'one to be always *there* [at Hagley] another always wherever I
am, and I suppose the rest for you'.[31] But Meriel, it seems, came round
to regretting that she had to live so much with the whole. 'Mother
always said this was a mistake', her daughter Gwendolen Stephenson
wrote much later.

> Though she was fond of her mother-in-law [the] presence of a very
> forcible character made her authority with her children difficult. Her
> self-confidence, encouraged in her own home, was, she always said,
> impaired . . . by Ganma.[32]

And her authority with servants, perhaps. For how could Meriel have
wished to hear (and, as it happened, after ten years' marriage) 'that
Ellen has not really been doing her best, and I should think it would
be quite as well that you should speak a little strongly to her'.[33] Mrs
Talbot was good in a crisis (the second baby was born so quickly that
only she and Johnny were there to assist) and most efficiently took
charge of Meriel's convalescence after a birth. But not entirely without
tension, it seems. In the fortnight after the third was born (a period
in which contemporary practice required that the mother should lie
flat and rest), a little struggle developed between them over Meriel's
wish to be allowed to read. In fact, 'with all her apparent calmness',
Mrs Talbot told Catherine Gladstone, 'she has always a strange
incapacity of lying quiet in that way without being depressed'. So it
had seemed best to let her read a little. 'I put her upon honor not to
read *continually* and amongst us we take very good care that she had
not much temptation to do so.'[34]

Such little spurts of independence apart, Meriel seems cast in a
passive role, driven by the active needs of others: of her children,

increasingly; of Johnny, who was hoping to get into Parliament; and of Edward, who consulted her on everything. Despite his interrupted school career, he had carried all before him at Oxford. In 1865 he got a First in 'Greats' ('Three cheers!' Lavinia wrote in her diary, 'Mrs Talbot will be over the moon'). He at once applied for a Studentship at Christ Church – though while the outcome hung in the balance this was to be between himself and Meriel. 'Wonderful that you have kept this from Mamma! I write assuming she is not with you. If she is you must not show her this.'[35] Edward was awarded the Studentship, and in 1866 took a First in History ('which now makes him *double* First man. He has never failed in anything', Lavinia noted). After very careful reflection he had decided to be ordained. 'I think he must turn out great', wrote Lucy: struck by 'his thoughtful, powerful mind . . . earnest reverence and deep feeling'.[36] Whether or not she perceived it then, his reverence was bolder than her own. He was exhilarated by the tone of the Stanley sermon which she found offensive: quoting to Meriel its exhortation, 'Be free, be liberal, be courageous!' Nor did he greatly seem to quail before the threat to the Oxford Movement (which had developed in his own lifetime) through prominent defections to Rome. Of course men wanted infallible truth, he reasoned in another letter to Meriel; but since God's truth was entrusted to depositories tainted by human sin and error, it would always be hard – perhaps impossible – to find it 'in brilliant and untainted clearness'. In this light he could not dismiss Anglican uncertainty as weakness.[37]

The kind of boldness reflected here is not apparent in another matter which absorbed him increasingly. He had fallen in love with Lavinia No declaration had been made, of course (Lavinia was then fifteen); nor was he so open with his mother as with Meriel, who bore the brunt of many an awkward confidence. 'I don't know when I have been so down', he wrote in January 1866, relieved that a sudden bilious attack on return from Hagley had concealed from his mother the true cause of his low spirits. 'You will not have much sympathy with my dumps [for Meriel had not undertaken to press his suit with her very young sister] but as . . . I have to bottle them up here I am glad to pour them out.' He then went on at very great length about Roman Catholic Mariolatry.[38]

'It must be no small comfort to you to have that profession . . . of a soother and comforter', Granny once told Meriel. 'It is what you are made for.'[39] Her father, who had been deprived for a year (ever since the Clarendon Commission wound up) of those opportunities to stay with her which official business in London permitted, had better prospects for 1865. He had been appointed to a new Commission, which in the first place would require his presence two days a week, he explained to Meriel, as he reserved his room in Great George Street. 'The everlasting Fates who sit in the clouds and spin have settled my doings for the next two months.'[40] They had in fact settled his remaining career.

Ever since the Clarendon Commission's report on Eton and other great public schools there had been pressure for a similar inquiry into the schooling of the middle classes. It was argued – for instance, at meetings of the Social Science Association – that the rich were all right, for steps had been taken towards reforming the schools they used; the poor were all right, for there now existed aided and inspected elementary schools; but the middle classes, the heart of the nation, largely relied on the ancient grammar schools, some hardly dusted since Tudor times, and on private schools of dubious merit. In the summer of 1864 Lyttelton and other leading members of the Social Science Association persuaded the Prime Minister to approve the appointment of a Schools Inquiry Commission to investigate middle-class schooling. This was hailed with great satisfaction at the Social Science Congress that autumn; where, among many papers debated on what the Commission should aim to do, the most novel came from Emily Davies, one of its very few women members, and the sister of the Reverend Llewelyn Davies, who was prominent in the Association. Her paper (for form's sake read by a man, for even this audience was not yet used to women appearing as public speakers) derided the superficial teaching offered in schools for *girls* of the middle classes and urged the commissioners to investigate.

> What are girls worth when their education is finished? What are they good for? . . . What is there that they care about? How are their lives filled up? What have they to talk about?[41]

Was any ideal presented to them beyond being amiable, inoffensive, always ready to please and be pleased? And could anything be more stupefying than such a view of the purpose of existence?

It seems likely that Emily Davies was the first feminist Lyttelton met – though the word feminist was not used then. Later of course she was to blaze a trail for the higher education of women by founding Girton College, Cambridge. But at this time she had just engaged in her first battle along that way. Rightly judging that tests conducted by a notable external body would be a means to raise standards in girls' schools, she had applied to Cambridge University to admit girls to the examinations which it organised for boys each year at a number of local centres (the Cambridge Locals, as they were called). The public examining of girls was unknown, but Cambridge at length was brought to agree to a private trial examination. It went off well and the question then was how to get the concession made permanent. At a special meeting, which Lyttelton chaired, it was agreed to send a memorial to the university with weighty signatures (he was able to promise Catherine Gladstone's). The point was won.

Did this new turn in his public life ever become a breakfast topic? Was he ever tempted to regale the family with some of the more bizarre objections to admitting girls to the Cambridge Locals? 'The idea almost takes one's breath away', declared the *Saturday Review*, in shock. 'The object for which girls are supposed to be brought up is that they may be married.' That all the girls who took the trial exam had behaved well and none had fainted was at least something, for opponents hinted at most dangerous mental effects – even insanity – if girls were encouraged to extensive use of their brains. 'What do *you* think of girls being examined?' Lyttelton might have asked Lavinia. For to every child at Hagley, girl or boy, it was quite a commonplace thing. Their father set them an exam each year. 'He never enquired what we had been learning,' Meriel recalled, 'but set us papers on what he considered we ought to know at our respective ages.' In retrospect, the Examination, like the Expedition or the Bromsgrove Match, had all the aura of a family treat. 'We were tremendously excited', said Meriel, 'but not the least frightened and I can well remember the scene in the study, all of us crowding in and clamouring to know what marks we had got.'

It must be said, though, that while Emily Davies looked on exams as an important step towards bringing the standard of girls' education somewhat nearer to the standard of boys', Lyttelton had scarcely thought of that. The formal education of his own children – true to the notions of his time and class – showed huge differences of cost, content and quality of teaching between the sexes. 'Cory' Johnson, the Eton tutor who had to do with the Lyttelton boys, was among the most distinguished the school had had: a classical scholar whom Lyttelton honoured with gifts of his own published translations. Not the ideal man, he explained to Meriel, to deal with idle or timid boys; but one who wrote exceptionally full and interesting reports on his pupils; had vast general knowledge, and would encourage any interest a boy had in studies outside school work. What could one say of Miss Smith, Miss Window, Miss West, Miss Merlet and the second Miss Smith in their tenure of the Hagley schoolroom? Much what Lucy actually said, after her Christmas visit to Hagley: 'Smith is not a being of a superior order whom one could lean upon or consult to any great advantage but she is an excellent good body'.[42] Granny, who had helped to appoint her, had found her churchmanship acceptable, 'her German . . . first rate, French above par and her talk quite simple and unvulgar'. Lavinia was very fond of her (as Lucy had been of the first Miss Smith). She took great pains to teach her to ride and did the same for her niece, Mabel, a girl about her own age of whom Miss Smith became unluckily the sole support, and who came to stay quite often at Hagley. From which one gathers that this poor creature, like many ladies, had come to teaching through family misfortune. Some might have better French than others, or be better pianists or better with children, but in Meriel's recollection most of those at Hagley had taken up the work because their fathers were ruined.[43] It was, after all, the only paid employment open to a lady.

Lyttelton, who had once hurried off to Eton when Johnson was ill, dismayed at the thought of his sons having a stopgap tutor, accepted the recurring deficiencies of governesses as he no doubt did the deficiencies of drains: with resignation. For what could be done? 'I go in governess matters', he told Lucy, 'by the advice of my feminine friends.' So at the beginning of 1864, when Lucy and Meriel agreed that Miss Merlet had become so disagreeable she should be got rid of, he performed his part and wrote the letter of dismissal (though 'as far as I know myself, which of course is very little, I should have no wish for it'); adding pessimistically, 'I much doubt getting another good one'. Yet even in those ill-provided days a thoughtful parent might have applied to Queen's College, Harley Street, which had been founded expressly to offer good education to the prospective governess; or have done some supplementary teaching himself. Lucy would have made an eager pupil. Even now she was 'delighted and proud' to be asked to copy out his *Samson Agonistes*, telling him, 'It always gives me the impression that I have written the Greek!' It is at least ironic that such a man, later a tower of strength to the women who were struggling to convince the public that girls deserved serious education, should have put his mind so little to the education of his own daughters. What it comes down to is that up till now he had been one of those 'thinking men' whom Emily Davies targeted. This was not a 'woman's question', she had said.

> Let me entreat thinking men to dismiss from their minds the belief
> that this is a thing with which they have no concern . . . The matter is

in their hands whether they choose it or not. So long as they thrust it aside it will not come before the mind of the nation as worthy of serious thought.[44]

And soon, she had persuaded Lyttelton to press for girls' schools to be included in the remit of the Schools Inquiry Commission – upon which, naturally, he was to serve.

'I do not admit that your education was wholly slipslop,' he wrote once to Meriel, 'as I think those old exam papers would show.' But Meriel in later life considered that she had learnt more from scouring his library in the years when she was in charge at Hagley than she had ever learnt in the schoolroom. From references in her diary at this time to reading Hume and Bacon's *Essays* and Hallam's *Middle Ages*, it seems quite likely.

In January 1866, Lavinia in her turn gave up lessons. 'My momentous birthday XVII. I walk out of the schoolroom!!!!!! Am now a creature that can have her time at her own disposal.'[45] But none the less, she did not mean to stop studying, she said. Her day seemed very full, May told Lucy, 'though I don't know exactly what she does as I am in the schoolroom mostly; she reads, practises, does Italian, German and singing . . . and is *always* at her table scribbling as you used'.[46] Later on Lavinia began to subscribe to a body called the Mutual Aid Society (which set its members essays to write), and was soon struggling with Platonism, 'with some amount of satisfaction'. Apart from 'cocked hat [formal] visits with Papa', her change of status was marked at home by her presiding at a large dinner party; and when they went to London, by her 'going grown-up to Lucy's dinner party in her own house! . . . My first *dinner* in my life', she wrote.[47] Soon after came the second, when she went with her father to a much grander one at Devonshire House. From London, there were delightful visits: to Falconhurst; to Compton Place in Sussex, where she tried sea bathing for the first time; to Oxford, with her father and Mrs Talbot, where Edward showed off all the colleges and his friends and the 'bumping' races and she had the thrill of hearing Liddon preach, standing two hours in a crowded church ('but I would have stood three or four . . . to have heard him').[48]

'How are their lives filled up?' was the question Emily Davies had dared to pose in regard to the host of middle-class schoolgirls who left the schoolroom with little behind them and nothing perceptible ahead. Lavinia, whose life these days was filled with any amount of interest, pleasure and congenial responsibility, would hardly have known what to make of that. In later years she did look critically, as Meriel had, on her education. 'All the books Papa so cares about, and the brothers, we know nothing of', she wrote in a forceful letter to May; urging her to make sure her reading was of 'the educating thorough sort'.[49] But now she revelled in having more time to follow her natural bent for music. Her first act at Hagley after long absence was usually to hire a piano in Stourbridge for assiduous daily practice; she also had a promising voice and when they were in London went for lessons to a professional, Madame Puzzi. But there was another bent – more felt than acknowledged – which brought her satisfaction: a bent for management, which seemed to come more easily to her than to either of her elder sisters. There is no sign that Lavinia worried, as Meriel did, over household books; nor that, like Lucy, she ever awoke shadowed by 'a sense of household cares'. On the contrary, one has the impression of the house ticking over while she turned her mind to adapting household arrangements to the changing needs of the family. Having already tackled the garden, she set her sights on the schoolroom now; with the idea that it could be transformed to make a new study for her father – once May (its only pupil these days) was 'out'. She also hoped to turn the morning room into a second sitting room. Having only one sitting room in winter was most inconvenient, she wrote to Meriel, 'with so many grown-up brethren'. The brothers too were in a state of transition. Charles and Albert had both left Cambridge: 'Albert *so nice* about his Third Class' (which had been a great disappointment); Charles, most creditably, having expunged his earlier indifferent performance by getting a First in the Law Tripos. 'It does one real good,' Lavinia wrote, 'and Papa is more pleased than I ever saw him.'

It was six years since Lyttelton had been troubled with any notable 'fit of the blues', though from stray remarks in his letters he evidently had not cast off grief. 'I daresay there are few of my age who feel so old in many respects', he told Catherine in July 1866, a few months after his forty-ninth birthday. 'It is partly the constitutional indolence and melancholy which I am seldom long without, tho' it has not been bad now for many years; partly my nine years' burden, which seems to grow heavier.' This sets him off on a familiar tack.

> Let no one envy the life of a widower who does not know it – its weary regrets, its vain self-reproaches for faults and misused opportunities, its loneliness, its privations! You can have no idea how fresh it all feels, and the constant longing to see Mary again.[50]

'I had lately the most strangely vivid dream', he confessed to Meriel that November, 'that Mamma was come back. She was very weak and pale; and I was holding her in my arms when I woke.'

In spite of all this, or because of it, he had got up a trip to Switzerland that autumn for Lavinia and May, himself and his brother-in-law. It was an effort, he wrote to Catherine. But Lavinia depicted him in bright high spirits: clambering to forbidden places on deck as they steamed along Lake Lucerne, chucking stones down into the valley on the descent to Chamonix and making up rhymes about other travellers, including 'the excellent Louisa Twining' (a well-known pioneer of workhouse reform) who struck them all as 'rather a quiz'. Lavinia of course was in her element: tireless, practically, in tramping the Alps (though on occasion they did resort to horses, mules or *chaises à porteur*); and quite refreshed enough on return to embark on her first visit to Chatsworth, which in its way was no less a challenge.

Lucy had been anxious about it beforehand, afraid that Lavinia with 'youthful severity' might find the Cavendishes uncongenial, 'so totally unHagley-ey as they are'.[51] And certainly on first arrival both she and Albert, who accompanied her, found them 'so excessively quiet and silent' as to be rather intimidating. However, the stiffness wore off later and Lavinia's account to Meriel from Chatsworth chiefly dwells upon Lucy herself, whom she found looking pale and thin: 'still rather on pins and needles with the Duke' and guarded in her talk when he was there. 'I do wish she could call him something, it would be so much more comfortable.' Then there was Johnson, Lucy's maid.

> She is pert to Lucy and last night when told to show a particular pattern to B.'s maid, refused flatly saying it was Lucy's duty to keep all her pretty things to herself! Of course Lucy had her own way in time but this sort of thing goes on every day. She lectures Lucy continually on the duty of being smarter than anyone else because she is the first here![52]

In the days when Lucy was in charge at Hagley, she had been bruised in her dealings with Wheeler, another intimidating lady's maid who, like Johnson, had bullied her, as well as upsetting the other servants. In the end she had nerved herself, as she did now, to dismiss the maid. But even with the infinitely greater standing of Lady Frederick Cavendish, she could not do this without much inner stress and misgiving. The dismissal of Johnson left her shivering. 'All I say and do, though it is not without prayer, seems to fail . . . with one maid after another.'[53]

Johnson was not her only worry. In two years' marriage her love had deepened to 'the feeling which is . . . like my own life to me'. But 'try as I will', she wrote to Meriel, 'I do get a little doldrummy when disappointments that shall be nameless recur'.[54] Visiting the infant school at Chatsworth, the bright little faces set her longing. 'Two pretty baptisms' in St Paul's were enough to bring tears to her eyes, 'so foolishly did I long to see a baby of our own christened'.[55] Meriel, now delivered of five, would have stopped '*very* willingly' at four, she knew; and would have been satisfied to have no children, 'which is all but inconceivable to me'.[56] For the dropping in on Meriel's nursery was one of her treats in London life. Anything so charming as the fifth little Talbot 'in a state of incessant springiness and kick' could not be imagined, she told her father (another impressionable baby-lover). And beyond the bounds of that happy spot, in places unimaginably less appealing, little children always went to her heart – as with the 'bright-eyed little pussy girl of five' whose plate she carried home from a poor people's dinner to a crowded tenement, for fear she should drop it. 'I felt ashamed of myself, coming back to this big house where there is not even one little baby to take up room.'[57]

In London now she involved herself, in the wake of Mrs Talbot and Catherine Gladstone, in a whole range of charity work: reading to patients at the London Hospital, where her aunt had done Trojan service during the cholera epidemic; regular weekly workhouse visits; dashing off to Limehouse to pour out tea at some 'do' for the Parochial Mission Women; shopping for crockery and utensils for Catherine's new convalescent home. There was much rushing between two worlds – for London naturally enmeshed her in dinners, concerts, balls and *politicums* (Fred had been elected as one of the Members for the West Riding in 1865). And then, the current year, 1867, was to see Lavinia and May's first Season.

'You are aware,' their father had written to Meriel in November 1866, 'that May is out after January.' She would not actually be seventeen for another three months but her first ball was local and she enjoyed it tremendously. 'Danced every time, except of course the valses. I found it rather heart-rending', she told Lucy, 'watching the twirling couples, knowing that I could valse; however my resolution is unbroken as to ever doing it. At least I think it is.' (Lavinia had walzed the previous year at her own first ball; but only with Charles.) It felt odd, she said, not having the schoolroom.

I enjoy the freedom greatly, but miss the good Miss Smith very much,

and the comfortable lounging places in the arm chair where we were
often to be seen in the last days gossiping endlessly.[58]

She was now Lavinia's regular companion, though naturally, as elder,
Lavinia answered whenever answers had to be given. And it was not
long before that happened. 'Papa says you were "much displeased" at
our going alone to the Foster luncheon,' Lavinia wrote to Meriel in
March, 'but I really don't think we could have done otherwise.'

> When Mrs F. asked us she said there would be no gentlemen whatever,
> not even Mr Foster and sons – so that Albert could not come – and we
> only met Mrs Hemming besides Mrs F. and her two daughters. It was
> to hear Miss F. play and sing and vice versa but perhaps we ought to
> have had Albert or Charles only they would have been such fishes out
> of water.[59]

While the informality of Hagley life and a superabundance of brothers
masked the extent to which the girls were chaperoned, clearly there
was a strict sense of propriety; with Meriel still, to an extent, in charge.
Lucy saw herself in the same position. 'I have always a painful sense of
responsibility when I come home', she wrote from Hagley to Meriel,
not long after the Foster episode, 'feeling that I ought to have nice
little talks and do good little deeds to each brother and sister. You
have the same feeling, I know'. She had seen a good deal of the two
girls. 'Lavinia does get nicer and nicer . . . and she has a brightness
about her now which she used not to have.'[60]

Lavinia's future was becoming a matter of pleasant speculation, given
that Edward Talbot's hopes, though undeclared, were now an open
secret. 'The two dear people', Lucy said, 'are certain to be guided right,
whatever happens.' May, on the other hand, she found 'a strange,
excitable uncontrolled old creature'.

> Gets carried away into noise as if she was a regular child, but is a most
> developed woman all the same. She is quite nice to talk to; only I am
> certainly impressed with the necessity of doing it with judgment!

Unfortunately, Lavinia and May had no Season in 1867 after all, since
Lavinia fell ill with peritonitis almost as soon as they came to London.
In November however they went to Coniston, to stay with relatives, the
Marshalls. But this did not turn out very well. 'How I should like to
have a talk with you . . . about the horrid Coniston business', Lavinia
wrote to Meriel.

I can't but think you are a little hard on May tho' I know she has been wrong in some ways – particularly in those nasty horrid confidences to and from Julia and in never feeling there could have been anything *not nice* in what has happened.[61]

So what had happened? Lavinia says only that May had been attracted by Jim Marshall and had been told by his sister Julia that he was similarly drawn to her. 'To be told outright that one was liked – what could May have done ?' she protests. It was the kind of thing that could not be unsaid, 'and I don't see what May could have done'. All the same, Lavinia did not feel easy. 'Perhaps there was something wrong in her manner that Julia could have told her such a thing . . . I wish so much that we had never gone to Coniston.' May quite clearly did not wish that. Was 'wonderfully un-shy', and dwelt on it. 'I don't understand her thinking so very much about a thing that has existed so very short a time.' And Jim, though 'taking', was an ordinary young man; 'not at all clever or what one would imagine May would be satisfied with'.

Meriel said it would all blow over. What she said of May we have no idea. Only it could never have been what Lucy had remarked of Lavinia after her successful Chatsworth début: 'I would trust her discretion and ladylikeness and sense of what is proper to the end of the world.'[62]

# 8

# *Courting*

'I can never depend on my spirits.'

Lord Lyttelton to Lucy, 1 December 1867

Meriel, the arbiter in such matters, was alleged by Aunt Emy to endorse her view that Lavinia and May led a giddy life with too much pleasure and excitement in it. The question arose because Lyttelton planned a five-month absence to visit New Zealand, starting in December 1867, and was busy canvassing views (in consultation with his elder daughters, Regan and Goneril, as he sometimes called them) on the family's situation while he was gone. It was nearly twenty years since he had become involved in launching the Canterbury Association. That body had been wound up in 1852 but the colony was there and he had long hoped to see it. 'One of my small passports to immortality is that the harbour town . . . has been named Lyttelton', he told an interested audience at Hagley. Through the *Lyttelton Times*, which was sent to him in England, and constant correspondence with Canterbury friends, he kept abreast of the settlement's progress. Now it seemed a moment to make the voyage which he had been pressed to undertake. It was also time that his fourth son, Spencer, should visit the estate bequeathed to him at the age of nine in the Canterbury Colony by Earl Spencer, his great uncle. 'At some future day he may be seen in loose clothing and with a tanned face', his father joked, 'meditating on scabby sheep and in a state of wool-gathering wealth exceeding that of any of his family'.[1] Spencer would soon be twenty-one.

Lyttelton's qualms about the trip itself centred on the prospect of sea-sickness and the fact that there would be no clergyman on board to celebrate either Christmas or Easter. But he had a great deal to do beforehand, including settling the vexed question of where the family should live in his absence. Aunty Pussy had generously offered to have them all for December and January; and Lavinia hoped he was going to accept. But, she told Meriel, 'Papa can't bear the idea of us being scattered at Christmas'. He also could not bear to settle the question without hearing everyone's point of view. 'If it is to be done, do it; if not, don't!' Aunt Henrietta had shrilled at them on another occasion, exasperated by the Hagley tendency to seek some kind of collective will. Lyttelton spoke to Charles and Albert and Nevy (back in England) about their plans; he wrote at enormous length to Meriel and took soundings from his younger daughters; from his mother; and from his sister, Aunt Coque, who hinted that the Gladstone cousins wrangled and did not think the children should be there too long – while his sister-in-law Emy opposed the idea so far as Lavinia and May were concerned, thinking they already had too much fun. '[She] wants a little more dulness for them', Lyttelton told Meriel. But *he* did not.

> They had no London season and no autumn excursion and have only slept out of this house once or twice since July. They . . . had one or two balls, the Coniston visit and the Church Congress.

He dismissed her view that when the boys were home in the holidays, even home life became more hectic than was desirable for Lavinia and May. 'I do not think it can . . . be called dissipation when it is only their own brothers.'[2]

A move to Hawarden, as Catherine stressed, would enable them to make economies by closing Hagley Hall for a time during the period he was away. Lyttelton was not keen on that. Would the saving be enough, he wondered, to warrant the upset to people's feelings. On the whole, as he told Meriel, he did not think economy should settle the question. Yet he complained that things were bad, sometimes hinting that a time might come when they would have to give up Hagley, sometimes saying he was hardened to it. 'I have been so used to moneylessness . . . that it is become to me like fire to the salamander or skinning to the cat', he wrote at one stage to Lucy.[3] But nearer the time of parting he told her, 'my spirits flag continually; and . . . any pleasure I might have in the excursion . . . is pretty near destroyed by the anxious state in which I leave my affairs'. One thing seems clear: he was never willing to economise at the boys' expense. 'Concerning Charles,' he had written to Catherine two years earlier,

> I have no great dislike to the old-fashioned notion that the eldest son should not have a profession and that he should see a little of the world before getting into Parliament. He does not lead an idle life here and

I cannot grudge him the athletic sports and exercises in which he so much excels.[4]

He had also been gratified by Charles's decision, after a poor showing in his first degree, to stay on at Cambridge and take the Law Tripos (and was over the moon when he got a First). Now, in the autumn of 1867, he told Gladstone that Charles was seriously thinking about his parliamentary prospects ('with a general adhesion to the Liberal side and to your leadership'). There might soon be a seat; in which case it would be hard on him if his father could not help with election expenses. It all came down to the uncertain prospect of developing a new seam of coal.

If the mineral speculation on my estate were absolutely hopeless, I doubt if I ought even to incur any risk; but that cannot be said, as I believe the tenant is sinking *lower*, which I cannot but believe to be the most hopeful plan.[5]

On 2 December 1867 Lavinia recorded in her diary: 'Today has seen one of our greatest family events – the starting of Papa and Spencer to New Zealand – at 11.30 they were off and I liked to think of them sailing down the Channel in this clear frosty weather'. 'Ah! this is Black Monday', wrote Granny to May on that same date. 'I can't think of it otherwise.' Charles had gone to Southampton with his father and brother. 'A pleasure which I don't envy him, for of all farewells, I think the most dismal is the watching a ship departing, till you see nothing but the blank horizon.' Still, the travellers had left in good heart. 'George so busy to the last', she wrote.

He had had an enormous amount to do. Up and down to London, as he told Lucy – and annoyed because the final report of the Schools Inquiry Commission on which he had served for the past three years was not yet finished, as had been planned. 'So I must sign in anticipation, which I can do as . . . the substance of it is pretty well settled.' In regard to the estate and the family, 'I took leave of all the people at Hagley; called on many of them, wrote very affectionate letters to the more distant ones and had up . . . the chief servants'.[6] He had written twelve pages of instructions for Charles ('in whom I have every confidence'), and had been to see the children in their various outposts: Albert, who was doing admirably at Cuddesdon theological college; Nevy, grumbling in the Chichester barracks because of the slowness of promotion; Arthur and Bob 'in great force' at Eton; Edward and Alfred in their last term at prep school. 'Rejoicing with trembling', as Lucy once put it, he admitted 'there is really not one of the twelve whom I have to tell that I wish them to do otherwise than as they are doing.' 'My last act here will be to write out the *Eton* prayer for Edward and Alfred whom Charles takes to Eton next month.'

He had already settled county matters. 'I have got a very competent Vice Lieutenant.' But, until he went, there was always the chance that he might be prevented from going by some Fenian outrage, he said: a not unreasonable speculation in a year when these forerunners of the IRA had attacked police barracks and tried to seize Chester. Ten days after Lyttelton sailed an attempt was made to blow up Clerkenwell Gaol that killed twelve people and injured a hundred. 'We are all over England in such a state that one is frightened by anything unusual', wrote Granny.

Christmas at Hawarden passed off pleasantly though it was not like being at home. They practised glees for the Entertainment but the audience was ill-behaved; 'unlike ours', Lavinia said. Nor did she esteem very highly the Gladstone style of church decoration – nailing holly leaves onto texts. They had a sociable time, however: danced and rode and sang with the cousins and like all guests were initiated into Uncle William's woodcutting craze. In quieter moments Lavinia researched and wrote an essay on the Indian Mutiny, set by the Mutual Aid Society as the assignment for December, and sent off letters into the void. For it was a void – until 12 January when cheerful news came from Panama. 'The horrid silence is broken at last.'

After Christmas there was more debate about how long they should stay at Hawarden. The Gladstones thought (and they *both* felt this, Lavinia was at pains to stress) that it would be a pity not to take advantage of the present opportunity to cut expenses. If they went with the Gladstones to London, Hagley could remain closed till Easter. Meriel did not approve of this. For one thing, she was anxious that they should do nothing in their father's absence which he might not like; and for another, these planned economies seemed to anticipate permanent changes in the home regime. 'I don't think Aunty Pussy's plan involves this', wrote Lavinia, 'I think what she wants is for Papa to see that we *can* get on living much more cheaply.'[7]

She herself felt painfully divided. For her own part, when they did go home, she would be glad, she said, to live more quietly, 'if you still think we can do nothing more positive in the old Dad's absence'. But as for the date, 'I find it difficult to take your side'. Though she was eager to get back to Hagley, if they went to London they *would* save

money. Probably not much; but, 'I don't see why this should be an
argument against doing one's very utmost'.

> Even without further dismissal of servants, I suppose not opening Hagley
> till Easter, entailing the absence of the March brewing – and having
> no horses on corn, would gain something. I know these are small
> particulars but I can't but feel strongly that almost anything – any
> amount of screwing would be worth while rather than leave Hagley,
> which is so terrible a prospect and means so much when one thinks
> about it.[8]

In the end they came home in February and were at once caught up
with a concert. 'We certainly think of and speak of nothing but glees,
quartets, duetts', she told Lucy. '*Nothing* whatever is alluded to but who
would be the best tenor . . . etc'. But like a good housewife, she had
worked out economies – down to saving on the library fire.

> We are being as stingy as we can, tho' it sometimes feels little use doing
> anything. The three peggies and footman are sent off some months
> longer, and Shirtliffe and Herbert, by dint of much speaking to, *know*
> how much we want them to be un-extravagent.[9]

'Days much alike – [now the concert was over] quiet mornings –
reading – singing – drawing and Italian; afternoon pottering about the
village.' Lucy sent news on 3 March that Lady Louisa (Fred's sister,
married the previous year) had just given birth to her first baby. ('If
only Lucy would follow suit.') They had still heard nothing at all from
New Zealand, though the travellers were surely on their way back now.
'One does long to know something about it.' But 30 March 1868 was
destined to be the red-letter day when they had a charming long screed
from Spencer.

> They . . . are interested and amused by the Colony which is . . . giving
> them a worthy reception – public dinners, balls etc . . . Spencer has
> played cricket and got 104 runs bowling 7 wickets in one innings![10]

Next day, arriving on his fifty-first birthday, came another letter – from
their father to Granny; whose delight matched her apprehension that
the 'anxiety which must belong to any sea voyage was not over yet'.

Easter carried them well into April. 'You will have a real quiet Holy
Week . . . I wonder when we shall all grow old enough to be quiet for
one week', wrote Lavinia to Meriel. Though she said the boys were
being very *good* – 'if only they would turn into girls sometimes!' When
at last they read the announcement of the date the ship had left Panama

they knew to expect it by the end of the month. So now it was a question of sitting tight; though Lavinia herself was very busy – struggling to complete the essay on 'Novels' which had been her April assignment, acting as riding mistress to Alfred ('and very pleasant it is', she wrote), coping with poor old, frail old Elly: still housekeeper, but so ill with flu that nothing would ease her at this time but last farewells and the sacrament. She did not die; but for the first time Lavinia had to do the Clothing Club on her own.

Spencer arrived on the 29th with news that his father would come next day. So next day Hagley was all *en fête*. 'Walked about, looking at various preparations . . . flags . . . bonfire . . . schoolchildren with banners and flowers and a whole crowd of people in the park.'[11] The train arrived punctually at 4.25. 'But the actual arrival of Papa in the britzka and post horses at full gallop was a most exciting well-managed thing and produced much éclat.' He was brown – and thinner – and in rousing spirits. Spoke from the perron with his family round him; then the crowd dispersed amid cheers and firing. The next day, Lavinia wrote, they all fell back into the old ways. 'Papa reading prayers – coming through the morning room – and going to sleep opposite Granny in the evening.' Quaintly, that night she forgot he was home 'and was glad to awake to the fact of his being lord and master again'.[12]

But three days later, a different story: 'Papa in low spirits'. The dark depression which he had escaped for the past eight years came upon him as they settled in London for the beginning of the season: he at Granny's in Stratton Street, Lavinia and May to stay with Lucy in anticipation of the Drawing Room and all the pleasures they had missed last summer. They knew he had serious money worries but Lavinia at least was not convinced that his attack was due to that. 'I think it is an illness', she notes in the diary, 'which one can only hope will soon pass off.' Much as he told his sister, Aunt Coque, that there was no point in calling the doctor. It had done no good in the past. 'This will go off.' Yet he sought reassurance. 'Asked me so simply, like his old self, "You think I shall get over it ?"' 'Hope I shall not be sent away. People think that does me good. It's no sort of use. What I want is to have people about me.' '[Meriel] always does me good.' But it was hard to see enough of her.[13]

He was terribly afraid of sleeplessness; and a good night's rest always seemed to signal a glimpse of light at the end of the tunnel. 'Your Father has had (by his own account) the best night's sleep he has had for a long time', Granny reported at the end of May. But it was not till the end of June that Lavinia wrote with confidence, 'Papa *entirely* himself again'. Luckily, the great thing for her and May – being presented at the Queen's Drawing Room – was in any case Lucy's affair (and in fact turned out disappointing, for the Queen left early and in the end they had to curtsey to lesser royalties). Their father put on his uniform to take them to the Queen's Ball a few days later, which was as regal as they could have wished; and the rest of that month they were all caught up in the news of Charles's electioneering. For owing to the recent death of Lord Calthorpe, his chance of East Worcestershire (the seat vacated by Calthorpe's son on succeeding to the title), had come at last. Or so they hoped. Though it soon appeared that the slipping into it would not be easy; for, contrary to their expectations, the seat was contested and expenses grew – it was costing a fortune, Lavinia wrote. Fred went to Hagley to speak for Charles, and her father went down in time for the count, while those of them in London hung on, waiting. Charles won. 'Wrote to my MP brother.' Six thousand pounds had been spent, she said; but there were hopes of its being subscribed by the Liberal interest.

Meanwhile the Season swept them on at a pace that would have concerned Aunt Emy. Though she still worked on the monthly essay required by the Mutual Aid Society, and homely duties were not squeezed out (Lavinia took a Sunday School class and did workhouse visits with Lucy in London), all such things were drops in an ocean of almost continuous entertainment. Not every ball received the accolade 'danced every time and enjoyed life'; but dancing was a delight to her. And Handel (glorious at the Crystal Palace), and the Opera ('could have cried when it ended'). Yet there was often so much done that one thing trod on the heels of another. Thus, Lord Dudley, who had kindly asked them to join his party for the Crystal Palace, laid on such an elaborate luncheon that they arrived too late for *Saul*. The pace was frantic.

> June 24: Papa read a lecture on N. Zealand. Afterwards rushed off to hear the Tyrolese singers at Ly James'. Charles and Spencer dined, and then went to Devonshire H. where there was a most pleasant party. Very sorry to come away but had to go w. Meriel to Ld Stanley's party at the Foreign Office. Foreign Office most splendid, well worth going. Then on w. Meriel to Ly Belper's ball where stayed only a short time. Have done enough today.[14]

'And so ends the long looked for 1st London season', runs Lavinia's diary in mid July. The journey back had been sweltering. 'Never was so glad to get home.' 'Delightful Hagley Sunday again . . . Dawdled round the park in the Sunday fashion', though the park itself was yellow with drought and her father was trying to find some means of getting water to the villages. Before she went away Lavinia had tackled the painful business of persuading Elly that it was really time to retire, and now she was much relieved to find that Elly seemed to have accepted this. 'Will I hope end her days peacefully here – much looked after by all of us and [by] Jane Brown' (a village woman whom she had installed for this purpose).[15] As to the element of economy, Shirtliffe, the cook, was now cook-housekeeper; and doing famously, she wrote to Meriel.

> Is evidently liked by the peggies and has done wonders in the way of cleaning. She and I get on. We troll for ever over the Co-operative stores and all sorts of household concerns. John makes a capital steady footman. With him and the beloved William Turner, I trust the man department is likewise turning over a new leaf. I can but hope that the house is altogether on a better footing and that we shall get on as in the halcyon days of Clarke and Elly long ago.[16]

It was not, however, in Lavinia's power by careful management to put the house on a better footing in a major sense, as she was more than half aware; though she would surely have been dismayed to have seen her father's dispirited account of money troubles that August to Gladstone – written at a time when he seemed to her to be 'in great force and spirits' again. He speaks of mortgage debts to be paid and more or less admits that the hope of finding new coal seams is unrealistic. 'As these mines are the only thing I have been relying on for thirty years, it must needs be a great embarrassment if they ultimately fail.' Bleakly he surveyed the options: letting the unlet part of the park, which he would not mind, ('but I much dislike the dismissing old labourers and gardeners'). Letting the house (but 'one must live somewhere and with such a family as mine it would hardly do to live only in London').

> To *sell* this place, which would fetch a fancy price, would no doubt make me a rich man and could be done with Charles' concurrence – but I hope he would not give it. Charles may not impossibly find some suitable lady with a tolerable fortune . . . but I have told him that I hope he will never 'marry for money' in the ordinary sense.

At the end he mentioned the unlikely prospect of an interest in the Althorp estate. The present Earl Spencer, he says, is childless; his sister, unmarried; there are two young children (the Earl's half-brother and half-sister). 'Failing issue from all these, it comes to me or my descendants. I wonder what is the worth (if it could be sold) of such a reversion?'[17]

In contrast, Lavinia's diary depicts the pleasant round of a Hagley summer: the Eton brothers home for the holidays ('Bob in Tails – what are we come to!'); her father presenting the school prizes at the school feast with its 'astonishing amount of beef and plum pudding, games, races etc.'; late August and the harvest home, with a dance in the barn, where, in spite of heat ('not to say *smell*'), they all danced vigorously. Meriel's children ('the Trots') arrived, requiring a good deal of entertaining and, in the case of the two eldest, regular lessons from Lavinia and May. Then with September came the Bromsgrove Match and the Expedition – this year to the Wrekin.

Edward Talbot participated in these last two important activities – happening to be there, as he often was: reading aloud to them, discussing Pusey, joining in the family's favourite walk – in the moonlight to the top of Clent Hill, to gaze at the distant furnaces. 'Edward very worthy of it', she comments. He was installed these days at Christ Church in the grand new rooms which Lavinia noted when they had lunched there a few months earlier en route for London to begin the Season. He appeared in town from time to time and joined their party – coming up from Oxford on one occasion specially for a ball where she did not expect him. For all that, nothing in the diary suggests that she wanted him to be anything more than the 'old shoe' which he had been for years.

That *he* wanted more was now well known. With all the intercourse of Lytteltons, Talbots, Gladstones and their liking for gossip, there had never been much chance of keeping secret the feelings he had once tried to hide from his mother. Granny, for one, had hopes of a match which she felt would be a blessing to dear little Win.

> The beginning of as happy and blest a life as could be granted. How could anyone who loved her feel otherwise, knowing him as we do. But the favorable termination has not yet come, and must be doubtful and at best, *so distant*![18]

Meriel still refused to be partisan: offering Edward her sympathy as always but no injudicious encouragement. 'You pray, my dear old Meriel, for both of us, don't you? If not quite in the sense which I would wish.'[19]

A very close friend of his, Arthur Acland, who had helped him to entertain the Lytteltons in Oxford, had fallen in love with Lavinia too. And who could say what else might occur in the autumn of 1868? She was off in October with her father and May to Lanhydrock and Orchard Neville; in November, to Chatsworth, in December to Hawarden – where the ball this year went off, she said, with immense *éclat*: 'room pretty and partners plentiful. Danced with all the gentlemen, I think, and enjoyed life'. But as she told Meriel, there is generally a cloud over even such jolly times. Her father was once again 'very low'. 'It is terribly disappointing coming again so soon.'

> One has ceased to try and explain it away by finding a cause . . . For we are all very prosperous and I do not know of any particular anxiety . . . It does make one rather wretched, one can but hope and pray it will pass off soon.

At least, it was *nothing* like so bad as in the spring: 'no restlessness or anything of that sort; and so very likely it will only last a short time and then we shall be all right again'.[20]

So far as one can tell, it did pass more briefly than his bout on return from New Zealand. From the Hawarden festivities in early December they went on to the overheated, over-luxurious Witley Court, home of Lord Dudley, where the company included the Princess Royal and her husband the German Crown Prince, the Duke and Duchess d'Aumale and 'hangers-on to the Royalties'. 'Greatly pressed to walze . . . Enjoyed life much', Lavinia wrote; and it seems unlikely that she could have enjoyed it quite so much if her father had been struggling. From Witley, Lyttelton wrote to Meriel, 'I have not been comfortable since I was at Falconhurst and it is rather disheartening; but it gets no worse and I rub on somehow'.[21] He gave the same sort of account to Lucy, towards the end of a jocular letter describing how 'Miss Win tomahawked her second victim and has got his scalp hanging at her sash. It is poor little Stumpy Acland'. For Edward's friend (who was extremely short) had actually proposed to Lavinia at Hawarden and she had felt obliged to turn him down. A few days later Lyttelton wrote again to Meriel, 'I think I am rather better on the whole, but I am puzzled and muddled, and vacillate almost from minute to minute'.[22] Which might have set her thinking, if she had not already, of his telling her in mid November – well before he and Lavinia and May had embarked on the social round which wound up at Witley – that he had just met an attractive young widow, 'whom I think you know something of'.

> She was born Clive, and left childless and very rich by her unhappy husband, young Humphry Mildmay, who died raving mad after some dreadful months for her and every one else.[23]

This seems to have been the first appearance of Sybella Mildmay on the Lyttelton scene. Meriel may not have been the only person, even at that stage, who was in the know (for though in many ways so reserved, her father was inclined to spread his secrets widely), but she had always been the daughter with whom Lyttelton felt most at ease. With a characteristic mixture of jocularity and misgiving he wrote near Christmas, mostly curious as to the chances of Lavinia being serious over Edward Talbot; then winding up with his own 'troubles'.

> I get on pretty well, and am seldom bad above half the day or so: and in the intervals I forget mostly about it. It gives me a strange apprehension of all that is coming, and repugnance to undertake anything; but I *do* go on as usual and it is better to do so.

He slept well, he said, which in one way was puzzling, 'as I lose the only clue I used to have as to what was likely to happen'. Whether the thought of Sybella Mildmay raised or depressed his volatile spirits at this time is by no means clear.

> In my own judgment such a vision as I have lately had before me would be a very good thing for me: but it is all dark and doubtful.[24]

On Christmas Eve he wrote again to Meriel, surrounded by the family ('all in great force'). 'We all wish you the happiest Xmas and New Year, in your new career' (presumably as an MP's wife, for Johnny, after previous failures, had got in, at the recent General Election). But the letter ends:

> As far as one may form such specific wishes, I do trust I may never live to see any of my children in widowhood – the heaviest sorrow and burden, apart from anything sinful, that is laid on man.[25]

One feature of what Lyttelton himself described as his 'queer mental constitution' was that, whatever his ups and downs, he usually managed to drive himself through an immense amount of work: and 1868 had been no exception. After his depression on return from New Zealand (which had lasted from April to June), he had quickly picked up the threads again. It was he who gave the opening address at the Social Science Congress that autumn – taking as his theme the Report – now published – of the Schools Inquiry Commission. Based on highly critical accounts by a young team of Assistant Commissioners, this revealed how neglect, incompetence – even corruption – had gnawed away at England's venerable grammar schools. Teaching was often bad, buildings squalid, many had sunk to elementary school level; some were empty (while the master continued to draw a salary from the endowment). These endowments – the individual legacies of countless benefactors over centuries – stood revealed as a wasting heritage, calling out for reform to make them the basis of an efficient system of secondary schooling for the present day. Fundamental reorganisation was what the Commissioners recommended; and what Lyttelton defended strongly.

Clearly his experience on the Commission had drawn him into a new crusade. At present, he told them, school endowment was lying crushed beneath a mass of 'stupidity, ignorance and maladministration', from which it could certainly not be freed if they were to continue guided by the wills of a host of long-dead founders. What they should be guided by, he insisted (like the *hodiest* he claimed to be), was not the literal will of a founder who had lived in a very different age, but what he would have thought if he were living now. The obligation on posterity ('supposed obligation' was what he said) 'ought not to be . . . necessarily binding . . . when it conflicts with . . . the best public use to which the property might be put'. He topped all this with the call to arms of Arthur Hobhouse, the radical lawyer: 'Property is not the property of the dead, but of the living'.

Nothing, in fact, in the whole Report was more alien to founders' wishes than the proposal that *girls* should be given some share in endowments for education. It had fallen to Lyttelton (who after all had been prominent in the struggle for their admission to examinations) to write the chapter which dealt with girls' schools: a task he had achieved with a whimsical flourish :

> Births: At 21 Carlton Terrace on July 11th, after a painful and protracted labour, Lord Lyttelton of a chapter on Girls' Schools. Friends at a distance will be glad to hear that this long-expected event has taken place & that parent and child are charming well.
>
> The Infant Chapter has a strong likeness in features and deportment to its parent. It is uproarious – squalls incessantly – and hopes to make much noise in the world.[26]

He liked noise, if the cause were good. A local critic, some years before – angry at his telling a Birmingham audience that their schools for the poor were the worst in England – accused him of being provocative. 'You made the statement deliberately, intending to give pain, which you believed wholesome.' Now the Infant Chapter conveyed a view of

schools which catered for middle-class girls that was far from flattering
to middle-class parents. The weight of the Commission supported the
charge made by Emily Davies and others that such parents were largely
indifferent to serious teaching for their daughters, though quite ready
to pay through the nose to have them instructed in the social graces;
and on the evidence, most schoolmistresses, themselves deficient in
education, were far too ignorant to make good teachers. Girls had
probably the same capacity to learn as boys, the Commission accepted,
and their exclusion from endowment was 'felt by a large and increasing
number, both of men and women, to be a cruel injustice'.

Lyttelton's speech to the Social Science Congress places him emphatic-
ally among that number. If nothing else comes of the Inquiry, he said,
he hoped for substantial rectification

> of one of the grossest instances of injustice – one of the most unrighteous
> deprivations, that can be mentioned: that of . . . the whole female sex
> of England, for a very long time past, of any benefit from the ancient
> educational endowments of the country.[27]

He closed his speech with the case of Christ's Hospital, which was a
gift for any reformer: for this celebrated Tudor foundation, endowed
for both sexes, was now providing for something over 1200 children,
of which no more than eighteen were girls. What he could not have
anticipated then was that he himself would become the man charged
with righting such ancient wrongs: that before Christmas a General
Election would have swept the Liberals to power with a majority that
opened prospects of radical change, and that some of these would
concern education.

In Lavinia's diary this historic election – the one that first made her
uncle Prime Minister – appears as rather a family affair. The family
Conservative, Johnny Talbot, to her great delight got in for West Kent.
The family Liberals had their ups and downs. Charles, who had begun
his canvass in August, got in again for East Worcestershire and Willy
Gladstone was returned for Whitby. The family Radical, to Lucy's joy,
was again successful in the West Riding. But his elder brother, the
Marquis of Hartington – a prominent Liberal politician – lost the seat
he had held for years; his younger brother Lord Edward failed, while
Gladstone himself lost South-West Lancashire, though he was sub-
sequently comfortably returned for Greenwich. 'Uncle William is getting
on very quickly with his Cabinet', Lavinia noted on 10 December; while
Granny, who called that day on the Gladstones at No. 11 Carlton House
Terrace, was amused to find that the entrance hall looked 'so Prime

Ministerial already   suitors and applicants, and messengers standing
or sitting about, instead of the well-known footman'.

> Your dear auntie was at home and I am happy to say much better,
> lumbago gone off and her spirits cheered. She is rather bored by the
> universal congrats – every body supposing she must be in unmingled
> delight – when in fact some anxious feelings she *must* have![28]

Lucy and Fred, who were rather low over Tory strength in the counties
that had led to the Cavendish disappointments, were restored by a
Hagley Christmas: to her as always a tremendous pleasure, 'especially
now that it is rare to have one's dear old eight complete'. She sent
Meriel a panegyric:

> Charles, Albert and Nevy are always very dear. Nevy I love better and
> better and Albert's immense development since Cuddesdon makes one
> feel that if the Bishop of Oxford had never done anything but Cuddesdon
> he would deserve everlasting gratitude.[29]

She thought Spencer much nicer since the trip to New Zealand. 'Arthur
is delightful, and my old Bob . . . is to my mind *greatly* improved, much
less stolid-looking, and . . . sensible to talk to. Edward is *silentissimus*
but his darling brown face is a pleasure to look at and "my tutor's"
letter raves of him.' Alfred, she concluded, was bewitching and apparently without a fault. As for the sisters, Lavinia had lately gained much
credit in Lucy's eyes for her tactful and modest handling of little Stumpy
Acland's proposal. 'May always shows least well in a houseful of mankind
but she is far less carried away than she was.'

The New Year made Lyttelton a Privy Councillor, which he was rather
taken with. 'I shall henceforth expect . . . different manners towards
me than any one has ever yet shown', he told Meriel. And in reference
to his private hopes, 'I am . . . well, but rather in a bubble and fidget'.
Another person in a bubble and fidget was Edward Talbot, whose letters
to Meriel early in 1869 show all the stress of an anxious lover – if
anything, more stressed after Acland's failure. Under such headings as
'Don't let this lie about, even in your own room!' he wrote at length
about blunders made through his having gossiped to the Gladstones,
his inhibitions when he meets Lavinia and the excitement which made
him flush so that she herself noticed how pink he looked. 'It quite
grieves me to see her worried so and to feel myself the cause . . . Oh
if she could but see her way to the remedy which would turn it all (DV)
into such happiness!' He tried to fix his mind on higher things. 'But

one learns, in presence of a strong desire, that the trust which implies readiness to take cheerfully either of two alternatives is . . . hard . . . to learn.'[30]

Lavinia recorded her January birthday ('I have turned my back on my dear teens'); the quietness of the house now the boys have gone; country balls, where she noted 'the phenomenon' of her father's dancing the Lancers (though she says that he mostly stood still), music, reading, and housewifely pleasure that, through Fred's kindness, plate glass windows had been fitted in the library and dining room. 'So the house is to be made fine on the verge of ruin,' was how Lyttelton put it to Meriel, 'like the victim decked with garlands.'[31]

Lyttelton's courtship continued. In March he told her, 'I think it is a little more probable than not'. The engagement was announced in April, though Meriel, Lucy and Charles at least had known for some time that it was in the offing and he was touched by the affection they showed. 'From my general temperament . . . you will not wonder that I am all ups and downs,' he told Lucy 'but not in the deep sense of the love of those around me, and the trust that it will be repaid to all of you a hundredfold.'[32]

It was not, of course, as simple as that. In fact, they had to put a brave face on it. 'There has been no managing or interference,' writes Lucy characteristically, 'and so one can rest in the certainty that it is God's hand that has led dear Papa to this "evening-time light".'[33] 'Papa . . . most happy,' Lavinia noted, 'and she seems to be almost perfect – only I have never actually seen her . . .' Later she added candidly that people were being 'very kind and nice to us about it, for *thankful* though we may be, it is not a matter for congratulation'.[34] Meriel was calm, in her usual way; so calm that even Edward Talbot was at first deceived. He was not himself particularly pleased with this new development; though as he told her, he could not help hoping that the changes it would bring to Hagley might make her wish a little bit 'for that which I wish for so greatly'. 'I know now how much you need sympathy about it, and my sympathy is almost too ready. But . . . there will be a bright side, after the first effort.'[35]

They glimpsed it a little when they met Sybella. Lavinia and Lucy both enlarge on the hideous shyness of this encounter ('even more awful for her than for us!') which took place at Meriel's house.

> She is not in the least pretty, and looks older than she is [thirty-three] but . . . has a dear good face, and nice, steadfast-looking kind eyes; a very sweet voice, and a manner at once dignified and gentle.[36]

She had met Lavinia and May first, alone: 'begged them to think of her as a sister and to call her Sybella; and to tell her everything Papa liked'. 'I am glad it has been done', Lavinia wrote, 'it don't seem now so thoroughly unreal.'[37]

They had a real enough task ahead: breaking it to 'the dear old eight' – or at least the seven who did not know – their father evidently assuming that they would sort this out for him. Spencer just then was on a visit to Rome, on the strength of his New Zealand money. Nevy, from Dublin (where he had been posted as Aide-de-Camp to their cousin, Earl Spencer, who had just been made Lord Lieutenant of Ireland) wrote that one could hardly avoid a *frisson* at the thought of the coming change. Meriel and Lucy went together to Cuddesdon Theological College where Albert was in the final stages of preparing for his ordination. Though his father had written to him, he was 'so unprepared and bewildered', says Lucy, 'that I am very glad we went'. Then there was the quartet at Eton, utterly in the dark so far. If she wrote to them, her father told Lucy, 'I hope you will be a little careful and particularly not lump them all together, for . . . there are great differences between them'. In the end Lavinia went to see them, with Charles. 'They were all great dears . . . and seem now to like it, though at first they were greatly startled.'[38] Arthur, the eldest, had found it hardest. Arthur in fact (now seventeen) poured his heart out the following week in a letter to his cousin Mary Gladstone, saying he was only just getting over 'the hurly-burly I was in when I first heard'. 'The advantages and the comfort it will be to Papa . . . outweigh every other consideration.' But the thought of going home to a much-changed Hagley 'knocked me down very nearly, and made [me] as unhappy as possible at first'.[39]

Prompted by some talk with his sister about the feelings of his elder daughters, Lyttelton wrote Meriel one of those long letters, as carefully worked as an official minute, in which he liked to explain his views to what he called 'the turbulent oligarchy'. 'She said you doubted if I was aware that this event was a trial to you and Lucy. But . . . no one has said more strongly than I have . . . of late years, that it *would* be a trial to all around me . . . to the children in particular, to the elder children above all.' And he understood that when his children told him – as she had especially – not to worry about that, it was simply out of unselfishness.

He did not try to gloss over the fact that his interest and theirs could not be the same.

For these long years there has been at Hagley . . . a *vacant* place . . .

an ever-aching void, a maimedness, a dull pain of a wound that heals not. Very seldom, perhaps never, as I believe, do the orphan *children* feel any wish . . . that that void should be supplied to *them* by such a step as I am to take. I think that . . . it is an essential difference as to lives between them and their father.

'I cannot but admit that I expect to feel soon a *return* towards past times . . . an undoing of change rather than a change, but I cannot suppose others to feel that.' At Hagley at least, 'except my daughters no longer being at the *head* of household affairs, I desire . . . there should be *absolutely no change at all*. And I am well-assured Sybella wishes the same'. Nothing could be further from his mind, for instance, than that they should feel shy of talking of the Record. And did she imagine he had ever thought of moving the *picture* from its present place?

Some people felt a new love could not coexist with 'undiminished . . . tenderness . . . towards her who is gone, and shining among the distant stars'. But while it was not for him to deny that he had conceived 'a great affection', he insisted that 'no shadow of change, no faint beginning even of forgetfulness . . . has passed over me these five months'.

What I have written may seem . . . hard to be understood by the young and happy. But . . . when the smooth course of domestic happiness has been violently checked and diverted, strange growths will come in . . . it is among the marks of our fall, and to a great extent the struggling effort of nature to repair the irreparable.[40]

They were married quietly on 10 June at the bride's home, Perrystone, near Ross-on-Wye (Meriel and Johnny representing the family). Lyttelton wrote to Lucy that day, 'I have entered on my new, or rather . . . my renewed life. I feel an intense confidence in Sybella'.[41]

# 9

## *Inevitable Change*

'Like you I have the thought of inevitable
change constantly present to me.'

Lucy to Lord Lyttelton, 7 September 1874

Though overshadowed by the central drama, there were other plots, other hopes that spring. Edward Talbot still looked to Meriel to help him interpret Lavinia's behaviour. When she wrote a note which need not have been written, did this mean that she was warming towards him – 'consciously or unconsciously'? 'Or that my behaviour satisfied her that I had put off . . . any serious thoughts of winning her?' One satisfaction he had, by now: that Meriel at last was entirely behind him. 'It was rather a trial to me to feel that you used to help me only from kindness. And I confess I used sometimes to wonder how you could give the help . . . without the wish, or how I could care for it so much knowing that it did not go deeper.'[1] As for Lavinia, he had no idea. Nor is her diary at all revealing: turning largely on the coming change – which was 'heart-pinchy' as Lucy said, for the two sisters left at home. 'It can't but be sad . . . just now', wrote Lavinia, brooding on the beauty of a Hagley spring almost as if that too were threatened. 'I have the last day-ums dreadfully.' She was also extremely busy. The household had to be rearranged; things were being moved now and carpets measured on a scale not seen since the Coming of Age. Her father was determined to have his study next to Sybella's sitting room, but the ante-room in question was too small for the easel on which Mary's picture stood. 'I suggested him putting it over the chimneypiece, viewing good light and being close to his table . . . I am getting moidered with the room-ums', she wrote, in these last days of her five-year reign.[2]

To May, whose nineteenth birthday occurred in the thick of these preoccupations, Granny wrote sympathetically:

I daily wish and pray for all good things for you. But *this* time I have even more of such feelings. There will be many little and some great trials, in this great change, *to all*. But I hopefully believe, *much* good to your Father and all belonging to him. The event has not been brought on by *any of us*, that's a great comfort. It is *sent*. And sent as a blessing and a good; and also, as all blessings are, this is *a trial*; and looking at it so, it must be a subject of deep thankfulness, earnest prayer and cheerful courage and hope.[3]

Most likely, May had a different kind of hope; for she had recently made the acquaintance of Edward Denison, a gifted young man who had just made his parliamentary début in the Liberal interest as MP for Newark, and their friendship, by the end of the Season, seems to have developed to a point where he was perceived as a suitor. Lucy in June 1869 describes a ball where she and Meriel shared the duties of chaperons. 'Fearful was the squeeze,' her diary notes, 'numerous the unknown maukins. But dear old Edward Talbot hovered about us, and while hooking me to the carriage, asked me what hopes I thought there were for him. I could not tell him!' (Though she knew, no doubt, that he was on the brink of big decisions, having been asked almost out of the blue to become head of the new college being built at Oxford in memory of John Keble, who had died three years before.)

Meanwhile Mr Denison was sitting and talking the evening through with May! Old Meriel and I superintended all this and had reminiscences of our last ball in this house, when Auntie P. told M. she must make up her mind as to Johnny and his marked attentions![4]

'Home in a state of mind', she wrote: but not, most probably, an anxious one; for Mr Denison's was not the kind of suit to revive doubts about May's judgement.

His father had been Bishop of Salisbury, but both his parents had died in his childhood and from fourteen he had been brought up by his uncle and guardian John Evelyn Denison, who was Speaker of the House of Commons. Though not yet thirty, Edward Denison had made some mark as a social reformer, especially by the pains he took to involve himself with the London poor. That his acquaintance with the East End was not just a matter of soup kitchens but of living there for many months; that he had built and endowed a school there in which he himself took Bible classes and gave lectures to working men, could only have appealed to Hagley interests and to that undirected zeal which one feels conscious of in May. 'How I longed to be a man!' she had once burst out, having listened, from the Ladies' Gallery, to an 'abominably flippant' speech in the University Tests debate. 'My blood boiled, but to what purpose?'[5] Denison was talented, enthusiastic, and in a hurry to get things done. 'I think it is no use living over seventy-five,' he wrote to a friend once, 'or if you have a weakness for round numbers, say eighty.' A week or so after the famous ball he and May were engaged. He was much in love. 'Poor E. Denison wrote me a letter which since the days of Ovid has not been exceeded', wrote Lyttelton to Billy at the end of June.[6]

But even by that time things had gone wrong. The Speaker, like some malevolent fairy, to everyone's astonishment raised objections. 'He has written to me very civilly . . . expressing much respect for all of us (*you* in particular),' her father told Lucy, 'and saying he has no objection to May . . . but what his objection *is* he does not hint, only saying that he had no idea that E.D. was thinking of "such a thing", which I construe to mean marriage generally.' At this time Lyttelton was still on his honeymoon and felt remote from the scene of action. Also indignant. For he took some pride in the independence he allowed his own children.

> I never heard of Meriel's engagement, or the possibility, till she announced it. Nor should I ever object to anyone marrying anyone, except on some moral or social ground, which is not alleged in this case. I should never dream of obstructing a marriage on the grounds that I had not been consulted and that the acqaintance had been too short.[7]

The Speaker's unexplained objection seemed to him a wanton giving of pain, 'as much as a boy torturing a fly'. The couple were not to communicate and no *terminus ad quem* was set. He worried about the effect on May, which he thought Lucy dismissed too lightly – and with too much regard for appearances.

> I have the utmost doubt of her bearing up cheerfully. Nor do I see how she can avoid 'suspense' and substitute some other state of mind for it. Whether it be called an 'engagement' seems little more than a question of words.

'When Damon and Phyllis are violently in love', he said, himself only two weeks married, 'I consider they *are* engaged, whatever we may please to call it.'

'So I hear you are both going to marry two Edwards', the Queen remarked to Lavinia and May at a Royal Breakfast that summer – ignorant, it seems, of the sudden cloud that had checked the happiness of one of the pair.[8] As for the other, that long story had by this time come to a head, for Edward Talbot had proposed to Lavinia the day after the ball and had been accepted. This was only accomplished, however, after much anguished consultation with ball-weary Meriel in the small hours. 'He goes into Meriel's dressing room', Lyttelton told Billy (for he found it hilarious),

> makes her sit down to talk to him and comfort him, *& lay on the floor with his head on her lap* (like Samson and Delilah) moaning and groaning. At last the infuriated John rushed out, about 4 a. m. and asked Meriel if she was coming to bed. This from a grown Oxford Don and Head designate of Keble College![9]

'Our dear old Ed. turned up after breakfast bringing me a note from M.', wrote Lucy, 'telling me to leave them together.'

> I . . . took off Aunt Coque into our little back room and we waited in desperate excitement. At the end of half an hour or so we could bear ourselves no longer and walked into the drawing room. There sat the couple . . . Darling Win, all her doubts and scruples gone into air and the tide of true love rushing into her little heart and he, the suspense of four years crowned at last with joy.[10]

Lavinia's diary account is brief. Edward, she says, had come to tell her that he had been elected to the Wardenship of Keble College, Oxford. 'And after talking a good bit on this, he said so tremblingly "would I like to come and help him" and I said *yes*.'

If she gave much thought to the life ahead, Lavinia's 'yes' might be rated 'blowing'. For this new college with its High Church ethos was most certainly a bold venture. At this stage nobody was sure if sufficient funding could be raised; and, even if it could, whether such a graft onto medieval Oxford would 'take' or not. Evidently, much would depend on the Warden. And as to that, it was hardly auspicious that Dr Pusey, the grand old man and icon, almost, of the Oxford Movement, had set his heart on appointing Liddon. Dr Liddon, whose renown was such that whenever he preached it was necessary to come hours early to get a seat, had been entreated to take the post and steadily refused: he felt, it seems, that he lacked the intellectual stature for it. A man who was much better equipped to put the college on the map at Oxford, he suggested, was Edward Talbot. So Edward was to take on an institution whose Anglican ethos, while pleasing some at a time when Oxford was under pressure to abolish religious tests, would most certainly frighten others who felt it went a good deal too near Rome. Many of all kinds would be opposed – if only for the reason that no new college had been founded at Oxford for 200 years.

Such anxieties seem far from Lavinia, writing a blissful letter to Meriel that July from Penmaenmawr, where she and May had gone on holiday together with Edward and Mrs Talbot.

> I hope it won't make me selfish and disinclined for home life and duties to be passing now through such a radiantly happy time . . . So much time for realizing one's own feelings besides the deep satisfaction I have, more and more, of getting to know Edward better and better.[11]

'I don't mind writing this to you . . .', she said, 'you can understand more than anyone what reason I have for such happiness, and I may feel sure of your prayers that I may not misuse it now or at any time.' Edward wrote to Meriel about his own happiness: saying it would help him to watch without grief 'the dear old Hagley of the past' give way to a new one, pleasant but different ('and, however we may enjoy ourselves there, having no halo like the old one'). He spoke of their reading *In Memoriam* in little nooks on the Welsh rocks and of Lavinia coming up from the sea 'looking pretty and rosy with all her hair flyng'. The trip had been 'almost honeymoonlike . . . in the constant intercourse Mrs T. and May were so kind in allowing us'. May was very brave, 'and . . . I think rewarded by enjoying herself very fairly'. Lavinia had written much the same:

> May is getting on famously on the whole tho' of course she has ups and downs. And she is very good and unselfish in always taking interest in what goes on, and in bearing her trial so well.[12]

Much sympathy had been expressed for May. A hostile verdict was passed in some quarters on the elderly Speaker for his behaviour and it was thought that friends might persuade him that the couple were seriously attached to each other. When one of these friends – Lord Taunton – died, Lucy half fancied this personal sorrow might soften Speaker Denison a little. But then she heard that young Mr Denison meant to go ahead with a plan made earlier to visit America with Sir Michael Hicks-Beach. This seemed to offer a breathing space and she wrote to tell him that he should not hesitate for fear of what any of them might think. 'We thought it would be right for him to go.'

May wrote cheerfully enough to Lucy when they returned from Penmaenmawr to plunge straight into the 'new' Hagley. 'It will amuse you to be met at the station by a barouche and pair. Drop a tear for the old britzka which has been sold for £5, poor old thing.' And not only that.

> Sybella brought with her a little chestnut about Toddy's size . . . and it is the delight of Edward and Alfred to ride about together on Toddy and Gilly . . . they have never been able to ride together till now and it is a great event.

'I am *very* fond of Sybella', she writes. 'I never saw anyone more devoted than Sybella is to Papa . . . She tells me things of her former life that make me shiver to think of, and make one so glad that she has come into smooth sunny water at last.' The boys were quite at their ease with her. She was teaching Bob Euclid and she and May were reading Mill's *Political Economy* together.[13]

Apart from this, May's account runs on through Hagley's usual summer events: the Flower Show, the family Expedition (which had been arranged this year for Ludlow) and the eagerly awaited visit of Meriel, Johnny and the five children. 'We are now in the full swing of Midsummer holidays . . . I am teaching Alfred music, and Lavinia does Edward's and I read aloud to them *David Copperfield*; it reminds me of the time when you read it on Saturday half holidays to Lavinia and me.'

Of Mr Denison's going to America, May said only, 'I think it is a good plan and . . . have partly got over the first feeling of dismay . . . I rub on very well and feel thankful and happy at the many bright things I have to think about'. Edward Talbot said the thing about the new-style Hagley was how well they got on with Sybella. This he thought due to Lavinia and May's generous-hearted acceptance of her, and to Sybella's open nature. 'One not only likes her but she is loveable.' And not only loveable. 'Sybella bids fair to introduce to Hagley what Mrs T. has long wished to see: more activity and variety of pursuits.'[14] In later years it was Edward Lyttelton who paid tribute to the greatly needed civilising influence of Sybella at Hagley.

> We became aware that there were such things as flowers . . . She was artistic, could talk three or four foreign languages, had a great gift for furnishing, and so by degrees lifted and enlarged the Hagley mind, which was in some respects uncultivated.[15]

She also, by enlisting the help of Charles (who was after all to inherit the house), stopped cricket being played in the long gallery. But she was tentative at first. 'Inviting us all to ride rough-shod over her', as

Lucy put it; though she says they tried 'to keep her on her proper pinnacle'.[16]

'If I was to guess what would jar you most', Edward Talbot wrote to Meriel of the newly-wed couple, 'it would be the semi-lover-like way of keeping near each other, walking tête-à-tête etc'.

> But the great thing that helps one over that is sympathy with her intense affection and admiration for him, and the sight of his placidity and content. We laugh at her for her quidgets about him, fitting him out with sandwiches for his journey, and such things.[17]

The journey in question had been to London, for Lyttelton had taken another appointment. Gladstone's dynamic Liberal government had lost no time in promoting a Bill for an Endowed Schools Commission with the drastic powers needed to reform the grammar schools. In June, he had invited his brother-in-law to become chief Endowed Schools Commissioner. To which, not surprisingly, Lyttelton replied that he had only just got married and did not seek commitments away from home. Besides, he argued that this new body, set up to introduce the controversial changes recommended by the Schools Inquiry Commission, should not consist of men like himself, who had been involved in that Inquiry and could hardly be thought unbiased.

> It seems to me essential that the new Commissioners should set about their numerous and very delicate negotiations with minds unfettered . . . I therefore regret that I must decline what I should feel as a false . . . position.[18]

But Gladstone persuaded him to take it; and there was one obvious advantage: money. On the day he accepted Gladstone's offer, which happened to be Meriel's twenty-ninth birthday, he promised her a better present than usual, 'for . . . I am to be First Commissioner at £1500 a year'. Lyttelton had often enough complained that the long and tedious hours he spent on Royal Commissions were unpaid. To the Lord President he had once joked that any Commissioner with more than ten children should get help from the Secret Service Fund. A sense, perhaps, of having fallen short of what had once been expected of him made him flippant about Royal Commissions. But this was different: not a Royal Commission but a body with executive power, an offshoot of that political world which he had sampled long ago as Under Secretary of State for the Colonies. Not that he aspired to politics now. And as he once told Gladstone, a lifetime spent 'in the tepid atmosphere of the House of Lords make[s] me a very poor partizan'.[19]

As to party politics this was true. But as to moral questions it was not; and by now the reform of endowments had become for him a moral question (as it was to his fellow Commissioners, Arthur Hobhouse, the radical lawyer, and the more temperate Canon Hugh Robinson, who had formerly been principal of the teacher training college in York). Before the official work even started, Lyttelton had thrown down the gauntlet at a Social Science meeting in July. The Endowed Schools Act, he announced – too frankly – laid stern duties on its three Commissioners; and as a result, in many cases, 'the "pious founder" would go to the wall'. This sent shivers through the House of Lords, some of whose members took an active interest in the grander City foundations. The Duke of Cambridge (a Royal Duke and President of the Governors of Christ's Hospital) declared that his faith in Lyttelton's honesty only increased his apprehension. So it had not begun very well.

Edward Talbot had different fears: claiming to have seen 'sufficient signs', though the Commission had barely met, that Lyttelton would find it all too much and risk another bout of depression – were it not, indeed, for Sybella. Poor Sybella and her sandwiches! And poor Sybella who May considered had come to 'smooth sunny water at last'. For in spite of her loving care the heavy cloud descended again early in September 1869. Lavinia describes the day to Meriel as one of the most dismal she had ever spent. They had tried the much-loved walk up Clent Hill but he had been 'beyond anything low', and Sybella miserable, naturally: 'coming to us at six thoroughly upset'. It chanced that some of her own relations were expected to dine that night, and she dreaded what might get back to her mother. 'This fear oppressed her enormously – it has however thank God passed off.' For he managed well enough before the guests; the effort seemed to be good for him. 'And today . . . he has got better and better.' In the afternoon he had gone to Saltey where Sybella had laid a foundation stone at the teacher training college and he had made speeches and was sociable and pleasant.

> I am nearly certain he is *quite* himself – full of fun and not in the least sentimental. Of course one can't be quite sure just yet, but I think one can judge pretty well . . . Dear much-enduring Sybella is radiant; and tho' prepared for a return tomorrow . . . will not mind it again in the same way.[20]

But he was not himself, alas. The illness teased them as it always had.

'Papa bad', she has to write next day. Though a week or so later Granny told Lucy, 'Your dear Father and his excellent wife, after many sleepless nights and rather miserable days, have recovered'.[21] She could hear Sybella singing next door. And he was well enough to go with Lavinia to Edward's ordination as a deacon.

'I wished you were there', wrote Lavinia to May, joyously describing how Edward had looked, how she was taken out of herself into that great body of prayer and how the four hour service did not seem tiring. She had also been to Oxford to see the rooms which she and Edward were to occupy when he took up his post at Keble. Now she was staying at Falconhurst. 'I really do feel selfish enjoying the quiet and should so like to think of you having some. Your letter was a cheery one, poor dear soul.'[22]

But May had less than ever to be cheery about. Denison's American trip was off; for he was ill, had seen two doctors, both of whom diagnosed consumption, and they were waiting to hear the verdict of a leading man, Dr Andrew Clark, Physician at the London Hospital. It proved damning. Mr Denison's lungs were injured beyond complete repair. 'My poor dearest May, I think I can realise better than anyone what this is to you – my heart yearns towards you. I so understand the feeling astray and objectless.'

May, she thought, was right to insist on seeing the copy of Clark's report which had been forwarded to Hagley. Though if the prognosis were very bad, 'I think even you, you poor dear, would see that Papa could do nothing but have it finally broken off'.

> The *only* comfort must be in dwelling on the higher greater Love, which so surely supports you . . . and it is this no doubt which so good and great a mind as Mr Denison's can in some measure feel . . . I think if you were less sure of his real and almost remarkable goodness, all this would be harder to bear.[23]

But what May said she found hard to bear was the thought of his being ill and lonely. She was cut off from contact with him. Lucy wrote to him but May could not; and it was to her father that Denison wrote to give the gist of Clark's verdict. 'I feel almost entirely hopeless about it', May admitted in early October, 'and live on . . . in a sort of unnatural state, laughing and talking as much as other people, with that weary, hopeless heartache always there.'[24]

The atmosphere at Hagley at this time was lowering. There was concern about Granny's health. Lyttelton was not yet in the clear and Lavinia urged May to try and stop Sybella talking to him so much about it 'It surely has become exaggerated . . . by so much discussion and sympathy.'[25] Perhaps it had, for as late as November Edward found Hagley's conversation dwelt on 'the Peer's health and Denison's prospects'. Sybella could talk of nothing else. They too had seen Dr Andrew Clark, who took the view that Lord Lyttelton's trouble had its origins in the digestion. He recommended exercise and a careful diet, and thought the Commission work no bad thing (seconding Lyttelton's own intention, which was, at all costs, to carry on). None the less Clark held out no hope of the depression not recurring.

Lavinia, when she returned to Hagley, found him cheerful enough at meals. And Sybella, who bore the brunt of his woes, was coping better, she wrote to Meriel: going to bed 'long before Papa as the only real chance of sleep she has is before he comes and after he gets up'. Then, May was wonderful, showing no signs of what she was going through, in public. But when they talked it was worrying to find how much she seemed to console herself with thoughts of an eternal 'widowhood'.

> Supposing, as she does, that they can never marry, the idea of ever thinking of anybody else is not only distasteful to her, as it naturally would be, but wrong. This is her greatest comfort, the thought she most likes thinking of. I don't say it will not be so. But it would be well if she did not 'legislate' so much for the future – it is all too dim to settle what may or may not be.[26]

To May the death blow had been dealt in the words 'mischief possibly arrested but not curable', Lavinia told Meriel. 'She has hardly taken it in yet; my heart bleeds for her. Turn where you will her future is dim and sorrowful, but one must have trust and faith more strongly.' May at least, said Lucy, had the comfort of knowing that, unlike the first obstacles to her happiness, '*this* grief . . . is straight from the Hand of God'.[27]

A long sea voyage being one of the things which Clark recommended to arrest the disease, Edward Denison sailed for Melbourne on 25 October 1869. He was quite alone and they had no news beyond a message on Boxing Day from a relative of his in Sierra Leone saying he was fairly well and comfortable. It seems to have cheered May up a little. 'None of us talk much to her about it.' She had gone on bravely through the Christmas period, 'not noticeable in any way for lowness', wrote Lavinia. Though her state of mind was not easy to judge, 'because she is so different with me, and to my eyes, even when outwardly cheerful, is unlike what I see others think her. This is a trying time to her; chiefly because it had once been Xmas which was to have brought Mr Denison back from America and been the time for a fresh appeal to the Speaker.'

May now looked 'very blankly' ahead. And Lavinia did not feel it wise to mention her own Edward's name too much, though 'I know she will like his coming when once here'. She does not seem to have liked it especially, and there were moments when Lavinia herself, 'finding it so hard to give her any comfort' felt her own happiness affected. Yet she was touched by May's warmth towards her.

> I suppose neither of us would ever have found out how fond we were of each other, but for the joy shared and then all this trouble. I see a great deal of her; mercifully Sybella is so placid and comfortable with Papa.[28]

*They* were very happy: Sybella now pregnant, and clearly overjoyed, in spite of sickness. Indeed, it was only Sybella's joy and the fact that this new development was 'so entirely of God's ordering' that reconciled Lavinia to it at all. It seemed, she told Meriel, 'to arouse old feelings only a few months ago about the whole thing'.[29] Meriel, in fact, was also pregnant – with her sixth child; but far from thrilled. Her sisters were delighted, and Lucy tried to provoke a more spirited response. 'I have meant to write my condolences, but . . . it is not in human nature to look upon the prospect as a pure calamity when one thinks as I do that the world will be all the better for multiplied Meriels and Johnnys!'[30] Meriel hated being pregnant, however, and had put off for as long as possible disclosing it to her mother-in-law. 'Didn't I know', wrote Edward sympathetically, 'that having written to me that you couldn't make the effort of telling Mrs T. you would . . . tell her within a few hours!'

> You and she get on better I think than if you had told her earlier; and you have got over a very great piece of the time, which is, I suppose, pleasant to you to think of as you are brave about the confinement.[31]

Unluckily Meriel, though she jotted down the drolleries of their infant life, seems not to have felt – or at least, to have shown – the spontaneous delight in her growing brood which was so marked in her own mother. She was not 'pre-eminently maternal', her literary daughter, Gwendolen Stephenson, came to decide in later years: and an extremely diffident person behind the orderly self-control. 'Dear old blessing, never mind', said Lucy. 'It is God's will and He *means* every child to be an everlasting joy to its parents.' But those few glimpses of Meriel and family which

come through to us rather suggest an indomitable anxiousness; and a
retreat. She was conscientious over the children's religious training but
otherwise often took a back seat. 'She never wished to choose our clothes
in childhood or take us to parties', her daughter wrote. Nor romp
about with them, evidently; for even the eldest (George was born when
she was barely twenty-two) could never remember having seen her run.
Meriel kept the many letters her mother had written through her own
childhood but it was Johnny who wrote most to 'the Trots' and 'made
little festivals of family happenings'.[32]

So in Great George Street there was a need to be filled; and it was
filled to overflowing by Harriet Fuller, the children's nurse, who had
come to them in the first instance out of regard for Mary Lyttelton
and became their idolised, trusted and passionately adoring 'Toody'.
'It is impossible', wrote Lady Stephenson, 'to describe the delight of
her companionship': adding that their devotion to Toody (towards
which, she made clear, Meriel showed 'a beautiful magnaminity') spoiled
their childhood relation to their mother. Gwendolen Stephenson gives
her view that between such forces as 'Toody' and 'Ganma' Meriel lost
a good deal of the confidence she had developed in charge of Hagley.[33]
Johnny (although his daughter recalls him as more the backbone of
their home than Meriel) very probably did little to boost it; for, to
judge by his letters to her whenever he had to be away from home, he
was also lacking in confidence. In Talbot circles it may well have been
Edward – confident (for all that he begged advice) and already on the
way to becoming an outstandingly pastoral Bishop – who did most to
encourage Meriel. He was only twenty-five and not yet ordained when
she asked him in July 1869 whether she should venture on the experi-
ment of attending a religious retreat, and there are other letters which
show that she turned to him for spiritual advice.

'It is the thought of the endless interest which belongs to the gift of
children that makes it most hard for me to bear the want of them',
Lucy admitted to her pregnant sister, 'yet I can understand how it
should be the main cause of your opposite feelings.'[34] Whether Meriel
was ever able to make a similar mental leap, who knows? The previous
year, 1868, Lucy had told her of a bleak disappointment .

> I was a day later than I had ever been for three years and after struggling
> hard not to be sanguine had just let myself begin building castles-in-
> the-air. I could not sleep for excitement! And then crash went all the
> hopes.[35]

'You can never know what a blow and pain it is at the time, and this time I can't get over it as soon as usual.' She had taken the waters that year at Ems; and in 1869 went to Kissingen, another German spa, where as well as being pickled, as she said, in salt water, she was ordered sessions in a curious gas bath where the gas, for some reason, never got through. 'It is such a quiz, sitting in all one's clothes in a converted tub, like the old woman who lived in a shoe, with a difference!' she wrote to Lavinia.[36] Lavinia's judgement in later life was that this 'difference' (which Lucy dismissed now as 'one little cloud in my great heaven of blue') came at length to be her deepest sorrow. She faced it, though, as she faced all sorrows, with a sense of being held in the hand of God. And on this question Granny assured her:

> You have shown by your patience and submission that all fit and Christian thoughts on the subject are ready in your mind and none need be suggested. May you be enabled still to wait, and to accept whatever is sent . . . as it seemeth best to your Heavenly Father.[37]

In the autumn of 1869 Granny, whose health was giving rise to concern, went to live permanently at Hagley. 'It *will* be a great change', Lavinia admitted, 'and in some ways a very sad one, but one forgets that most people at eighty-two are apt to remain almost entirely in one place.' Granny herself took it realistically and wherever possible with humour. 'It does not tire me to write', she told Lucy; saying she was not 'inconveniently weak', although unable to go to church, which made Sundays rather unpleasant. Apart from that, though, her strength was kept up 'by such quantities of wine and brandy as I am ashamed to think of'.[38] There was one great blessing: 'your Father . . . sleeps well, and the megrim cloud has faded away'. Edward wrote to Meriel a few weeks later of a very contented chat with her, 'her interest keen and her manner bright . . . She talked of her own state, treating herself as near to death . . . but not closely so'.

Christmas seemed to give her a shot in the arm, for she wrote an energetic letter to Meriel about the delightful crowd there had been; and as vigorously to Lucy in February, hoping that she would find a post for 'a little pet of mine, Emma Smith' who was then employed as maid-of-all-work 'in a *very* hard place . . . with *very* poor wages'. By March, though, Sarah could only dictate her blessings for Meriel's new baby, Jack; yet she still enjoyed a good conversation, discussing Motley's *Dutch Republic* clearly and ranging in these last days over every one of them, full of love and interest, as she always had been. 'Last night', Lucy wrote to her father, she spoke of you with intense feeling that almost overcame her and made her voice tremble. 'The one I love best in all the world – tell him all about me . . .' And of Sybella, 'Tell her what a comfort it is to me to know she is *what* she is and *where* she is'.[39]

Granny's condition had not been such as to have prevented Lavinia and May from going to London in February (though May was much depressed at the thought) and that is where they were in March 1870 when it was reported that Edward Denison had died on arrival in Australia. 'One of the most promising young men of the day lost to a country that could ill spare him', declared the *Times*. And lost for so long while May still hoped, for he had died in January. 'My old May . . . God grant you His Help day by day and hour by hour', wrote Lucy. At Hagley Lavinia dreaded the moment when May saw Granny – who felt so much for her that it seemed likely to make things worse.

> But it was very quiet. 'Much tried very good May' she repeated. She thinks she has been so brave; likes dwelling on her sight of Mr Denison – on his goodness, on the certainty that it will have raised May's standard for ever, that it will beautifully chasten and refine her.[40]

Granny died at last on 14 April; after some restless, painful bouts which were pitiful, Lucy said, writing to Meriel who was still convalescent. 'Papa leant over . . . holding her right hand, Aunt Coque . . . on the other side . . . held her left hand. Uncle Spencer stood near . . . Uncle Billy read the Commendatory Prayer and the Blessing.' 'Oh it is such a sad . . . feeling I have of hardly knowing what to pray for!' she had told Aunt Emy previously.

> It can hardly be right to ask for longer life when such great age is reached . . . and yet one's love clings as much as ever to the dear dear life which has all through one's own life been such a precious possession among us all.

'And to me especially it is terribly sad to feel all hope of any little child of ours seeing Granny fade quite away.'[41]

'The poor old past time – how *all gone* it is!' Lucy wrote to May and Lavinia on 23 April 1870. Dear old Elly, who had housekept at Hagley long before any of them were born, had just died; a week after Granny. And Lavinia was soon to be married. But *what* a past it had been, she added, fresh from rereading Granny's letters. On 20 April May embarked on a new volume of her diary. Of the volumes that went before, we know nothing, for none survive. Looking back on the last, May wrote, made her dread what the year might bring.

She sought comfort in reading letters Edward Denison had written to a friend, who kindly copied them out for her. That apart, she found it hard to settle. She had started reading *The Woman in White* and Wilberforce on *The Incarnation*, but 'my thoughts are rebellious'. And she felt the weight of the prospect of Hagley without Lavinia.

> May 1   Lavinia's last Sunday here unmarried, a day full of pathos and sadness . . . Glad to get to bed out of the way of thinking and feeling.

> May 4   Going back [to London] will be terrible. I am clinging desperately to these poor last days.

> May 6   . . . impossible to realise that Lavinia and I shall never be here again in the dear old way.[42]

Lavinia had her own pangs, of course. That last Sunday walk with the boys. 'Sad most sad day in many ways.' 'Began the packing up; visited the gentry.' 'My last Club day.' ' Visiting poor people.' 'She has so many roots in this place, and among her own people', Edward had written to Meriel some months before, 'that all this . . . with the . . . pain of leaving May desolate, will make the parting . . . a great wrench.'[43] All the same, Lavinia was growing impatient. 'I am getting tired of saying goodbye to him!' Her future was rapidly taking shape in the 'pretty little rooms' at Keble College which she and Edward were to inhabit and which she went to inspect with May on their way to London – with an eye to furnishing.

May reached London feeling 'dazed and blue', after a journey which exhausted her – and with such a headache as seems to have excused her from going with Lavinia and Mrs Talbot to look at sofas and Turkey carpets. 'That atrocious London!' Apart from riding, there was little that pleased her: certainly not 'the eternal drive' which set the pattern of their afternoons; nor her twentieth birthday – 'rather wretched, in spite of . . . Ascension Day thoughts and services'. One relief was the safe delivery, soon after they arrived, of Sybella's baby, putting an end to the dreadful worry they had felt since Granny's funeral day, when there had been alarming signs that Sybella was about to give birth prematurely. 'A girl, I am thankful to say', wrote May (presumably feeling that a boy might have threatened the interests of 'the dear old eight'). 'She is my god-child, poor little mite.' The baby, Sarah, was christened by Edward on 15 June, and soon whisked off to the country by Sybella while London roasted in a terrible heatwave. Sybella's going reminded Lavinia that

she would never again be with her '*en qualité* of step daughter'. 'I do
indeed begin to realise my year of probation is over.'[44]

May never ceased to think of that. 'It doesn't do to have a minute to
oneself or I become wretched at the thought of Lavinia's marriage.'[45]
Days of preparation ran through their fingers. They were driven out of
their minds, she said, with the quantity of things to do. Apart from the
wedding, two other occasions of particular importance marked this June.
On the 22nd they were all in Oxford, boiling hot and deafened by the
noise of undergraduates in the Sheldonian, to see the Chancellor of the
Exchequer, Mr Lowe, the eloquent Dr Liddon and their father receive
honorary DCL degrees. May had started out with a shocking headache
and found the Latin boring but was pleased with the scene. At All Souls
later, as they waited for lunch, a strange thing happened. For Speaker
Denison came out of the throng and asked Mrs Talbot if she would
introduce him to May; to whom he then said, very kindly, 'I wish to
have the pleasure of shaking hands with you'. She thanked him. 'I was
indeed much pleased.'[46] It seemed amazing to have happened that day –
'the *very day year* of her engagement', wrote Lucy. 'The poor Speaker!
one can never feel anything but grief . . . for him now.'

A change of weather during the night improved things greatly for
the second, and undeniably greater, occasion – though in surroundings
far less splendid: the official opening of Keble College and installation
of Edward as Warden. 'The excitement . . . has not left me yet', Lavinia
reflected some days later. She and other ladies had gone in advance
to decorate the little temporary chapel, which she could not help hoping
some rich patron would very soon feel bound to replace. Although the
college had received its charter, its hall was on a par with the chapel,
its library non-existent. It consisted mainly of undergraduate rooms in
bright red brick. But in the unfinished quadrangle that morning there
assembled a splendid host. 'Beautiful . . . with its white clergy and
choir, its scarlet Doctors and Bishops, its golden-robed Chancellor',
wrote Lucy, who had watched them processing before she hurried to
her seat in the chapel, from where she heard the chanting coming
nearer and nearer. The service of installation followed. The *Veni Creator*
was sung in Latin while Edward knelt before the altar: a valiant knight
for this congregation of Talbots, Lytteltons and High Church clergy;
for Dr Pusey, who had dreamed the dream and Lord Beauchamp who
had paid for the bricks and Charlotte Yonge, the writer – Keble's friend.
For all, this college was an act of faith.

Later, there were speeches. Edward spoke 'with the greatest possible
earnestness and fervour'; and Lavinia was proud to have overheard

from her place in the distinguished throng 'That's a speech worthy of the first Warden!' As for stature, who on any count could better face down Oxford snobbery than a tall man with a double First; a Talbot married to a Lyttelton who was also a niece of the Prime Minister; a confident and optimistic man – attached with all his heart to the Church of England and convinced of its historic role at a time when many minds were unsettled by Anglican defections to Rome?

'I must write no more of Lavinia Lyttelton', Lavinia entered in her diary. May observed that she seemed quite calm. 'Lavinia's wedding day tomorrow. This is all I need say to describe what this day and night have been to me; full of inexpressible sadness.'[47] They had shared for the last time the 'dear old bedroom', and had breakfast on their own together. At eleven Lavinia was dressed, and then walked with her father the very short distance from the house to Hagley church, 'under a lovely green erection'.

> Uncle Billy married us, Albert helping. After the marriage service Edward and I received the Holy Communion quite quietly with Mrs Talbot, Papa and a few others.[48]

After lunch they set off for Ingestre (lent by Lord Shrewsbury, Edward's uncle) where they arrived to bells ringing. 'And so I have begun my wonderful new life.' But she could not get the thought of May out of her head.

> The last I saw of the darling old home was a vision of you . . . alone in the morning room . . . and that's the vision I have had ever since; so . . . you must write directly and send it away.

At Ingestre, she said, they were well set up in a charming sitting room full of roses, and much amused at 'the stately little meals when we . . . feel on our hind legs in the presence of a flunkey'. But she had left behind her travelling clock and felt very shy with her new maid, Down, who handled hair badly and spoke so little.

> Tell me . . . how you are getting on. I know how brave you will be as you always have been and fight on thro' all the shadows. Those are lovely lines Edward put into your book – two of his most favourite ones. He told me afterwards he thought you had behaved so beautifully thro' the great yesterday – and he has been touched more than you know by your manner to him of late.[49]

'Good-bye, my poor – shall I be able to think of you as thankful to

God for the intense happiness of your real – though certainly very unreal loving sister, Lavinia Talbot.' May answered at once; but perhaps not frankly, for her diary after the wedding runs, 'Anything like the desolation of this afternoon and evening I have never felt'. The next day, 'terrible . . . one-legged feeling'; the Sunday, 'Lumpy-throated, more or less all day'.

Lavinia wrote urgently of things to be sent ('I am umbrella-less, watch-less, clockless, workless and hat-less') but left no doubt of her married bliss. 'I am in my wonderful lilac silk – quite "b was a bride".' (Though she hardly meant it; for that was an unflattering Glynnese expression – adaptable to context, but always meaning someone who was very much a 'type'.) They had been driving in a pony chaise; worked at her Greek (a routine started when they were engaged); and had 'nice little potters' over guide books for their foreign tour. The great thing was that there was now no need to cram everything into a very short time. 'You have no idea how delightful it is.' As soon as they got on the train, she went on, she had felt that lack of time 'would never again press one or bring about misunderstandings'. And then there was 'the daily delight in being able better and better to know one's man, to be able with GOD's help to suit better, to be a greater help as that knowledge becomes deeper'.

'It is the blessedness of happy marriage which makes it more Heavenly than earthly', Lucy had written to her after the wedding.

> All that is agitating and overwhelming gradually loses itself in a love that learns more and more to trust and give itself up to the great answering love . . . As our own Mammy used to say, there is a halo round the honeymoon that . . . can never come again.'[50]

But Lavinia felt ashamed to dwell too much on her own happiness in letters to May. 'You know how earnestly I pray for you, and [hope] this travelling will be a means of *some* happiness to you.' For May was also about to embark on a foreign tour. They could look forward to meeting in Switzerland, where their paths were due to cross at Murren.

May was to go with Aunt Coque, Mrs Talbot and her cousin Gertrude (the surviving daughter of her mother's brother, Henry Glynne, Rector of Hawarden). And while she left Hagley with little zest for it, her letter from Dover gave Lavinia the sense of 'a spirited and rather jolly start'. So, apparently, it continued. Perhaps too jolly – or that was the impression which seems to have got back to Lavinia eventually. May's diary throws a patchy light on that. From Ostend they had travelled to Brussels; thence to Cologne for the Rhine steamer. At Cologne was the astounding cathedral and the terrace where she watched reflections in the river as the lamps were lit; on the steamer was the good-looking youth who followed them on deck, 'talked to Mrs Talbot, then to G. and me . . . Got rid of him at last'. When they disembarked, the next train journey – to Heidelberg – was enlivened, she says, 'by the courtesies of a Chivalrous Being, who though an American spoke French and German . . . beautifully and was more polite than anybody I have ever seen'. He helped Aunt Coque in her efforts to retrieve the clock and umbrella which she had lost. Heidelberg had its breathtaking castle and 'a fascinating German youth who showed us our way down'. Then as they settled in the train to Basle there was the pleasant young ticket-collector 'who flirted beyond with Gertrude and slightly with me . . . named by Aunt Coque "The Spark from the Engine".' Jolliness was dimmed, though, at Interlaken ('lovely . . . but horribly cockney and smart'), where out of the blue they heard the news that war had broken out between France and Germany.

It was very sudden: on 19 July the French had crossed the Rhine and taken Radstadt. Switzerland was obviously not at risk but every *table d'hôte* buzzed with worry about how to get home if the trains were stopped. They went on to Grindelwald as planned, and enjoyed a visit to the Mer de Glace, but against a background, as May noted, of 'much anxiety over the war'. News of French onslaughts was expected daily (though in fact the French army was so badly organised it could not profit from its early initiative and the last days of July were lost). 'But we get only vague news', she writes. She was also worried about Lavinia and Edward, travelling through France on their honeymoon tour, from whom she was awaiting a letter with the date they were supposed to meet at Murren. 'Last in the morning room, next in the Alps!' Lavinia had promised. To May's relief, on 21 July the letter came.

It was astonishing to look from the window of the hotel dining room in Murren and see a tall man in a Panama hat, accompanied by a very small lady, walking up the road from Lauterbrunnen. These two had heard of the war at Amiens. Moving on to Rheims and then Auxerre, they had found themselves caught up in troop movements – experiencing what Lavinia described as 'the first thing in my life which could be called an adventure': a night in a station waiting room full of smoking, singing, talking, snoring and generally tipsy French soldiers. 'The war is occupying all minds', wrote May, 'and one is afraid to look forward a week.'

For all the general noise and laughter and conviviality over dinner, sitting tête-à-tête with Lavinia later felt too odd to be snug, she wrote.

They met at Thun again, two days later, and 'toodled about in the pretty old town till my legs nearly came off'. But all the same, she felt 'un-intimate' with Lavinia; and when they parted, was forced to conclude, 'The meeting hasn't been altogether satisfactory'.[51]

They had no delays on the homeward journey, nor any sign of war, beyond an old French organ-grinder who was playing the *Marseillaise*. None the less, May's attitude to France at that stage – like most English people's – was very hostile. 'There is . . . a light-hearted ferocity about them which revolts me', she wrote, as England drew near. But, again like others, she softened in August when Prussia inflicted so many defeats, culminating on 1 September in the slaughter of 20,000 French soldiers at Sedan.

May had been home a month by then and was able to savour 'the sensation of snugness and security in this dear old England while such horrors are raging round us'.[52] Hagley had not seemed so snug at first. 'Find myself walking from room to room, trying to find and settle things.' But gradually it wrapped itself round her, though she did not care for the morning room (which had been a sitting room for her and Lavinia) and often sat in her bedroom now. In spite of the all-too-familiar headaches, she had made a start on serious reading (Leopold von Ranke's *Popes* with Sybella, De Tocqueville's *Democratie en Amérique* with Charles); she practised, took charge of Alfred's practice and showed off Baby to the village ladies. Lavinia, when she came in September with Edward on her first married visit to Hagley, did not think that she looked very well. They had what May called 'trolls on the surface'. Given the busy state of the household, the presence of several tedious guests, the garden party in Lavinia's honour, the Bromsgrove Cricket Match, the Expedition (fourteen, including the baby, to Bredon), there were few chances of a tête-à-tête. And then, Lavinia's second going was like June 29 over again.

Lavinia – very unhappy too, when it came to turning her back on Hagley – was on the other hand now absorbed in helping Edward with correspondence arising from the first admissions to Keble, and positively enjoying the thought of taking on a new kind of work. One cannot easily imagine her saying (as Lucy had said before she went to Court) that she was very much looking forward to being relieved of responsibility. 'I have had enough of my own way', Lucy had told her, 'and the cares it entails.'[53] Lavinia's cares were of a different sort; and, alas, were revived that autumn by an account she had from Meriel of May's flirtation with a Captain Mildmay.

# 10

# *May*

'Funny mixture my life is to be sure'

May's diary, 30 March 1871

'I am of course sadly disappointed', wrote Lavinia. 'I never thought that her piteous romance would take away the power of enjoyment, or even of liking someone fresh, but I had thought it would . . . have quieted and settled her, disinclining her to jump down any stray Captain's throat.'[1]

While this kind of head-shaking went on, May's diary dwelt on the simple pleasures of being at home with one or two brothers while her father and Sybella are away on a visit; and on Meriel's four-year-old Medge, 'twining herself round and round my heart' while the little Talbots are staying at Hagley. 'Played with the Trots. Put my sweet Medge to bed. Very snug and happy with Charles and Spencer . . . I can't describe the charm of these last days. I've not been as happy for ages.'[2]

Then there were visits: in early November 1870 to Albert, her devout and unworldly brother, now a Curate in Hillingdon. She mothered him a little, making blackcurrant tea to warm him after his parish calls. It had been such a nice week, she told Lucy, 'enjoying the snugness of his wee bright rooms, hearing of his work, in which he is . . . absorbed'.[3] He was extremely well looked after and on friendly terms with his Vicar. A short time later she went to Oxford to spend a week with Lavinia at Keble.

May had already found that seeing her sister renewed the 'horrid hankering' after her. But of course it was the greatest fun to go round chaperoned by Lavinia, linger over their tête-à-tête meals and seek out services in college chapels of rare beauty and heavenly music. Lavinia was putting down musical roots – sang in the Philharmonic

Choir and, to her pride, had been invited to lend support to a Keble Glee Club. May now joined her in practising anthems with some of the undergraduates – 'Killing!' From the tow path they watched bumping races and gave support to the Keble boat. They went to one of Ruskin's lectures and to a dinner in the great man's honour at which he took Lavinia in while May was placed on his other side. She found his singular talk amusing but not so funny as the journey home – full trot with her sister in a double sedan chair which was a tight fit. 'Died of laughter!'

'Enormous fun having her', wrote Lavinia; who still liked fun, for all her dignity as the wife of the head of an Oxford college: a role which, according her mother-in-law, she had taken to 'wonderfully well'. Most young brides, in Mrs Talbot's opinion, would have grumbled at having to eat alone (for Edward usually ate in Hall) but Lavinia had adapted to this strange way of life with a truly unselfish devotion. She had made their small rooms *so* pretty ('her little drawing room perfect in taste') and won the confidence of the undergraduates, who often came to seek her advice, 'quite treating her as "Mother Keble".' On this theme Lucy teased her in verse.

> The Warden goes trotting upon his gray mare
> Bumpety bumpety bump
> Mother Keble beside him her nose in the air
> Bumpety bumpety bump
> Thorough moor, thorough wood, thorough bush, thorough briar
> Bumpety bumpety bump
> While deans, dons and fellows all rush to admire
> Bumpety bumpety bump.[4]

Certainly Lavinia enjoyed her role. None the less, by her own admission, she sat 'perfectly glum and silent for a whole hour' after May had gone.

'Coming home nowadays isn't what it used to be . . . Miss Lavinia acutely', wrote May.[5] She felt low at the thought of Christmas; yet her London life was gathering pace – largely owing to the presence of Spencer, who was now Gladstone's assistant private secretary but seemed to have a good deal of time to indulge his passion for music. He had a very fine baritone voice and it was highly agreeable to May to be included in his circle of intelligent, musical friends: among them John Strutt (later known as an eminent physicist and Nobel Prize winner), Hubert Parry (the future composer) and Lord Salisbury's nephew, Arthur Balfour, not yet launched on the political career which led him to become Prime Minister and very ready to enjoy himself. Though

May thought Mr Parry rather 'y was a young man' on the surface, his piano playing was by itself for tenderness and power, she wrote; while Mr Balfour (no great performer – his only instrument the concertina) set the pace for intense performance in any household where he happened to be and was 'quite unlike other people'.[6]

'Music and madness on the part of Mr Balfour', she records that December at Hawarden. In January 1871 he visited Hagley where all the first morning May played Handel, his favourite composer. Most of the next day was 'sadly frittered' in the same enjoyable way. 'Mr Balfour dangles about and does nothing to an extent which becomes wrong.'[7] But she liked him very much and did not agree with those of the family who found him affected. Lavinia, for instance, on a New Year visit, though taken with his dreamy, amusing manner, thought him spoilt from too much visiting and too many admiring young ladies. One was their cousin, Mary Gladstone (like May an excellent pianist), staying at Hagley at this time; while May she considered at times to blame in too loud talking across the table to him 'and in her . . . absence of all shyness'. This lack of shyness (or, as she saw it, the seeking to be picked out and admired) Lavinia had always found distasteful. But May was trying to improve, she told Meriel, 'and now fails not so much in act as in manner'.

> Even in this I sometimes feel a word from Sybella would set her right, but Sybella takes strangely little part in the young man and young lady arrangements here.[8]

Despite a feeling that it was useless trying to influence May from a distance, Lavinia tried. There is hardly a letter without its paragraph of moral guidance: which May even seemed to invite – at one time anxious that her 'standard' was slipping, at another irked by Aunt Emy's complaint that she should defer more to her elders. 'The old faults of independence have been given to us both', Lavinia told her. 'I can never feel I shall quite rid myself of them.'[9] All the same there was room to improve. 'I know Aunt Emy sees the difficulties . . . of such a life as yours and wants to warn you afresh.' She herself had not given up hope of May's being 'permanently . . . quieted and settled' by the memory of Edward Denison. Having known such a man it could not be 'as if so . . . holy a perception of happiness . . . had never been granted you', she said.[10]

But what May chiefly sought was distraction. A glamorous and exciting visit, such as she paid that January with Charles to Belton in Lincolnshire, home of the Brownlows, carried her up to the seventh heaven.

She was enraptured with the striking beauty of her hostess, Lady Adelaide Brownlow, and of Lady Gertrude Talbot, her sister (cousins of Johnny and Edward Talbot); played wild games of hockey on the ice and saw, at nightfall, the winter scene grow less hilarious and more romantic.

> When dark a huge bonfire was lit and we had tea by it, then started to skate madly till 7.30, delightful to see Lady Gertrude's enjoyment, she and I flying along with our respective brothers for horses; the scene like one in a play. The pond lit up by the fire, the rest in darkness; curious effect of the figures appearing out of darkness and vanishing into it.[11]

'Lady Brownlow came down', she wrote, 'looking like the Queen of Night, in long black dressing gown, hair streaming down her back.' And later, 'Lady B. and I sat on G.'s bed talking. It's wonderful how much there is to say to them both.' ('I do wish', Lavinia wrote, 'you would not make confidants of so many people.') But May described it as 'a rare pleasure finding new people to love . . . as I love Lady G.', and allowed herself to be persuaded to stay at Belton a day or two longer.

Her new friends gave a fillip to London, where she had long since ceased to care for any of the great set-pieces. ('To Queen's Ball bored . . . stayed very short time'; 'To the Drawing Room an unmitigated nuisance.') Rather, 'To the Gladstones, to see my beautiful ladies, Lady Brownlow and Gertrude Talbot'.[12] 'Luncheon with Gertrude Talbot and Adelaide, as she tells me to call her.' In London she caught up with Spencer's circle, some or other of whom were apt to descend on the Lyttelton house in Portland Place, or on the Gladstones' in Downing Street or on Mr Balfour's in Arlington Street – as the wind blew – for music-making. They were all naturally zealous fans of the Saturday and Monday Pops ('Popular Concerts' in St James's Hall, London's main venue for chamber music). With an insatiable appetite for Handel, they made up parties for the Crystal Palace; and, as Mary Gladstone was of their number, had the privilege of hearing such artists as Joachim, Gounod, Madame Schumann, Jenny Lind and others in the Gladstones' drawing room. May worked hard at her own piano, as she always had, in town or country, practising endlessly in Portland Place – especially if the family were out – 'It being too great a luxury having the house to myself to resist'.[13]

Of course the interests of Spencer's circle were not wholly confined to music. 'Messrs Strutt, Balfour, Parry etc.' partnered May at almost every ball ('Mr Balfour . . . two valses tea and interesting talk'); met her at the Gladstones'; appeared, as she did, at Professor Tyndall's lectures on Sound (for at this time she had taken up science), and still more certainly in Rotten Row. A day without riding was death to May. 'Rode with Spencer, rather nice, with the Balfours amongst others.' 'Rode pleasantly with Agnes [Gladstone] and Mr Parry.' 'Rode in the evening . . . Being chaperonless with Hubert Parry and Mr and Miss Balfour we got into childish spirits and went at a tremendous pace.'[14]

Mr Balfour stands out in the diary. In early March, at a dinner party, May is delighted that he shows interest in the Parochial Mission Women, for whom she now does regular work. A day or two later they meet at the Gladstones'. 'Much talk as usual when Mr B. is present; he has lent me a pile of delightful music.' And the next day,

> Mr Balfour to luncheon; how we have lived and died with him these few days! The poor man was exhausted and Spencer and I played and sang to refresh him.[15]

Towards the end of June Mr Balfour hosted three hilarious luncheon parties from which they went on to the Crystal Palace to catch the rest of the Handel Festival. 'All very low at its being the last day', May reports after *Israel in Egypt*. The festival occurred only every three years. 'Mr Balfour says there are three years of misery before us! . . . Very nice day but the time has reached a climax.' Two of their number were now engaged: Mr Parry to Lady Maude Herbert and Mr Strutt to Mr Balfour's sister, Evelyn. It would hardly have occasioned wild surprise if May and Mr Balfour had done the same. However, they did not. 'What a long, long season it has been,' she wrote, at the point of leaving, in July, for Hagley, 'but I've liked the last part in some ways greatly.'[16]

In the last part, June, through the sort of chance that might have done for a romantic play, she had fallen in love with Rutherford Graham, whose father was a wealthy Scottish MP and patron of Pre-Raphaelite painters and whose sisters often rode with May. Owing to their parents' Presybyterian scruples, Frances and Amy never went to balls but they knew May well in the Row; and in the spring of 1871, sheltering in their house from rain, for the first time she met their brother. After that his name often appears in her lists of partners, for no earnest scruple kept Rutherford Graham away from balls; indeed, though only just down from Balliol, he already had a wild reputation. 'An odd attractive youth whom one instinctively mistrusts', May wrote early on.[17] But she was not put off. And though it was soon clear that this attachment ran counter to her family's wishes, her moods at home betray the impatience of one whose daydreams remain elsewhere.

'The London life is growing distant', she wrote. Yet by the time she had arranged her books and taken a pleasant ride in the hills she felt 'fratched and restless beyond measure'. Croquet at the house of a favourite neighbour left her 'very actively bored'. Watching falling stars from the perron, as they did these summer evenings, saddened her. The diary shows her greatly afflicted with inferior dinner partners, the maddening click of billiard balls, the deathly tedium of archery meetings, and household guests who drive her sometimes to take refuge in Newmany's room. When Lavinia appeared it was a great relief. 'Talked satisfactorily to Lavinia who is more to me than all the rest of the world.'[18] For all that, Lavinia does not seem to have given her complaisant advice. 'If I have been at all hard on you', she wrote in November 1871 after May had returned to London, 'it is only because I have been too anxious . . . and one learns to dread anything *wrong* in the wonderful chapter of one's life which love and marriage entail.' Lucy had been paying her a short visit.

> She seems to me more *deep* and strong than ever . . . and it is rather a beautiful thing to dwell on how she and F. have helped each other, for . . . the want of congeniality etc. in her new people and him have made her fight out the reasons of things.

They had of course discussed May's problem. 'You need not be afraid of her being harsh about it, though she is painfully anxious about you.' 'GOD bless you my darling sister and keep you strengthened and helped to do right.' 'Don't get into a despair', she wrote, a week or two later. 'Just now . . . ought not to be a time for depression . . . when you are conquering yourself gallantly about Mr Graham and know now what you ought to do clearly.'[19] Her father too made his wishes clear, and by the time she came home for Christmas May had broken with Rutherford Graham.

So that was the end of the first chapter. But it was not the end of the book. Back in London in the New Year 1872 ('Beastly place it is'), May was very low. 'Indescribably fratched', she wrote. 'Days drag . . . The everlasting drive . . . Drove, drove, drove – oh for a blessed ride.' She put herself through the usual motions: thorough-bass lessons, lectures on Handel; boring dinners (as well as a good one where the great Joachim took her in and they talked music all the time). But she kept an eye open for Mr Graham and marked each glimpse with a blank in her diary. 'Saw ——', after going to a lecture. 'Watched —— all

the time' (at a Monday Pop). At length they spoke; and when he asked
her, 'Won't you shake hands?', of course she did.

Lavinia was not impressed by this.

I mean, those words really set things going far more than little civil
conventionalities, and belong – please don't mind my saying it – to the
character we have so often heard given him: *slippery*. Doing something
on the face of it [right] yet meaning, and intending to mean more.[20]

It was not honourable, she said. 'My old dear, you won't deceive yourself
and make yourself believe things which are not probable?' If the rela-
tionship had not been ended she thought it difficult their both being
in London. 'But if it is to be so you will have to fight hard perhaps
and – win at the end. For GOD will show you how.' In fact she and
Lucy were appalled by May's judgement; quite unable to understand
how she could seriously consider a man 'so very very different' from
Edward Denison. Sybella, too, whose brother had given her most unfavourable reports of him: 'Wretched talk with Sybella', May wrote, the
day following the shaking of hands.

Though it is impossible to trace in detail how things were going in
this affair (now and again May used code in the form of a minuscule
German script – effectively indecipherable), there can be no doubt of
her frustration. 'No thoroughfare at every turn.' 'Arranged flowers, was
fratched beyond measure.' At a concert to which she went with Sybella
the music touched her 'like spoken words' and in some passages left
her throbbing 'with want and weary, hopeless longing'.[21] 'Music has
wings on which one can mount into a much higher, purer atmosphere . . . only it ended', she writes, 'and then . . .'

Easter soothed her, as it always did. But back in London she was low
again. 'To Tyndall's Lecture . . . didn't understand a word.' 'To Lady
Phillimore's beastly party.' After the Drawing Room in early May ('unmitigated evil') to a ball, with Lucy. 'Mr Graham was there. Saw him
for a long time.'

To Lucy, it seemed like a long nightmare. 'You won't blame me for
being . . . against her ever allowing Mr G. to come to an explanation',
she told Lavinia afterwards. 'I could not conceive her having strength
to be firm.'

And I must confess that I was never sure that she *herself* was convinced
of her duty: I thought it was more as a matter of obedience that she
had brought herself to give up thinking of him. So when Auntie Pussy

came up to me . . . saying May was bent on my allowing her to speak
to him, I was in despair and I am afraid angry.

But when May came and asked herself, she weakened:

> I could only make one thrust . . . saying, 'O May, you never distrust
> yourself'. To which she answered . . . meekly that indeed she did, and
> I must pray for her. Well then of course I could say no more and I did
> try (seeing she was bent on doing right) to call up my faith. It was very
> strange, sitting on my bench in the middle of the . . . dancing, praying
> with all the heart I could! I saw her disappear with him and as time
> went on and she did not come back I got more and more frightened . . .
> I could not tell if I ought to go down to the rescue or what.

Then a friend asked to take her down to supper – 'So I thought he
was sent on purpose!'

> Down I went, and saw the poor things . . . together. In a few minutes
> they got up, and the sight I had of poor Mr G.'s face . . . showed me
> May had gone through with it.

'Nobody can tell what peace [it is] to feel that I can respect the old
child and approve of her, as well as love her . . . Never had I a clearer
sight of the power of prayer.'[22] And Lavinia's words ('Well it is over')
in a note to May convey the same relief and finality. 'It must have been
a very terrible time . . . Thank GOD for what he has enabled you to do,
and remain confident in His strength.'[23]

There seems no reason at all to think that May had less confidence
in God than Lavinia. She was as likely as any Lyttelton to seek and
find refreshment in church; took her duty of Sunday School teaching
and teaching the servants and the younger boys seriously, and was
uplifted by the great festivals. 'Nothing can spoil Easter Sunday', she
wrote. But obviously faith allowed for the prospect of Rutherford Graham's being reformed.

'I do believe in the possibility of good in Mr G.', Lavinia conceded;
some months after the famous ball.

> But . . . you of your own free will having refused him, not because you
> had no feeling for him, but on the higher, nobler ground, it must be
> right to stand aside patiently and not . . . dwell more than you can
> help on a sadly vague and uncertain future.[24]

But less uncertain, it seems, than before. For the final parting had not
been final; and the ball not the last where they danced together. And
May quite soon had rushed off to Oxford. 'Comforting endless jabber

with my L. . . . Things settled as I wished.'

So what was settled? What arrangement would have satisfied May – as it clearly did – while leaving Lavinia (as she herself admitted) more hopeful and bright? Whatever it was, there seems to have been no irreversible rupture with Graham. Edward Talbot complained that summer that he could never get through to May. 'One knows that all her brooding is occupied with Graham and that that precious influence goes to colour everything.' But soon the matter was taken out of their blundering hands (as Lucy put it) by God Himself. For Rutherford Graham died of diphtheria on 28 October 1872.

Pity for May in this second tragedy; pity for the Grahams (those afflicted people slightly alien to the Hagley mind and, above all, Presbyterian) did not exclude immense relief that a great problem was now no more. As Lucy told Meriel when the news came out, 'One can't be exactly sorry'. But when she saw May, she reproached herself with not having understood before that her love had been *very* real – 'strange though it will always seem to me'. Indeed her feeling for Edward Denison had perhaps been 'less of an "in love" thing' than what she had felt for Mr Graham. 'I do think the poor darling is being tried in the fire and that it will turn to wonderful good for her.'[25]

May, when she heard, had clung to Newmany. Next day, like a stricken child, she fled to the arms of Auntie Pussy at Hawarden, where she was allowed to make the schoolroom her burrow till she felt equal to general company. Lavinia wrote to her three times in a week, infinitely wretched and quite unable to summon up the usual sound advice 'My poor darling, I can say nothing to you. GOD's most blessed pity and mercy come to you . . . in this desolate moment.'[26] 'I would do anything [but] can do nothing, only you know how deeply all this is with me – in me all day – and how much we pray for you.' 'It seems sometimes hard to understand why GOD lets you have so much sorrow and trouble.'[27] For the contrast with herself was as marked as it had been at the time Edward Denison died. She was immensely happy and satisfied with all their life and progress at Oxford. Only that summer they had visited Hursley and stood together by Keble's grave in what seemed almost a rededication: 'Edward with his hat off [and I] half bewildered when I thought that above anyone living *we* are bound to keep Keble's memory honoured.'[28] It seemed almost too much that a few days later a benefactor offered all they needed to build the college a worthy chapel. To May she could only reaffirm her trust that one day they would know God's purpose.

And today's glorious lessons tell one something of the privilege of
suffering . . . and of what the road is we shall all have to walk before
we can see fulfilled the prayer 'Make us to be numbered with Thy
Saints'.[29]

'I have a sort of feeling of reverence for you, as one chosen out by GOD
to be chastised.' Lavinia begged May to come and see her. And when
she came, kept her as long as possible, to shorten the time May would
have to spend 'tête-à-tête with Sybella' in London before the whole
party came home for Christmas.

May spoke warmly of Sybella's kindness, Lucy announced with relief
to Meriel: sure that they were on 'a comfortable footing'. But though
Sybella was kind by nature they had hardly ever been 'comfortable'. At
least, not since Lavinia left home, when May had found herself in the
front line for all the myriad preoccupations of 'poor Sybella and her
Martha-like life'. (Lavinia's words; for she thought Sybella was too
engrossed in domestic cares 'from the park and garden to the scullery'.)
And May – so restless, with disabling headaches that must have reduced
her usefulness: clever, disatisfied, not quite to be trusted – especially
over Rutherford Graham – was not easy to be comfortable with. It is
not true', Lavinia had once said, 'that Sybella has no respect for you'.

> I can tell that if she lacks confidence in you, it would more than come
> back if you were quieter. Consistently working at one thing and avoiding
> all possibilities of having anyone admiring you by your manner. Con-
> sistency is what Sybella, like most of us sees most plainly in a life.[30]

Lavinia made what seems to have been the only practical suggestion
for helping May onto her feet again: that she should work with the
London poor. 'I am very glad to have such definite work', May had
written in March 1871; having spent an afternoon cutting out shirts
for the Parochial Mission Women, and rather pleased to have been
appointed a Supplemental Lady to a district in Lambeth. There were
many signs that she felt a need for something more disciplined and
demanding than family life alone could offer, especially after her father's remarriage.

'Something of the sort might perhaps be arranged', Lyttelton told
Meriel: without much force. 'Sybella fears infection', he said.[31] (Which
was understandable, for two-year-old Sarah had a seriously infected
knee.) He himself was anxious lest May get morbid, but his one idea
for preventing this was that she should not 'mope with the Grahams' –
the only thing that she wanted to do.[32] Letters from Francie and Amy

Graham and from their father about his son's death had been her solace. Such beautiful letters! 'They must be angels and the odd-looking father a saint', declared Lucy, who took May's part and was strongly against attempts to 'hurry away' her grief. 'I hope you will agree with me', she wrote to Meriel, 'and that we shall both try and impress . . . on Sybella that she ought . . . to be allowed to see the . . . Graham sisters and to correspond as *much as ever she likes*.'[33] Lavinia too thought it would be harmful to keep May away from her friends just now. 'I wish her to have every comfort, poor [darling] I'm tired of the sad discussions over her . . . She says so funnily she feels like an illness prescribed for and consulted over.'[34] The upshot was that when May went to London she was more with the Grahams than in Portland Place. Which was irritating to Sybella, who knew she suffered but conceived of suffering, at that moment, mainly in terms of the abscess on the knee of her two-year-old.

Sybella had a great deal on her plate. Various doctors had shaken their heads over poor little Sarah and could not say when the child would be able to walk properly. In January 1873 she was taken to London to see Sir James Paget, the leading pathologist and surgeon, and Sybella poured it all out to Meriel, perhaps as the only other one in the family equipped to understand a mother's trials:

> You see, the abscess is *in* the knee and on its management the whole cure depends. There is very great difficulty about carrying her up and down stairs, in and out of the carriage, washing and dressing, to all of which I attend myself. And it requires the eye of some one who can say as I did today to Baldwin who wished to take off the splint *before putting her into her bath* that it must not be done.[35]

Eight months pregnant, she was much relieved that Paget said worrying could not harm the baby. For she did worry. Apart from Sarah, the shock of her husband's depressive illness in 1869 had left her anxious. Since then there had been some minor 'blues' which she evidently took in her stride; though that autumn of 1872, the return of symptoms recalling those of three years before had frightened her. He had been low again in December; and in January, when Sarah was taken to Paget, he wrote a most dismal letter to Lucy.

> I have but feeble hopes that she will return here – unless it be when fallen asleep, to be borne from this door under a little white pall, with a few white-robed children following her.[36]

'Darling daddy, I am *sure* you need not have such hopeless forebodings about sweet little Sal.'

> But I know how you have always 'rejoiced with *trembling*' in the blessings that have been round your children; and perhaps it is wrong to take away that trembling. If only God may help us all, whenever heavy sorrow does come upon us, to bear it as you have done.[37]

She wrote at the end that he must not let Sybella see this letter. 'It might set her off crying; which, just now, she had far better not be allowed to do.'

Lucy did not worry as much as Sybella over her father's fits of the blues. In 1869 her view had been that one ought not to fret, that it would pass 'like a cloud'. In the event he had gone straight on to head the new Endowed Schools Commission – the most demanding, controversial and publicised venture of his career: through it all, suffering nothing worse than what Sybella called 'little bouts' that she said could be controlled by watching and discipline. Many a buoyant man might have faltered before the near-universal hostility which met him and his fellow Commissioners trying to apply the Endowed Schools Act. One of them, Hobhouse, later said that the Act itself had been premature; got through Parliament with no understanding of the radical changes it implied. Indeed, the three of them were like those Commissioners who applied the New Poor Law in the 1830s: 'missionaries sent to lighten the heathen and to be persecuted and perish at their hands'. The opening lines of a long ballad lampooning Lyttelton, Arthur Hobhouse and the Commission's secretary, Roby, which appeared in the *Bedford Times* when a Scheme to reorganise Bedford's wealthy Harpur Charity was published, pointed the way to trouble ahead.

> When first Queen Vic in court began
>   To wear half-mourning sleeves,
> She entertained three serving men
>   And all of them were thieves.
> There was Hob the resurrection man
>   And Rob from the North countrie,
> And Littlejohn that drew the long bow
>   The biggest knave of the three.[38]

The Commissioners' efforts to adapt endowments to the needs of their own day often involved (as they did at Bedford) abolishing the *free* education willed by benefactors in the past, laying them open to a telling charge of 'robbing the poor', which was unpleasant. Against it, however, they were armoured by the Schools Inquiry Commission's findings on waste and corruption in the ancient system, as well as by the new attitude to charity which had developed in the nineteenth century. New ideology was driving out old; and charity, which had once seemed pious, now seemed inimical to personal effort. When the Commissioners tackled those foundations which most embodied the old charitable ethos – the formidably wealthy hospital schools – the clash of ideology was extreme (faintly presaging the modern conflict over the merits of the welfare state), and much was said about robbing the poor by the Dukes, City Aldermen and other grandees prominent among hospital governors. Blue Coats, Grey Coats, Red Maids and so on were well content if their vast endowments clothed and boarded a few poor children in the manner of Tudor times: giving them uniforms with brass buttons and appropriately modest schooling. When the Commissioners urged their view that the poor these days would be better served by providing grammar schools where some poor children might rise in the world through scholarships, the answer came back that hewers of wood and drawers of water would always be wanted. In 1871 the Lords threw out their Scheme for Emanuel Hospital, London, and this was fêted throughout the land as if it were the news from Waterloo.

'Our duty is to act for the future', Lyttelton had written in an early report. But the procedures were laborious. Schemes (i.e. legal constitutions) had to be made to adapt endowments and these were open to be rejected at various points as they passed through Parliament. The hospitals, naturally, blocked their way; while Anglican hostility was all-pervasive. For grammar schools had been a church preserve where religious teaching meant Anglican teaching, schoolmasters were in holy orders and only Anglicans became school governors. The Act abolished these privileges in all but a few exceptional cases; and when it was found how few these were, and how strictly the Commissioners defined them, clerical fury knew no bounds. 'The Church was to be harassed, humiliated, robbed . . . the clerical profession . . . discredited.' 'I love you . . . all ways but E[ndowed] Schools way,' joked one of Lyttelton's clerical friends, 'and that way I hate you exceedingly.'[39] For many clergy the hatred was real: of Lyttelton, the noted Churchman, who was betraying Mother Church; of the Dissenters, who stood to gain; and of the Liberals who had passed an Act so deadly to the future of Christian England. It was rough ground for a pious Anglican and Lyttelton admitted that it was not pleasant to be obliged to express opinions which, in the eyes of many people, were 'impious and sacrilegious'. But it did not stop him hammering home (notably before a Select Committee) his view that, in their own generation, the old church privilege could not be defended.

Lucy and Meriel came to hear him, proudly thinking what a lion he was. He had looked forward to the grilling, wrote Lucy; 'announcing that he would "make sport for the Philistines"'. 'And so he did!' To her admiration, he was 'in his best vein . . . wonderfully brilliant . . . letting fly especially at the notion that "founders' wills" were to be reckoned all prevailing'; and triumphantly clearing the Commission of the charge of being hard on the Church. 'But can't go into it all', she wrote. 'He kept everybody amused and good-humoured.'[40]

As if it had been some lark at Hagley. Whereas in fact it was more like a trial – with the verdict uncertain. The Select Committee did at length propose that the Commission's term of office be extended for another three years, but some at least of its members doubted whether Lyttelton should remain in charge. His frank expression in public speeches of strong commitment to the terms of the Act had from the first antagonised people whom it would have been wise to placate. In any case, the wind was changing. In political terms, the following wind that had bowled the Commission into existence after the Liberals' landslide victory of 1868 had dropped. The Tories, fortified by Anglican anger, were able to sense their own time coming. In the summer of 1873, when an Amending Bill reached the Lords embodying the Committee's three-year extension, Lord Salisbury ensured that it was cut to one. So began what Lyttelton spoke of as the Commissioners' lingering death: 'to live for a year with a halter round our necks, and be hanged at the end'.[41] For, once in power, the Tories would surely get rid of them.

The question was, when? From this time on their work was hobbled by uncertainty and it is not at all surprising to find Lyttelton in 'the blues' again. 'It has been worse before', he told Lucy in June, 'and I think it must run its time.' He was sleeping quite well, but with the aid of pills. By August he was able to joke about it.

> Your phrase 'three cheers for the departure of the Blues' is like a description of the famous departure of the Guards for the Crimea in 1854, the Queen looking out of the window and all the people cheering. They returned, somewhat forlorn and dwindled.[42]

In October Sybella told Meriel that she would really be glad if the Commission ended. 'There is no time in this rush for any pleasant intercourse or any book but Bradshaw [the Railway Guide].'[43] But nothing happened. In November Lyttelton wrote to Gladstone with a request which seems so odd that in the circumstances one may wonder if it was not also a sign of stress. In a letter which rather illustrates Gladstone's affectionate allusion later to the childlike element of his character, he applied to be made an Earl. 'I have only one reason why I wish for this, which . . . I fear will appear a foolish one.' Typically, before stating it, he felt bound to state the reasons against: *viz.* that since the 1832 Reform Act, earldoms had not been awarded 'except on the ground of eminent public service or great wealth'. 'To the former, of course, I can make no pretence; nor to the latter at present.' 'I hope I need not say it is an object for which in itself I do not care and for which, without a particular reason, I should not think of asking.' The reason was that the Duke of Buckingham was likely to die without an heir; and if that happened, like it or not, he himself would become Viscount Cobham. 'I greatly dislike the rank of Viscount.' After enlarging on this, he ended, 'You will not suppose that either I look for any sort of personal bias on your part, or that I should feel anything worth the name of disappointment if you refuse'.*

In February 1874 the Liberals were routed in a General Election. But the future of the Endowed Schools Commission remained uncertain for another six months – the Commissioners effectively sent to Coventry, while the government made up its mind whom to get rid of and what to alter. Lyttelton at length received an offhand note from the Lord President, the Duke of Richmond, saying that a Bill would be introduced to transfer the powers of the Endowed Schools Commissioners from the end of that year to the Charity Commission. 'Poor Papa and his fellow Commissioners have been viciously attacked', wrote Lucy, when the amending Bill reached the Lords, 'and very philosophically has Papa borne it.'[44]

He spoke well in the debate, and recanted nothing: taking them again through what he believed, and had long been known to believe, on the subject of founders' wishes.

> My Lords, people may call me what they like . . . revolutionary, impious . . . I know not what – I cannot depart from what I have maintained – that this supposed right of perpetual bequest has no foundation in right reason, in the principle of law, or . . . any other sound ground.

They had often been accused of failing to compromise. ('We lent them

---

* For the full exchange of letters, see Appendix, pp. 221–24 below.

a pruning hook', one angry Member had protested in the Commons debate, 'and they turned it into a sword.') Where, asked Lyttelton, in the Act, was there any indication of compromise. 'What I find there is not compromise but thoroughness.' They had fallen victim to their own exertions. All the same, he was inclined to think that the future would judge them differently.

> However ill a savour our doings may have in the nostrils of some of Her Majesty's Ministers, of newspaper writers and Governing Bodies, we may even be reckoned among those just persons, I do not say who need no repentance, but of whom it is said that 'the actions of the just smell sweet and blossom in the dust'.[45]

To some people (though not very many compared with the number of their detractors) the Commissioners' actions had already blossomed. The Women's Education Union praised them for all that they had achieved for girls, whose claims to education had been considered 'in a way they have never been considered before'. Certainly they had done what they could, under the authority the Act allowed, to prise endowment from the richer grammar schools in order to start up schools for girls: again, in the teeth of much hostility. The balladeer of the *Bedford Times* had amused himself a little with this, bringing in the name of Lydia Becker, a prominent campaigner for women's suffrage.

> Littlejohn shall build a Ladies' College
>   Miss Becker President;
> Like dew upon the tree of knowledge
>   Is petticoat government.[46]

As to government, had he not been ridiculed, Lyttelton was asked by the Select Committee, for ruling that there should always be *women* among those appointed as girls' school governors? He replied that he would like to see them as governors of almost any school.

> I believe women are often highly qualified for it, and when I see the admirable part which such women as Miss Davies . . . take in the highest educational questions, I cannot tell that there may not be ladies equally qualified in many parts of the country.[47]

In the ten years since Emily Davies made her appeal to 'thinking men', Lyttelton had evidently thought to some purpose. Apart from his work with the Endowed Schools Commission, he had been one of the most active supporters of advance in women's education: presiding, in 1871, over the meeting that inaugurated Maria Grey's Women's Education

Union, and securing it a royal President, the twenty-three-year-old Princess Louise. In 1872, at the Albert Hall, he had launched the Union's successful offshoot, the Girls' Public Day School Company (to the council of which Lucy was appointed). And from the first he had been a supporter of Emily Davies's college, Girton. Lord Lyttelton was ahead of his time, the Women's Education Union now declared, and his loss would be a serious blow to their cause.

'I certainly shall not much mind if he has to give up the Commission', Lavinia had written to May early in 1874, after the Tory election triumph. She had been talking to a 'Mr Bernard' (evidently a Worcestershire man) who thought the Commission work could be done just as well by somebody else; and that 'Papa's genius lies chiefly in influence and the power of affecting the tone of others round him in the county. Mr B. talked enthusiastically of his old Worcestershire position . . . and he with many others would be very glad to see him return to this'.[48]

When he addressed the House of Lords, Lyttelton had spoken lightly of the change in his own affairs:

> *Moribundus vos saluto!* but I am certainly not about to make any Jeremiad on the subject. I like £1500 a year as well as anyone else; I have more cause to like it than most people. But the official work I do not like at all, nor this particular work. As Falstaff says, 'Rebellion lay in his way, and he took it': so I suppose I must say, 'Confiscation lay in my way, and I took it' – but not from any particular pleasure I have in it.[49]

May reported a few weeks later that he was in very good form at Hagley. 'Sybella still will fancy he is not content here, of which . . . I see no symptom', she wrote to Meriel in September 1874. 'He is in especial force and spirits.'

May herself was in better shape; finding this a more tolerable year than 1873, which had had to be faced so soon after the death of Rutherford Graham; and had begun as a calendar of wretchedness that even music could not assuage.

20 January: To the Pop with Bob. Couldn't bear it.

10 February: To Pop with Mary and Spencer. A trio of Schumann's with an Adagio the like of which for expressing utter hopeless unresting misery I never heard . . . A poor note began on the violin and went wandering about in vain longing for rest, and sank away wailing into utter despair

1 March: Too much disembowelled to enjoy thoroughly a wonderful quintette of Mendelssohn.

She had had no heart for things. 'Rode, lovely day, but did hate the sun and the horrid smirking people.' 'Henley Regatta . . . quite too tiresome . . . horrid dull races, idiotic people.' Her London circle was unluckily depleted by Spencer's going to Egypt for a time with Balfour; but she was a great deal with the Grahams. If anything could be called a watershed in the process of her recovery, it seems to have been her stay with that family in Scotland in October 1873, the first anniversary of Rutherford's death. Her own family had not been pleased. Lucy, over-conscious of the *look* of things, worried because May made no effort to hide her attachment, nor seemed to realise 'how cynically' the world would view it ('people only know . . . she was engaged before'). But the great welcome she received at Strathallan ('Talked and talked and feel filled up and warmed');[50] the salmon fishing and highland scenery, the cold without and the comfort within, had sent her back to Hagley glowing. Of course she returned, Sybella said, with the Graham halo around her; but was, all the same, 'very *nice* and companionable. I only wish we had some quiet time together'.[51]

However, in the Hagley of these latter days, quiet time was in short supply. Three-year-old Sarah (now on crutches) and eight-month-old Sybil kept Sybella busy. There were many other preoccupations. They missed Nevy, who had recently set sail with his regiment for India. In September Meriel, to her own dismay, had given birth to twins. 'What a delightul light-as-cork feeling . . . to be writing to your own precious old self on the *right* side of the twins instead of on the wrong!' came Lucy's greeting. 'I had for so long been heavy-hearted over you, thinking you sadder and iller and more oppressed than usual.' She did not fail to add the old encouragement.

> The poor little unwelcome couple are God's gifts, after all, and we know He means them to be blessings and there is nothing for it but to love them and surround them and all their brothers and sisters with prayers.[52]

Lyttelton had also written to Meriel. 'You could not be told how anxious we all were . . . I hope that the three years before and after Jacko [her previous baby] may have been . . . enough as far as your own strength is concerned: though one cannot but feel, with the Frenchman, a wish that it "may be put a stop to".'[53]

May had settled down again with Sybella; seeming to them less of a loose cannon (though the diary shows how much she enjoyed any little gap when Sybella was absent). January 1874 involved them all in a shocking tragedy: the deaths, of typhoid, within days of each other, of 'our nearest neighbours, tenants, friends', Mr and Mrs Firmstone, leaving fourteen children in a state of financial ruin. May took four little Firmstones in, and one or two older ones by the day, amusing them as she did the Trots. 'Emy and Lucy such ducks', she wrote; and felt it terrible to go away. ('Kept feeling little Lucy's clinging arms.') But London of the Pops and the Crystal Palace and the Grahams and the Balfours again received her.

Whether she had learnt, as Lavinia hoped, 'to acquiesce humbly' in her present lot, she took up the Season with the same vitality and fitful zest that she had always shown, and with the same headaches and frequent tiredness. 'Tired.' 'Overtired.' 'I'm going to break up soon.' For all that, she was reading Maine's *Ancient Law*, working two hours at a stretch on Harmony and spending a lot of time with the Balfours learning to play the concertina. Spring brought 'a noisy racketty party' with the Brownlows at Ashridge which she much enjoyed. The riding 'as usual perfect bliss', the gallops furious, and the company addicted to that sparky new game – lawn tennis. But for her, the highlight of the year, undoubtedly, was going to Switzerland in July as one of the Keble College reading party.

There were ten of them: six undergraduates and Edward, Lavinia, Mrs Talbot and May – settling with their books in a friendly pension at Abendberg, above Interlaken. Their days were regular: the hours after breakfast given over to serious reading (which May devoted to Mill's *Logic* and Lavinia to Mommsen's *Rome*). Dinner was at one. But from 12 o'clock Mrs Talbot read *Peveril of the Peak* out of doors to a keen audience, with smoking permitted to men who sat on the windward side. The afternoon was for expeditions, the evenings generally for music. 'The days will be short to describe', wrote May, who did not think then of how mountains, sunsets and their own antics would demand description.

> Most absurd descent, L. and I in a sledge, dragged by Mr Thatcher in front, and behind by Messrs Sanctuary, Ottley and Walter . . . Fearful excitement round the corners.[54]

'Laughed a great deal' (coming home in rain). 'Afterwards the gentlemen went wild and had the maddest bear fight I ever saw, ending with Mr Walter jumping gravely on all fours over two chairs as lightly as a cricket; we shook the whole place with shouts of laughter.' None of which apparently provoked complaint from the old German ladies who

May had labelled 'the terrible quizzes of the *table d'hôte*'. Indeed, they seemed to derive much pleasure from her piano-playing in the big salon and the Mendelssohn part-songs and violin pieces which she accompanied with keen delight.

'Am enjoying myself.' 'Felt springy and fit.' And though, unlike Lavinia, she did not venture on the great expedition to the Grindelwald Glacier (which meant difficult guided walking with a stay overnight in a mountain hut), she loved the regular demanding walks and was always ready to view the world from the top of the Abendberg. 'Horrid grind there, but such views of Thun all along the beautiful wooded ridge. Watched the steamer trailing her . . . train across the lake, looking so indescribably stately.'

She felt chilled as the prospect of return drew near: dreaded losing, with all this beauty, the long companionable study hours which had seemed so stiff at first, and the camaraderie of those young men who had so gaily hauled her and Lavinia over the most impossible places. 'Even my tea appetite has gone', she noted. The party had had its photograph taken and spoke of reunion, but what of that! Unluckily May was the first to go. 'Another shawl', cried someone as they saw her off, 'it keeps the heart warm!' 'But it didn't', she wrote.[55] Lavinia had already put in her diary, 'She hardly looks forward to anything in England.'

However, May had not been home three weeks before she had made a lawn tennis court. On it she played with her brother Albert, who said he must lay in a stock of heat before setting out to go back to Hawarden (where he was working as Curate now). He seemed very well, she wrote to Meriel, and she herself felt much better than usual, thanks to the weeks at Abendberg, 'which have done me good in more ways than I can say'.[56] She found it cosy at home just then – liking to read in the morning room alongside Arthur; for at Abendberg she had got so used, she said, to someone else working. With Spencer she had always had music in common; but with Arthur, 'I've more interesting talk . . . than with any'. He had also, it seems, been 'nice and gentle' when she confided in him at the time of trying to break with Rutherford Graham. Arthur had thrilled them the previous year by coming out first in the First Class of the Moral Science Tripos, and was now preparing Extension lectures to be delivered in the Pottery towns. In contrast to Lucy, who told her father she wasn't sure what Moral Science *was*, May had read many of his Cambridge books. 'Metaphysics have a wonderfully calming effect on me', she once alleged. So it was a joy to discuss with

Arthur, though Abendberg would have been good for him, she concluded, to Meriel, for he was becoming a bit dogmatic.

Early in November May went to Keble and the Abendberg reunion
came off well, together with a great deal of lawn tennis. 'Got very hot,
and bottled up from not being able to scream, great fun . . . Oh how
I minded coming away!' Then Chatsworth: but Chatsworth had never
drawn her. 'It's not worth writing a long description of a singularly
uneventful visit . . . had some good lawn tennis', she said. She also
developed a throat infection; and returned to London feeling tired and
ill. Nor was she well in December at Falconhurst, though she carried
on 'playing with ducky twins' and producing a charade with the older
children. In the run-up to Christmas she found time for music-making
and lawn tennis in London with Spencer, Mr Balfour, Mary Gladstone
and others. After Christmas her returning strength is evident in the
stand she took to restore necessary peace and order in Sybella's bedroom, where a few days earlier a third daughter, Hester, had been
born. Imagine – the day after the birth, she told Lucy,

> having both children scouring the room and Papa tossing Sybil till
> Sybella started with terror. Monday she had the children in *five* times . . .
> On Tuesday when I arrived I found Sybella unnaturally lively and to
> the fore, sending down orders, fussing; Papa like a tornado in and out.
> I *am* happy to say I lost my temper and lectured right and left with
> such energy that everything since then has been beautifully quiet.[57]

Sybella's condition was now satisfactory. 'I should have thought Papa's
slight experience might have taught him better,' said May, 'but no!'

The New Year found May unwell again and she began to dose herself
with 'mad little homeopathic powders'. Which had probably done harm,
her father told Meriel in an exasperated, anxious letter of 22 January.
She was now ill.

> I am greatly put out about May . . . and I fear, from what Sybella says,
> it has been from constant neglect and inobservance of advice . . . We
> know how particular Clark's regimen is and I fear there will be a deal
> of trouble in even getting her to mind it.

The greater part of his annoyance arose from his being stuck at Witley
Court as the guest of Lord Dudley, the important neighbour whom he
had never found congenial. 'A stupid and utterly needless visit . . . but
it was on account of May.' For she had refused the Dudleys so often
that it was thought she should accept this time, especially as there was

to be royalty present. 'Then she . . . breaks down, and the Royalty too, for he had to go off to the other Prince.'

> I should have stayed at Hagley had I known all that. I have played ill at billiards, worse at chess; and [am] bored to death by Lord Dudley's incredible unpunctualities.[58]

'This is an exceedingly X letter; as it ought to be', he concludes.

Lavinia went to Hagley three days later, in response to a telegram from Aunt Emy saying that May had had another bad night. She was being nursed at the Rectory – where (because of building going on at the Hall) she had been lodging when the illness struck – and 'was so pleased to see me', Lavinia writes. 'She asked me how my neuralgia was and of the Keble people and made us laugh over her account of [Dr] Giles carrying her.'[59] None the less she seemed very ill; her manner was odd and she appeared at times to have difficulty in expressing herself. 'I hated leaving her so.' Next day, she heard of May's calling for her all night, 'Send a man to tell her *Miss Lyttelton* wants her!'

Dr Giles had talked of low fever at first; and Dr Wade, when he came from Birmingham, found none of the usual typhoid symptoms of spots and diarrhoea, and thought May's fever was 'of the "nervo-bilious" type', which might or might not become typhoid later. (Though typhoid was common and its symptoms familiar in 1875, the bacillus was not discovered until 1880. And, as for treatment, another fifty years passed before the discovery of penicillin.) Lavinia and Newmany took turns in the sick room: May often struggling to get out of bed – delirious, and so weak it was not hard to restrain her. But it was an immense relief when the two experienced nurses came. 'Her pretty hair was all taken off – beautifully', by one of them, Lavinia wrote.[60] And the same day, 'Papa came up and we were able to comfort him a little'.

Characteristic of the whole nine weeks of May's pathetic struggle with death were the extremes of her condition (eventually confirmed as typhoid) and the corresponding extremes of feeling which these produced in all around her. She rambled often: her voice quite odd then ('just like *Punch*'). But this would alternate with lucid times when she seemed to be returning to normal and her manner was 'so docile and pretty, so grateful to the nurses and so graceful . . . to us'. 'Please nurse, move that screen. I should like to see my sister. I always like seeing her', she had said.[61] 'We are a pair, as you and Mamma were', she told Auntie Pussy who, valiant as ever, had come to Hagley to help nurse her. And Mrs Talbot wrote to Catherine Gladstone, 'They do so cling together, those two. Does it not seem strange to think that poor little Win is in *your* position of seventeen years ago?'[62]

Seventeen years ago had been much calmer. No delirium, no frantic calling, 'Newmany, Newmany – come and find my back hair!' And with May, they worried what to do about prayers. In one of her clear times, says Lavinia, 'she asked me how Uncle Billy was, and then when I told her he would come and pray with her when she was stronger, she said "I should like him now, I think"'. But she was never, alas, in a state to be able to receive the sacrament.

So they went on: the sad days measured by pulse rates and temperature readings. 'Temp. 105 – it has never reached that before – couldn't stay, it felt so awful' (Lavinia). Then it fell to 101 and the hoping started all over again. 'February 26, Midnight', wrote Lucy: 'We are in the thick of the *lung* fight now, and I fear it must be a long one'. She was in charge (with Aunty Pussy); and most relieved to think that Lavinia (who had gone home for a rest to Keble) had missed 'the horrid fright' of the blood-spitting. For there was now an abscess on the lung. 'It has only proved its presence by the matter coughed up . . . If this abscess is all coughed away . . . they speak of getting her into plain sailing.'[63]

There was no plain sailing. They were up and down – as it had been from the very start. Lavinia insisted that Lucy summon her at once if things got badly worse. Others were not so easy to summon. Nevy was in India and did not know; Spencer, who had cancelled plans for Florence (and had indeed been extremely shocked by a glimpse of May on 10 March when she looked so changed he could not recognise her), rather oddly took them up again, only three days before she died. Lyttelton was in London mainly. At Hagley his family conspired to protect him, softened things a little or kept them back, as had been done that earlier time. On one occasion he arraigned Mrs Talbot, 'complaining . . . he had never been told the truth'.[64] When he knew it, he seemed to face it: on his own idiosyncratic terms.

He had been pressed to go down to Hagley to persuade Aunty Pussy to go home and rest, which he doubted being able to do. As to May, he wrote to Meriel on 13 March,

1. May may be able to see me now . . . In that case, I could come down on Tuesday.

2. She may be *unable* to see me now, but *probably* able in about a week. In that case I should leave the time open.

3. She may be unable now and impossible to say with any confidence

*when* she can see me. In that event I should still leave the time open . . . But I wait to hear what purpose it can answer that I shd fix a time for coming at all.[65]

May never managed to clear her lung. Indeed, at one very dreadful moment she had been at risk of being choked by the phlegm. Her form grew skeletal, her skin discoloured: terribly shocking to all who came. But though they tried to nourish her with milk and water and sips of port, she could keep nothing down. Lavinia took charge again towards the end, with Auntie Pussy, who never wavered. May died on 21 March 1875, Palm Sunday: fairly peacefully, with everyone round her – apart from Spencer and of course Nevy. Spencer, whom they telegraphed in Florence, managed to get back in time for the funeral, picking up in London his great friend Balfour who at the service broke down completely. What was not known then, outside the family, was that he had given to Edward Lyttelton an emerald ring that had been his mother's, asking that it should be placed in the coffin. He had meant it for May's engagement ring.

# *A Fall*

'May the Holy Angels lead thee into Paradise: at thy
coming may the Martyrs receive thee . . . and with
Lazarus once poor, mayest thou have eternal rest.'

Prayer of Commendation used by Anglo-Catholics

'It is sad to see the Peer,' Spencer put in his diary, 'it brought back
such a vivid remembrance of that morning in August '57.'[1] On the day
May died, Lyttelton had written to a clergyman who, a day or two
earlier, he had heard preach on the subject of sorrow.

> But you did not know, nor did I, how the sermon suited my case. While
> you were preaching, the message was on its way to me that my daughter
> was dangerously ill . . . She died this morning.[2]

His thoughts went back to what had been so much on his mind the
previous year, when the Firmstones died: the temptation to doubt the
love of God in the face of great personal loss. 'If we lose . . . our belief
in the love of God,' he had said then, 'what is there between us and
recklessness, despair and madness?' Yet he told the minister, 'I cannot . . . think it always a sign of spirituality that one's faith and love . . .
are not shaken by sorrows'. Gladstone wrote in the same vein to Catherine: 'I must own that events like this bring the greatest shock and
strain to faith.'

> That she should have died . . . that for her this long struggle, these
> pains, these . . . wanderings should have been appointed – How – why
> is all this ? I can find no answer but in remembering my own weakness
> and incapacity to judge.[3]

From the heart of anguish the family's prayers went out to Nevy in
India: his isolation underlined by letters full of hope for May's recovery
which arrived after she was dead. 'The sorrow is very great to all of us

who can comfort each other', his father wrote, 'far worse for you in your distant solitariness'.[4] 'We do all think so much of you just now', wrote Meriel, 'when this heavy burden seems to draw us all who are left so close'.[5] To Lucy, Nevy unburdened himself of wretched memories that he and May had not parted on very good terms. 'How well I know what the pain must be of thinking over your parting', she wrote, 'and wishing vainly that it could have been . . . different.'

> But I think it will comfort you to know that, in her journal, where she mentions it, there is not a word to show that she thought you cold.[6]

The circumstances though had not been perfect. They had parted (not long before he left for India) at Stourbridge station where he saw her off at the start of her journey to the Grahams in Scotland. Nevy had never felt much sympathy over the Rutherford Graham affair: had even been 'rather rough' towards May, 'both in his own opinion of her and in his manner', according to Lavinia.[7] Lucy's efforts now to console him were backed by Mary Gladstone's assurance that May (whom she had seen so much of) greatly admired him, 'though for a long time that did not seem to include all the sisterly love which she poured out so freely to the other brothers'. But it had blossomed, she insisted, in the summer of 1873.[8]

May's death took them in different ways. Spencer ('very much cut up', said Sybella), turned his back for a time on London and its Monday Pops and Crystal Palace and set off round the world with Mr Balfour. Bob told their cousin Mary Gladstone that he wished she could live with them and fill the vacancy 'which we all can hardly recognise the reality of yet'. Arthur, the brother who had joined with May in lively discussions on metaphysics, also wrote to Mary: in his case asking if she could get May's scrap-book from Sybella, who had taken it – unaware that he had set his heart on it and had no other personal memento.

> I don't think she will object when she knows how much it is bound up with my memories of May, as one of the chief points of interest between us.[9]

Edward Talbot set himself to consider, in a long and earnest letter to his friend Mr Illingworth (who had been at Abendberg), what he called 'the doubleness' of May's character. There had certainly been times when, in his opinion, 'rather a hard view of her conduct' (harder, at least, than her father and sisters seemed capable of taking) was the right one. He had thought she looked for too much indulgence in her mourning for Rutherford Graham; and had pointed out to her at times the gap between the lofty aims she professed and her fitful pursuit of them. But now, 'refined in God's discipline of suffering', he had no doubt which side had triumphed. He had learnt from May, as he wrote to Illingworth, the intrinsic value of high aspirations, even if they were unfulfilled.

> 'Whatsoever things are lovely, whatsoever things are pure, whatsoever things are of good report . . . think of these things', has seemed to me to express the grace which she showed us.

He praised 'her loving instinct of goodness', her love of beauty (which he perceived as 'God drawing her . . . by different cords') and, above all else, her faith.

> You know she read widely and talked freely so as to have realized most of the difficulties which beset and trouble so many. And I used to be alarmed about this, and caution her about the need of watchfulness in handling tools so sharply edged. Yet one felt these things were not laying hold of her, that her faith remained as it were untouched.

'Why was this? Was it not because she had not tampered with her love of goodness?'

'She drew one out intellectually and morally – she drew out one's best self', Edward wrote. 'I suppose it was this that enabled her to radiate brightness greater than she always had herself.' The gift of sympathy had laid her open to being unduly *influenced* by others and brought 'a difficulty in moral consistency which perhaps was the great oppression of her life'. But it also gave her a power of influence which 'purified and disciplined (if God had so willed) might have borne very lovely fruit'.[10]

Few attempted such analysis. 'The old quartett will never be the same again, for we have lost our leader', wrote Mr Ratcliff (a young man whose name crops up often in May's accounts of music-making). Johnny Talbot lamented simply 'the quiet brightness' that had gone from Hagley (in his view continuing a process begun when Mary Lyttelton died); and Mary Gladstone summed up her cousin as in turn 'a care, a sympathiser, a wonder: admired, scolded, consulted, praised, petted, pitied – but . . . always loved'. 'Oh Nevy', Meriel had written, 'I do miss May so with the children. She knew all about them and helped me so much with them.' Sybella too: 'She was just like a sister . . . and in the last two years she had softened so much and was so affectionate and nice, and I consulted her on *everything*.' Lucy was quite cast down to think how little she had really seen of May in these two years when she had made such progress. 'I shall have unavailing regrets over this to the end of my life', she confided to Auntie Pussy. Aunt Emy was not ready to go so far. Although accepting the moral improvement ('she . . . fought against her faults'), and the mental brilliance, she felt May's future had been so 'tangled' that there seemed a kind of peace in the struggle ending. And Mrs Talbot's main comment was that May at last was 'safe in the Home that can really shield her from . . . falling back'. Her own concern was for 'poor little Win, whose life can never be quite what it has been'.[11]

Outwardly Lavinia's life was less affected than the lives of those who remained at Hagley. Her diary, which makes harrowing reading all the time she was nursing May, settled back into Oxford again with preparation for the Ladies' Lectures;[12] for Eights Week (Keble bumped three nights running), and for visitors. Mr Balfour was shown round Keble in a lovely sunset, and young Prince Leopold was given tea after admiring the new chapel. Benefactions poured in: one for a hall, another for a library, a third for scholarships at Keble College; while plans were already under way to build them their own house – the Warden's lodging. All of this she longed to pass on to May, whose 'twenty-fifth birthday' came and went. ('Felt the great shadow all through the day.') When a drawing of May was commissioned, she wrote, 'How wretched only to look for ever at the shadowy black and white things!' In August she went with Edward to Hagley, and up to the Rectory when everyone was out. A very close friend of theirs, Henry Scott Holland, who had recently lost a friend through typhoid, had written to her, 'How *hungry* one is for the joy death takes away!' And in the room where she had tried at the last – and failed – to make May say her name, Lavinia wept for the lack of it.

'I never wish her to be in this bad restless world again', she told Meriel after that visit. 'But the missing her dear pretty presence . . . her advice, sympathy and spiritedness is so sore still – it feels like a . . . silence fallen on what was bright and young.'[13] Her thoughts, however, increasingly turned to something that, through those dreadful weeks, she had not been able to share with May: that she was pregnant, after five years' marriage. 'I lean much upon you for myself and for L.', Edward had written early on to Meriel, in fear of Lavinia's being over-stressed by her involvement in the ordeal at Hagley. Now that was over he wished above all for her to lead a 'quiet healthy routine life'. 'I see she thinks a good deal of her own time . . . and dreads it.'[14] Edward was with her on 2 October through the many hours of a painful labour – for all that she had chloroform and 'soothing draughts' (neither of which I should . . . care to have again'). And at length the 'little brown shapely girl', whom she at once called May, was born.

To Gladstone on the day of his tragic loss Lyttelton had written that for him, the father, it was like being torn apart. His fifty-eighth birthday followed soon after and he broke down then, although next day he wrote to Meriel that her letter had helped him.

> The little pussies [are] in black frocks. They have taught Sybil to say 'Poor May's gone' but I have not heard it. Sybella talks to Sarah about it, but I cannot yet.[15]

To Nevy he recalled how May had had 'just that mix of dignity with attractiveness and grace' that appealed to people. 'I was so proud of her and had such confidence in her . . . and her little waywardnesses counted for so little.'[16] Now, as on Mary's death, he asserted that something of the sort had been bound to happen. May had not been robust since her scarlet fever; she had neglected her health and so on. Though what it came down to was his ingrained sense of the fragility of happiness. 'Now that my fairest flower is gone . . . I keep wondering which will be next.'[17]

He was deeply touched when Lucy wrote saying that the family wished to share in the expense of May's long illness. 'I send you Freddy's and my contribution as the rich ones among your children, with our loving love.' They wanted to help him. 'And in a sort of way, it seems, even now, like doing something for our darling.'[18] It was Lucy also who proposed for the headstone an epitaph that pleased him greatly: 'We asked life of Thee, and Thou gavest her a long life, even for ever and ever'.

As usual her father's outward manner was no guide to his inner state. Lavinia had found him 'very lively and funny' when he and Sybella came to Keble in May. But hardly more than a week beforehand he had written to Catherine Gladstone, 'I have always had that feeling of the precariousness of all earthly things . . . Yet I cannot reconcile myself to the loss now it has come'.[19] In August, during the cricket at Hagley, Lavinia recorded him 'roaring about' and Lucy observed that he had recovered all his usual spirits and fun. However, May had become 'a sealed subject'. 'Poor dear daddy,' she wrote to Meriel, 'I don't mean but what I can . . speak of May to him, but he does not begin.'

To show you what a sore spot it is in his heart (almost *physically* sore I think) I found he had put his photograph of May where the window-curtain hides it, and he said 'I can't bear to look at it yet'. I said, 'O daddy, you always liked to see Mamma's picture'. And he said, 'Yes – but not at first'.[20]

In September, writing for Lucy's birthday, he touched again on 'foreboding fancies'. ' "The clouds return after the rain" and I feel no confidence, now that the first link has been lost.' 'Darling dadorums', Lucy answered, 'I think I have rather the opposite feeling . . . We have had years of great peace after sorrow, and I trust it may be so again.'[21] Though it struck her that this earthly life – '*waiting* in wavering hope and fear' – would seem pathetic to look back on when they were in 'the Better Land'. And as people arrived at Chatsworth and the long dinners began again, her heart grew heavy with thoughts of May, 'who came here just this time last year'.

In October Lyttelton introduced Alfred ('captain of everything at Eton – house, Pop, football, fives, cricket') to Trinity College, Cambridge, with pride. 'Having taken all the seven there myself,' he told Catherine, 'I should be sorry to miss the last.' In November he went with Sybella to Keble on a happy visit to admire the baby and be conducted round the chapel, which was nearly ready for consecration. He spoke of grief and its long shadow in a letter to Catherine after Christmas, but said that otherwise all looked bright. Charles had come to the end of a year of agriculture at Cirencester; Nevy (who was still in India) had passed two staff examinations; Arthur at theological college and Alfred at Cambridge had pleased their tutors; while his youngest daughter (one year old) had bright red hair but was undoubtedly 'the finest baby in the planetary system'.

He and Sybella had made arrangements to visit Italy in January and it gave him great satisfaction to hear before he went from Spencer (now in New Zealand on his world tour) and to visit Bob on the farm in Yorkshire where he was acquiring experience with a view to becoming a land agent. 'The . . . wellbeing of the children that remain', he told Lucy, 'is very wonderful to me.' He wrote from Florence, 'It was time for me to come, for I am lazy about sight-seeing . . . and bored at leaving all the babies'.

Every one above the rank of a tinker ought to see Rome – the only town, beyond all comparison, of equal and paramount importance in ancient and modern history.[22]

To Meriel he wrote a fortnight later that the Coliseum was very sublime and that they would be paying it another visit to climb to the top, and yet another to see it by moonlight. They had not yet been round the Vatican but St Peter's was worthy of all its fame and they had seen many other churches. Charles was expected to join them soon.

Charles however found nothing sublime. He depicted Rome to Mary Gladstone as a tomb which was still being excavated, and could hardly bear to talk of his father, at least in a letter, for there had been another awful fit of 'the blues'. ('What he knew in Rome gave him heavy forebodings', Lucy concluded later on.) 'The Peer's distressing state had better be forgotten now that it is (I hope . . .) passing away', he wrote at the time to Mary Gladstone.[23] His father and Sybella had returned to England.

'It is too wretched about Papa – quite a miserable feeling at the bottom of one', wrote Lavinia helplessly to Meriel, 'and I had hoped the real bad bouts were never to come again.'[24] Her father had gone at once to the doctor. 'Clark thinks to get him right', she put in her diary, but his progress was very erratic.[24] On 29 March she wrote, 'decided improvement', but two days later, 'wretched account' – and this in fact was the day that Spencer came back from his travels to find 'the Peer' in an 'absolutely deplorable condition'.

Dr Clark suggested he stay in London, within reach of his medical advisers – and, it seems, would have preferred an asylum. An attendant, Thomas Barnes, from the Clapton Asylum was in fact engaged as 'valet'. But in deference to the family's wishes and to the opinion of Dr Monro, a specialist in such cases, it was agreed that, for the time being, Lyttelton should be treated at home. At first he was at Lucy's (for the previous year they had sold the house in Portland Place). Then they rented No. 18 Park Crescent, where Lavinia and Edward took charge, assisted by Aunt Coque and available brothers; with Lucy and Meriel also involved until they left London for the Easter holiday. Mary Gladstone dropped in often, as did Sybella's sister, Kathleen Clive, who sent reports back to her at Hagley. 'I like to feel that my people too are with your dear father', Sybella admitted.

'You know what sort of things you can be useful to Papa in', her mother had told Meriel long ago – when what they now faced had never been dreamt of. They did their best. Though the trend was downwards, there were many little 'normal' patches such as often raised Lavinia's hopes; and the general aim was to keep things normal. Easter was approaching; and some of them went to hear the *Matthew Passion* performed at St Paul's. Her father was too restless to have sat through that but Lavinia and others rode with him daily. In early April he still dined out – though not unaccompanied, and it fell to Spencer to walk him home ('a depressing occupation'). On 3 April he took his father to the House of Lords. On the 9th (Palm Sunday) Edward Talbot was preaching at St Paul's and they all went to hear him. Her father had been wretched that day, said Lavinia, but was quiet during the service, and liked it.

He himself clung – so far as he could, and as he always had done in depressive phases – to the framework of duty and obligation. 'Never in all his life of duty did he fight a nobler battle', wrote Frederick Cavendish, 'than he did during these weary weeks.' On return from Italy, although unwell, he had at once sent Dean Stanley of Westminster, recently widowed, 'a word of sympathy from one who . . . went through the same affliction'. More surprisingly, two or three weeks later when his own condition was very much worse, he wrote to the captain of Bromsgrove School regretting that he would not be able to be present at the school sports that year. Yet his general behaviour was no longer normal. People noticed, it was said, at the House of Lords. Home or abroad he was terribly restless and often overwhelmed by floods of remorse which he would pour out to all comers. A few days after the move to Park Crescent it was felt that these maudlin outpourings imposed too much of a strain on Sybella, who (mistakenly) thought herself pregnant again. There also seems to have been a feeling – or quite possibly Clark advised – that Sybella's abundant compassion imposed too much of a strain on *him*, as some had thought happened in 1869. At any rate on 11 April she was persuaded to return to Hagley. 'I don't in the *least* mind being alone. With children and Newmany I am as happy as I can be', she wrote to Meriel. 'But I don't see that my being away does your father any good.' And it was a blow, his taking chloral again. 'I don't believe he will ever get well till he leaves it off altogether and it strikes me as the time to try, now that he has someone to sleep in his room.'[25]

Edward and Lavinia's time in London could not extend beyond the Easter vacation. Indeed, for Edward to be there at all had meant his reneging on an Easter commitment to the Vicar of Markbeech near Falconhurst – a man with whom he had the strongest ties. But 'Your Father is more guided by him . . . than by anyone', wrote Aunt Coque, who had found, to her sorrow, that she herself could achieve nothing. '[On] Friday morning he would not eat his breakfast, nor open Sybella's letter, till Edward quietly enforced it.' One can see in Edward all the qualities needed. He was young but had the authority of orders, of the place he held and of natural confidence. He was perhaps bolder, less

disquieted than if it had been his own father; but he had loved and
revered from childhood the man who became his father-in-law. To
Meriel at Falconhurst he wrote on 12 April about the deepening melancholy.

> There was one paroxysm of it after lunch when Aunt Coque was with
> him and he poured out about 'poor Sybella' to her. But when I went
> in and perseveringly read Bishop Gray with an occasional question to
> him, he got gradually quiet, subsiding into his book and snoozing. Then
> came a ride with Lavinia and Bob and then a melancholy time.[26]

'This miserable remorse is wretcheder than what I imagined', said
Lavinia, though Edward thought it differed only in degree from the
kind of thing they had seen before.[27] 'The . . . thoughts round which
it revolves this time [are] only one channel for what would find a channel
anyhow . . . Now that he is more occupied about Sybella she takes her
turn as the subject of the melancholy and the other is less thought
of.' (It is not clear who or what was 'the other'. An otherwise cryptic
note of Edward's indicates a woman in the family circle but not one of
his daughters or his first wife, Mary. Auntie Pussy, Aunt Coque? Whoever
it had been, the unfortunate object of his obsession was now Sybella).

On the 14 April, Good Friday, Spencer and Alfred took their father
to church in the morning and he went in the evening with Lavinia and
Edward. 'Papa very wretchedly restless and low.' Edward saw Clark, who
was still convinced that the illness would pass; but also clear that, as
treatment in the family was not succeeding, they should try the course
he had always thought best, though he had originally waived his opinion
out of deference to Dr Monro. 'I fancy Monro would now agree', wrote
Edward to Meriel; adding that he meant to get a third opinion the
following week from Sir William Gull. 'You would probably wish to be
here for that.'[28]

Next day Lavinia had a great fright, riding. Her father had lagged
behind herself and Spencer. Scraping along as he did these days, close
to the palings, his leg was caught and he got knocked off. He had not
been hurt. Indeed, she said, he had got up quickly, but 'in the horrid
indifferent passive way which has grown on him', and which so upset
her. 'He is talking now . . . about resigning offices.'[29]

On Easter Day he went to the service and she stayed close by him.

> He was fidgetty and scared looking and fancied he had not repented
> enough afterwards but my little talk with him seemed to soothe him . . .

I am getting nervous over Papa – one can only say he is *changed*, not better. He is wretched now about his Lord Lieutenancy.[30]

Alfred, she said, as well as Spencer, had begun to hope that, when Gull came on Tuesday, their father would be advised to go away. Looming over them was also the question as to who would take charge at Park Crescent when she and Edward returned to Keble for the beginning of the summer term. Edward wrote to Meriel again that night.

Because I think you must clearly realize that on Wednesday or at the very latest Thursday you must come into command. There is simply no option. Sybella must not have the charge of this. The only way in which you could be relieved . . . would be by the doctors' deciding to send him away sooner. I think all of us who are here feel that it must come to that, unless by God's mercy there is a sudden and real turn.[31]

The next day, Monday, it looked as if there might be. To Lavinia at least he seemed 'more himself' and she felt 'ridiculously over-pleased'. He wrote his letters so fast, she said, 'and was so *compos* in all his old ways'. However, that evening came a miserable scene about resigning his Lord Lieutenancy. 'We had one of the wildest moments we have gone through', Edward told Meriel.

He was quite ungovernable by me . . . and only got calmer after a sedative and when he had written a letter to Mr Hardy 'Immediate' resigning Lord Lieutenancy.[32]

He and Alfred had tried unsuccessfully to persuade him to dress for dinner. However, as they went in, Lavinia called out to him to come and he came,

ran upstairs to wash his hands, eat [sic] his dinner as usual, *repented* of his letter to Mr H., burnt it [Edward had not let it be posted] and spent an unusually quiet evening reading much of Macaulay's *Life*.[33]

But going to bed he was bad again, 'and we watched him creeping upstairs, taking I should think *ten* minutes going up – talking to himself. Did not like it', says Lavinia, 'but Barnes was at hand'.

Another person present had been Mary Gladstone, also witness to the 'awful storm' which was 'far worse than I ever saw'. 'If you had seen him then', wrote Edward to Meriel,

I don't think you would have thought that it would be fit for a person in Sybella's position to be in charge. And if you had seen him nearly in tears when Aunt Coque asked him . . . about S. and the children you would see great reason for thinking that she must be the most unsuitable person for him.

Lucy meanwhile, now out of touch, wrote to Meriel from Lismore, the Duke's seat in Ireland where she and Fred had been spending Easter, 'I hope there will be no sending of poor Papa away from us . . . without a clear opinion from both [doctors] that it would be better for *Papa*'.

> I know that you and I feel . . . how greatly the feeling of being outside everything harassed him and what he wd do without any business or interests I can't imagine.

Dr Clark, she thought, was probably thinking of the problems for *them* of his staying at home. 'But I am sure we would all contrive anything rather than pack him off on *that* account.'

> I am all for Syb. keeping away till he is more human; but if Aunt Coque and any brothers can go on keeping house, when we are back in London you and I and our dear faithful husbands would relieve guard, wouldn't we? I would go out bumping on horseback as regular as clockwork and . . . have him to dine as often as need be. The same sort of thing might go on if Syb. is able to go to Park Crescent and we would get the doctors to insist on her only being with him at stated hours.[34]

'There is no reason, I hope, for thinking he has gone back at all', she went on. When Edward and Lavinia returned to Oxford, might he spend a few days at Falconhurst? 'Let us oppose passive resistance to any *precipitate* plan of hustling off poor Papa', she urged.

The decision, of course, was expected to be made the following day by Sir William Gull. But that day Lyttelton killed himself.

Just after eight on the Tuesday morning he fell from the second floor in Park Crescent down the stair well to the hall below and died in the early hours of Wednesday without regaining consciousness. The inquest, held in the house on Thursday, was given a very clear account of what had happened by Barnes, the 'valet'. On Monday night Lyttelton had not slept well.

> And when he rose, shortly before 8 o'clock, witness helped him to dress and began shaving him. He had shaved one side of his face when Lord Lyttelton, who had previously asked for the razor and had, of course been refused, desired the witness to stop for a little . . . His lordship then   walked quietly up and down the room in a melancholy and reflective manner. With great suddenness he then dashed at the door,

opened it, and rushing out, closed it behind him. Witness followed as fast as he could, but was only in time to see his lordship grasp the banisters, and vault or roll over them, hanging for an instant and then dropping down the well . . . to the hall beneath.[35]

This is what confronted Edward Talbot when he returned from his morning walk.

Clark was sent for, and the surgeon Paget, and Sir William Gull. But nothing could be done. Though he lingered unconscious for eighteen hours, the skull and pelvis were badly fractured and he died after midnight, 'in the calmest way', wrote Edward to Meriel, 'just a few fluttering breathings and then a sudden change'.

> I read the Commendatory Prayer and gave the Blessing and kissed his forehead . . . We watched by him till one. There was something grand in the face . . . Grand like the character and the life before they entered into this dark overshadowing cloud.[36]

The inquest jury delivered a verdict of 'Suicide While of Unsound Mind'. Thomas Barnes, with his seven years' experience of lunatics and 'persons of suicidal tendency', said he had no doubt that the act was deliberate, 'as deceased had often told him he wanted to die'. He repeated that Lyttelton had asked for the razor and gave his opinion, as did Clark, that in these last weeks he had been insane. They did not speculate – and why should they – on the fact that Lyttelton had killed himself on the day appointed for Gull to call to decide if he should be sent away. This, which he had feared in the past, had grown certain and would promptly have settled the question he had brooded on and dreaded – of giving up the Lord Lieutenancy. Lord Lieutenant of the County of Worcester he had been appointed at twenty-two and to be seen unfit for that, to have had his roots torn out of the County, would have been something of a different order from being thrown off the Endowed Schools Commission. In her mourning, his sister, Aunt Coque, liked to hark back to his early glories. 'There's something too pathetic in the change,' she told Meriel, 'his becoming an object of compassion and care.'[37] And no doubt, sane or not, he had felt it.

After the inquest, the family foregathered from its various locations for the funeral at Hagley. Not Charles (for he was still in Italy and they had no Italian address). Not Nevy of course, in India. Spencer, summoned from the home counties by news of 'an accident' had hardly grasped the reality of its dreadful end. Alfred had been detailed to go to Cambridge and tell Edward, who knew nothing at all. Lucy and

Fred, who had been in Ireland, arrived with the Gladstones on the day of the funeral. In this sad house were the three little girls: all quite bright, Lavinia noted – even Sarah (six) seeming not to realise. 'The coffin lies under the perron', she wrote, 'just like last year.' 'People streamed up the park.' The Bishop of Oxford – with Edward assisting – took the service in Hagley Church. And Meriel pencilled in her diary, 'My darling Daddy was buried today.'

'Of the mode of death I think nothing,' wrote Dr Vaughan, Head-master of Harrow (he who had once been bracketted first with Lyttelton in the Classical Tripos), 'only as I would of a stroke or of an accident. But of the precedent suffering I think much.'[38] In so vigorously dis-claiming any moral repugnance Dr Vaughan was ahead of his time, for suicide in England was not only a crime (as it remained till the 1960s) but also a sin which could justify clergy refusing the rites of Christian burial. It is true that the barbarous practice of burying the corpse on the public highway with a stake through the heart had been outlawed in the 1820s. The relation of depression and insanity to suicide had come increasingly to interest doctors, and most clergymen took account of 'Unsound Mind' in a jury verdict. But there remained a strong moral aversion, especially among devout people; and Lyttelton's suicide be-queathed to his family the painful task of squaring this circle on behalf of one who, as Aunt Coque said, had been 'the centre and stay of us all'.

In the first shock they could not accept it. The impression that came through to Lucy in Ireland, before the inquest, from those in Park Crescent was that the death had been accidental. A few days later she put in her diary, 'We shall never know if it was . . . or not, but we *do* know he was as unaccountable as if a lightning-stroke had fallen on him'.[39] It had been a lightning-stroke to her. 'Oh I can't believe the words as I write them!' she poured out in a letter to Nevy (for her thoughts had flown at once to him and what he must face, so far away). 'At first', she wrote, 'it seems as if all was utter misery and darkness, but darling Nevy, we must not think so. God help you in your loneliness and heavy sorrow to find the one comfort.' The horror, she insisted, was just external – not really worse than May's constant delirium. 'Both were illness.' And the fatal impulse came as a messenger of release.

Dear, dear Papa – we must remember how terrible it would have been for him to have this awful depression on him for longer . . . and then as he grew older, the attacks might have become worse. Often too I used to think anxiously how little fitted he was for old age . . . and how heart-breaking it would be to see him go through more sorrow.[40]

'Once when he was in great distress, he said he could not attend to his prayers. I said, "But you know the prayers of a life-time are around you." He answered gently, "That's a good thought".' 'I spoke to him of all he had been to his children . . . and he said with a little faint pleasure, "I hope I may have done some little good".'

Meriel too sought to comfort Nevy, telling him how her father had told her that 'whatever comes of this' he would never forget the love which all his children had shown him. 'I like to think how we all took our share in trying to help him, all the boys did their very best, walking with him and talking to him.' 'It is all so difficult to understand.'

> One can only cling to the thought of the Cross and of our Lord having suffered the horror of being deserted, which must have been something like Papa's misery.[41]

'The souls of the righteous are in the hands of God and there shall no torment touch them', runs the inscription in Hagley churchyard. 'I think as time goes on', said Mrs Talbot 'the special horror of the event will fade.'

> The memory of his noble life will not be tarnished and I think no one's faith in it . . . will be shaken – though it leaves one now with a feeling almost as if one had been present at a personal conflict with the powers of evil.[42]

This sense of an evil but *exterior* power is evident in Gladstone's tribute to his much-loved brother-in-law in the *Guardian*. Lyttelton, he stated, 'repelled, condemned and repeatedly mastered the impulse which he knew to be upon him rather than in him, *an alien and guilty thing*' (my italics). And when at last it had proved too strong for his 'shaken and enfeebled system', a noble life was ended 'by the action of an impulse foreign . . . to all his past and all his latest thoughts'. He wrote of Lyttelton's sense of duty and of the integrity which 'lifted him far above jobbery and intrigue'.

> His time and energy were constantly applied to all the interests – social, moral or religious – either of the general or of the local public. Devotion of such a kind, little known *except in this country*, has rarely even in this country been carried so far . . . It was rewarded by the affection and indeed the reverence of the community and the county in which he lived.

He spoke of a character 'in the highest degree childlike and in the highest degree manly'; of a blunt manner which concealed 'a temper of remarkable sweetness'; of 'a bright, genial and joyous life'.

> Nor was the performance of his daily duties ever interrupted by the few fits of dejection with which at very rare intervals it was chequered. Even in the latest and by far the worst of them, his perception of duty and his resignation and love to the giver of all good, were . . . active to the last days of his life.[43]

Frederick Cavendish wrote to Nevy, 'We are sending you a *Guardian* with a sketch which we all like of him by Mr Gladstone'.

Two days later there appeared an article of a very different kind in the *British Medical Journal*, which cited Lyttelton's case to illustrate the false economy of the upper classes when caring for an insane person at home. The thought of an asylum, it was acknowledged, 'even in these enlightened days', generally evoked a feeling of horror. But if the patient were kept at home, proper precautions must be taken.

> It is to be hoped that those who are afflicted with the presence of an insane patient will take warning from the misfortune which has happened to Lord Lyttelton's family – a misfortune caused, doubtless, more from ignorance than from any intentional neglect.

Acknowledging the eminence of Dr Clark, and of Dr Monro ('whose experience of the treatment of private cases is perhaps unequalled in the kingdom'), the writer felt obliged to point out that only one attendant had been employed, whereas day-time and night-time attendance was needed.

> The lessons to be learnt from this sad disaster are, that we should not grudge employing a sufficient number of attendants if the patient be rich; and that if he be poor, he should be sent to a well-organised asylum.[44]

The medical evidence, declared the *Standard*, explained why Lyttelton's life had been 'to some extent a failure'; why, with great powers, he had not played a greater part in the affairs of the nation. Dr Clark at once refuted this – saying that the earlier depressive attacks had been very few and widely spaced. 'Looking back . . . a few months, I can say with . . . truth that I knew of no healthier, happier, busier or more useful life than Lord Lyttelton's.' He had never aimed at a political career, declared one resolute friend, in *The Times*; and had been too just, too blunt, too kindly ever to have made a politician.

His detestation even of the appearance of insincerity caused him sometimes to give offence by an abruptness which was misinterpreted. But the roughness was all on the surface. No woman ever possessed a kinder heart or would have shrunk more from inflicting pain upon another. To perform in the way he did the duties of a great local magnate, of the father of a family and of a representative Churchman – to win the respect of all classes in his county, and the ardent affection of a host of friends, cannot be regarded as a failure in life.[45]

'Hardly one but calls it "a noble life" ', Lucy wrote as the tributes poured in.[46] Some, by implication, mourned the passing of an old ideal of nobility. Canon Robinson, one of Lyttelton's colleagues in the work of the Endowed Schools Commission, found England poorer for the loss of one who 'joined nobility of rank to nobility of nature' and wished to leave his country better than he found it. The *Spectator*, praising a career of honour 'and remarkable public usefulness', considered men of Lyttelton's stamp 'the pride and safeguard of the English aristocracy'. 'It is an immense blessing to you to have known your Grandfather', Meriel's fifteen-year-old George was told, 'and to understand and value what all England says about the worth of his name.' 'We live in the midst of titled people', the Birmingham *Town Crier* stated bluntly, 'who profit more by us than we by them'.

> They are Presidents of this and Presidents of that and our limited intercourse is very pleasant, doubtless owing to its limits. But Lord Lyttelton did know something about us and cared something about our aims and objects.

'He was wide-souled.' And had seen the need to free poor men from the curse of ignorance. Wherever any knot of people gathered in a good cause 'he was at home with them'. 'Lord Lyttelton was honoured for his own sake,' the paper insists, 'not because of the title; which owes all the honors it can give to such men as he was. In no part of the kingdom was his death more lamented than in this rough town.'

If public service took pride of place, courtesy also played a part in the old ideal of the nobleman. W.E. Forster, who as minister concerned with education in Gladstone's first government had had frequent contact with Lyttelton, said they had not always seen eye to eye. 'But with what rare beauty of temper and with what real courtesy he used to put up with contradiction!' Maria Grey looked back to the time when she had been seeking Lyttelton's support for her Women's Education Union, and some who knew him well had assured her

of his readiness to listen and give full weight to the opinions of others, of his modesty . . . of his genial humour, and the real . . . sweetness that underlay his somewhat rough and burly exterior.

'Amid the countless opportunities presented by . . . daily or even hourly intercourse', wrote young Mr Richmond, who had worked under Lyttelton on the Schools Inquiry and Endowed Schools Commissions, 'I have never received from him one unkind word.' A clergyman, once a young Curate at Hagley, wrote that he had never met anyone who came 'so near to my idea of a perfect English nobleman'.

> Who had such a high standard before himself and yet was so gentle in his judgement of others, who could be so full of fun and humour, and yet so free from any tinge of ill nature, whose piety and goodness were so undoubted and yet so unobtrusive and so unmixed with anything approaching to cant – and whose great intellectual gifts made smaller people feel their own inferiority so little.

'I never used to mind if he was in church when I had to preach', Mr Johnstone said, 'as I felt sure that, though he was the most capable, he was sure to be the most indulgent critic.'

'Is there, I sometimes ask myself, such another generation behind?' wrote Dr Vaughan. Maria Grey claimed, with some justification, that nowhere outside his family circle would the effect of his loss be greater than it would in the Women's Education Union, 'to which he was a friend when friends were few and which even now can ill spare such friendship as his'.

> The services Lord Lyttelton rendered to the cause of the education of women . . . date from the time when that cause had not outlived the phase of ridicule and reprobation: when the claim of women to any knowledge beyond that which could make them more pleasing in the drawing room, or more useful in the kitchen, was the easy theme of every witling.[47]

Things had changed. And so much so, that a younger generation, 'enjoying . . . the privileges so hardly won by this, may forget what they owe to him. But we, whom he helped through the heat and burden of the day, can never forget'.

# 12

# *The Last Chapter*

'HE is not the author of evil and the thought came to
me that all these dark troubles are not meant but
permitted . . . Behind them is the Eternal Goodness,
bringing who knows what blessings out of it all.'

Lucy to Meriel, 1870s

Lucy and Fred had stayed on at Hagley for a week or so after the
funeral, doing what they could to comfort Sybella; and Lucy persuading
six-year-old Sarah to attend to 'a little grave talk' about her father.
Sybella had flustered outbreaks at times, but was very touching, Lucy
thought, in her unselfishness and patience. 'She has constant tears to
relieve her, and clings to his children, and turns to the religious
thoughts and words which were "the strength of his life" to comfort
her.'[1] If he had lived, Sybella said, the consciousness of having been
deranged would have destroyed his happiness. 'The mode of death
does not affect me – it never has', she affirmed to Meriel. 'Only the
yearning longing for his return, and the loss of that great love – just
too as I felt that I was growing up to him – and learning to understand
him fully.'[2]

Lavinia at times had been inclined to pity Sybella's 'Martha-like'
existence. She may even at some level have reacted against the tendency
to wifely adoration, feeling, as she said once of a cousin, that it was
'unreasonable for a woman to surrender opinions, conscience, will to
a man'. At any rate,

To me, to be a *mère de famille* over a big house, with delicate children,
a vast array of step-children and relations, not very sufficient 'means'
and a husband who took *none* of the responsibilities upon him . . . would
be a life of such incessant cares that I sometimes think Sybella puts a
good face on it.[3]

Sybella painted a different picture. 'You see', she told Meriel, 'from that chivalrous feeling that every woman was an angel, and I one of the band, he never would teach me anything (and it was not for the want of asking but I think it bored him).'

> So I had to find out his life's work for myself, and in many ways the train of thought was so different to any that I had in any way lived with, that I did not at first appreciate it. But that was all over and I had fully taken it in, to find it all snatched from me!

'Still the example will remain . . . and help me through the many weary years . . . in store.' And she had his children. 'You will all help me to bring up these poor little things as he would have wished. Hester is growing absurdly like him.'[4]

Charles arrived from Naples on 28 April, four days after the funeral. To let him in gently they had arranged that Meriel should meet him in London. And evidently, 'all the poor little steps we had taken to soften things' paid off; though at Hagley, 'the sitting tight for his arrival was terribly sad and nervous work'.[5] Lavinia, in the morning room with Lucy, noticed how white and strained she looked. Sybella ('wretched') had taken to her bed. Edward Talbot met Charles at the station. Albert greeted him in the hall and took him to the morning room. They had tea; then Charles went to the library and shook hands with the household. 'It was just dreadful the half hour before he came – then it was all right,' Lavinia wrote, 'and the blessing is great to have a head again.'[6]

Charles said they had all had more shock than he had. But the next morning he disappeared for a long time and Lucy saw later that he had been crying.

> He was for three-quarters of an hour with Sybella and we found her quite composed and stilled by him. They talked over the illness, and he said some quiet strong kind words about the mercy of what Papa may have been spared.[7]

He and Bob talked estate business. 'I always knew he could buckle to it if it ever was . . . incumbent on him to do so', Bob confided to Mary Gladstone. And Charles admitted to Meriel later that even if he hadn't had a sense of duty,

> I think the high-pitched estimation of me on the part of those nearest to me would be enough to keep me fairly straight. And this is very important to me, having lost one whom to pain, or even to disappoint, was a thing to be shrunk from.[8]

He could certainly not expect to be well-off. At first it was feared that he might not even have enough to enable him to live at Hagley. 'But it is pretty clear now', wrote Lucy to Nevy, 'that with careful economy and shutting up half the house, he may do it, so as to keep up a home for the brothers.' His household was to be 'Howe and footman, Wordsworth and k[itchen] maid, housemaid and "scrub", Daphne and a boy', Lavinia noted; much relieved that he was staying on.[9] Lucy reckoned that Charles would have about £1500 a year to live on and house-keep, when he had put aside £1000 a year towards the debt,

> and paid us all our charges on the estate. The brothers are . . . tolerably off his hands. Albert, you and Spencer are all to some extent provided for; the Glynne money that has come to us pays Arthur's remaining time at Cuddesdon, and then he will have a curacy. Edward's Cambridge, Spencer says he will pay for, and dear Sybella, Alfred's. There only remains Bob's expenses at Escrick.[10]

'What strikes me about this family', Edward Talbot had said to Meriel when he was about to marry Lavinia, 'is . . . an unusually strong patriotism for the place and for the clan.'[11] The present circumstances brought this out: though the word 'clan' obscures a little the individuality of its members. Each – though comforted by the others; by Hagley even, and by Charles's return – had to face up to the painful task of reconciling the death with the life. 'I need never say anything about these two days', Lavinia had written, just afterwards. 'The time feels burnt into one's mind and it is hard not to feel pain and bitterness.'[12] An event which they had long looked forward to, the consecration of Keble chapel, took place three days after the funeral. Edward was 'a good deal worn down in spirit', and very conscious of the changed gathering and the chill of having hardly any family there.[13]

Nevy wrote from somewhere in the Himalayas, 'bewildered and wretched', Lavinia said. 'The central figure of my life had vanished', was how he put it in later years. He also had too much time to brood, for the news had reached him on his way to Kashmir where he was about to spend six months' leave. 'I know well that he was not responsible', he had insisted then, to Meriel. None the less,

> The recollection of the end would be frightfully bitter, were it not for the knowledge that all his life for which he was responsible was so different. In my present lonely life I think of nothing else.[14]

Bob, on the distant farm in Yorkshire where he was learning land agent's work, also felt very isolated. 'When I first faced the bustle and noise of the world', he confided to Mary Gladstone,

> I felt rather like a wild beast, for I was conscious of being stared at by everybody and . . . I felt wretched to the last degree. I didn't feel as if I could ever take an interest in agriculture or anything again.

He plunged into work, but it did not protect him from people's embarrassment – or good intentions. 'Well sir, I hope you are pretty well after your bereavement!' called out one acquaintance, sitting over his beer in a pub. 'This in the public bar with several other people present together with a ringletted barmaid – he meant well, poor old man, but it was painful, very.'[15]

'I think my people here must think me very cheerful', wrote Lucy from Holker that September, 'but the great grief in its various aspects goes aching on underneath.'

> I don't yet find the thought of the 'brilliant happy life' overcome in me the heavy pain and humiliation of the last weeks – except by way of most piteous contrast. And sometimes fear this particular acute pang will keep me 'mourning to the end'.[16]

She had learnt, though, as she explained to Meriel, what she had not understood on her birthday in 1857, when she said there could be no more happy returns. 'That was like the sorrow of sixteen . . . Still less could I have then conceived how deep sorrow can coexist with deep happiness . . . I have such immense blessings that one main part of me is happy indeed (and so it must be with both you and Lavinia).'

They, alas, had had the extra shock of Mrs Talbot's unexpected death from pneumonia – only six weeks after their father. Summoned by telegram, Lavinia and Edward, with Meriel and Johnny, were powerless to do more than witness the dying. Edward again had the solemn task of reading the Commendatory Prayer and the Blessing. The Talbots, Gladstones and Lytteltons, who had recently assembled at Hagley, reassembled at Falconhurst. Lavinia made a great cross of flowers ('like the two others we have lately made'). 'All those lately gone from us have gone . . . straight out of life, without a word', she wrote later. Meriel's summer was taken over by the great change at Falconhurst. Feeling 'sadly helpless and astray' in that familiar place without its guiding spirit, she was yet 'so busy all day long that I sometimes feel as if I had hardly leisure to . . . realise the great sad days in our life'. With all the complex business entailed in Johnny's taking over the estate, there was the worry that he did not know yet what his income was likely to be. 'Big bills keep coming in (I don't mean arrears but the regular payments of this place).' But she was heartened by the news of Hagley.

How thankful the thought of the old brothers' earnest home life does make one, with the light of Papa's example shining in every part of it, bless him.[17]

In October Lavinia spent 'a most snug week at the darling old home – as home it still feels'. Sybella was away, and it was like old times, 'when May and I were alone with Charles and some of the brothers when Papa was on the Commission etc'.

The impossible thing was to realise that he would not come straying through the library to listen a bit while singing went on, or with his lamp in the evening. It was not Sybella or the children I missed, but just Papa.[18]

It would surely have pleased him to see Charles trying to follow in his footsteps, 'down to minute points: he is an old *dear*'. Spencer, Arthur and Edward were there, and there was singing and walks and talks and she gossiped with Newmany and village people. 'The whole place seems steeped in associations and how I do love it!' She had felt 'the old pinching feeling' when leaving; and yet perhaps a stir of hope that Hagley would exorcise Park Crescent.

Back at Keble, and reunited with one-year-old May, whose amusing antics were a constant source of delight, Lavinia observed to Lucy, 'I begin to feel I ought to have another' (and in fact did so the following year). This, however, did not diminish her sense of responsibility for Hagley. She and Lucy discussed at length what could be done to avoid the brothers being split up this first sad Christmas; which in fact was made successful by Lucy and Fred going there to join them. 'O the blessing', Lucy expostulated, 'of their being so truly his own sons!'

So that there is no jar or bitterness in seeing Charles at the head and all of them at home as usual. Charles is such a tower of strength to the poor old home.

Lavinia pondered other problems. What was to be done about Spencer's future? Spencer, alas, had lost his job as Gladstone's assistant private secretary when the Liberals lost office, two years before; and after her pleasant October visit, Lavinia had returned 'more bent than ever on his being given something to do'. 'It is so wretched', she wrote to Lucy, 'to hear him mapping out the coming months without a view to a soul in the world but himself. I am sure he don't like it, but he has no power of looking out and *making* objects of work.'[19] A few weeks later she returned to this.

> It is bad for him to live such a piece of his precious youth [he was twenty-nine] in having no *musts* in his life and no one to live for . . . It's a thousand pities we are none of us clever enough to put him on the right road for finding something.

Aunt Coque had suggested the librarian's post at Althorp, but Lavinia did not think that a good idea – 'even if it were offered which it won't be'.

> There are so many first rate men to whom such a place would be riches, and I should feel Spencer was almost taking the bread out of someone's mouth. And then, would it be at all uphill work or disagreeable? I don't mean that all work must be . . . one or the other – but it should not be too luxurious and charming. A real great Librarian is a wonderful being, but I fancy they have been people who have had to work hard through drudgery and real work in such places as the British Museum.[20]

Charles concerned her in a different way. No one could have faulted his application to the tasks of his appointed role. 'I begin to feel the family allegiance to the head', Alfred admitted to Mary Gladstone; while Sybella praised his kindness to herself and to the children – for whom he had built a great tower of bricks 'which came down amid shrieks of excitement'. But it exercised Lavinia that at thirty-four he showed no sign of seeking a wife. Two years earlier she had noted that his friends were rapidly doubling themselves, and now she told Lucy she would like to see a suitable lady presiding at Hagley.

> Our brothers have always wanted gentleness of manner . . . and I can picture such a happy state of things if Charles was to marry a gracious warm-hearted woman. But that 'if' makes one almost thankful to leave things as they are![21]

In this way the graceful figure of a new Lady Lyttelton entered their minds: tall (for Charles was well over six foot), handsome (as he was) and in every way worthy. But Charles played his cards very close to his chest. 'It *is* odd Charles being again at Latimer, and what is in the old fellow's mind who can say?' Lavinia observed to Lucy in February 1877. 'But Mr Balfour comes here tomorrow and as he met him at Latimer I shall pick his brains judiciously.' In September that year Aunt Emy died. Lucy could not resist observing how Charles would miss her help in the village. 'I can't help hoping it will make him feel very strongly the need of a wife', she told Auntie Pussy, 'the poor old place will be quite womanless now'.

It was still womanless the following summer. 'It is very peaceful here', she wrote to Meriel, 'and there are many things to make it bright': not least, the presence of little May – who loved her dearly and liked nothing better than squeezing *tightissimus* into her armchair to look at pictures and be cosy.

> Charles is busy most days: Board of Guardians, Bromsgrove School speech day, audit, magistrates' inspection of allotments. It does one good to see him but how he can help being driven into marrying I can't think.[22]

The change at the Rectory made it worse: 'everything feminine withered up and gone, grievously to the loss of the place'. Charles told her she wanted him to marry to get the district visiting done. 'How poor! and how unlike the speech of a man who had any *objet aimé* in his view!' Here she was mistaken, for three weeks later, on 23 August 1878, Charles informed her that he was engaged to Mary Cavendish, Lord Chesham's daughter.

'Oh my darling old Creature – what would I not give to get at you at this memorable moment!' she wrote to Meriel from Bolton Abbey: railing against the cruel fate that put so many counties between them ('so that unless the great things all happen during London, we can only scream thro' the post'), but thankful for the rain that gave her time to write. Charles had come out with it just before leaving. And never, since that very time twenty-one years ago in 1857 had she seen him so moved. 'There are just five minutes to tell you what I want to tell you', he had said. 'Do you like Mary Cavendish?'

> It must have been Providence that put things into my mouth . . . for it *was* a thunderbolt; but I am glad I had no preparation. My love of him, and his happy look . . . and the feeling that he must have been led into it by nothing that was not good and genuine and right-minded – all came to my rescue.

'But the *cons*', she said, '*will* make themselves heard.' As well as she could (people wandering about, Duke writing letters, small nephews fighting), she set them down. Mary Cavendish was short; and not at all pretty; and hers was not the name they had ever expected (having thought him interested in someone else).

How *can* the little plain woman ever be within 100 miles of being worthy of him! Has he really found the strength and goodness and brightness which one would have for him for his wife?[23]

'I did not think I should be such a fool about looks but . . . this one *can't* look in any degree like what another Mary, Lady Lyttelton ought to be!' 'And last and perhaps least,' she says, 'the money!' 'I did ask him a little about that, but he only smiled brightly and said Mary Cavendish would be able to "keep herself".' ('He is far gone, you may imagine', Lavinia wrote to her brother Edward, 'when he takes her poor little fortune of £10,000 so mildly . . . possibly there will be more at Lord Chesham's death.')[24]

'Well, I don't mean to let myself be foreboding . . . I am sure it is the real thing', Lucy wound up, 'and that the dear, dear old brother has done all in the fear of God. You could never doubt it if you had seen and heard him.' Lavinia had commented long ago that Lucy had 'a wonderful way of literally *liking* what she knows to be right'. Which was true here: for three days later she wrote again to Meriel – full of delight in the thought of this new happiness for Hagley, 'which for so long had sunshine in the very sound of its name'.

> How little one ever dreamt of such an event without darling daddy to tell! Such things make me picture so vividly that look of his, that bright, bright smile full of vivid interest and delight which no other face ever has.[25]

And how little they had dreamt of Charles himself – so deeply reserved – being so much in love! 'She is no bigger than you', he told Newmany (now in her eighties), 'and quite as good, and nearly as fond of me as you are.'

The wedding was to take place in October. Lavinia had at once begun discussing bedrooms and carpets and curtains with Sybella – joined by Auntie Pussy, who arrived at Hagley with an Aubusson carpet for the morning room. Lavinia described it at length in her diary. 'Never felt so desolate in a childish way without May when looking at it', she wrote. But in general these were happy times. She approved very much of Mary Cavendish. True-pointed, warm-hearted, a real trump.

> She will stand up to him and understand Hagley and old times and associations and enter into the life there and be a dear little sister-in-law. *Plain* I am afraid I do think her, but if she don't get fat I don't mind.[26]

Lucy spared a thought for poor Sybella, now to preside at Hagley no more, and yet so generously delighted that Charles was making a real love match. 'It will be such unmixed happiness to a nature so full of real deep feeling . . . From my heart I rejoice at it.' She had already bought the house in Bryanston Square which was to be the London home not only of herself and the children but of Edward and Alfred for the time being; and a focal point for all them for many years. Still, she found it hard to leave Hagley.

> But I am . . . grateful it was not *last* year and that a little time has been given . . . to help one . . . tide over the Sad loved Past before the scene had again changed.[27]

She had just been sent a photograph of the tomb in Worcester Cathedral which some of Lyttelton's friends in the county had erected to his memory. The likeness was exceedingly good; 'and its deep peace seemed almost to check the longing intense desire to have him here. It is so heartbreaking not to have him to speak to . . . not that in reality I miss him more at one time than the other', she said. 'Still at these exceptional moments . . . it does seem hard to be alone.'

19 October 1878, Charles's wedding day: 'a golden day within and without!' and certainly an exceptional moment. 'Thank God for this great happiness that has come to him, and thro' him to us all', wrote Lucy, 'after the heavy sorrows of the last two years.'[28] She gives it the atmosphere of a beano: the sunshine and the family's arrival 'in a great army' by sundry vehicles. 'Very plucky of old Meriel!' (who was nine months pregnant with her tenth baby). 'She and I, Bob, Edward, Spencer etc. drove up together in a bus and had ridiculous jokes. Behind us came a trap piled with the Reverend gentlemen [including her brothers, Albert and Arthur], who appeared to be equally jovial. Latimer looked lovely: the walk to the church all of a glow with golden sunshine and autumn tints.' The service was taken by Uncle Billy; Nevy was best man, brown and grave after his four and a half years in India, and performed his various duties with 'a military spirit all his own'.

> The little bride looked her very best, her face so softened with deep feeling and joy; Charles glorious! At breakfast afterwards Uncle W[illiam] made a most faultless little speech, and Charles answered very perfectly: his face a sight to see, as he looked down at his little wife with that smile of his that is like both Papa's and Mamma's . . . They drove off to Cliveden in the glowing afternoon.

Afterwards it occurred to Lucy that they should have used this unique occasion to have 'the old eight' photographed together. 'The saddest . . .

missing of Papa', she had once said, 'is when good or pleasant or amusing news of the boys turns up and we can't tell him.' The wedding, for instance. Or Edward's getting his Trinity scholarship just the year after his father died, which had made her long for 'that delighted face . . . which his eight sons have so often called up'. Or, 'little pig Arthur', as his father had called him, being offered the headship of Selwyn College, a new college to be founded at Cambridge on the same High Anglican lines as Keble. 'O what it is not to have Papa, May, or Mrs Talbot or Aunt Emy to tell!' There were to be many such occasions. True, unless he had lived into his eighties, her father could not have known Arthur as a Bishop, or Nevy as a General, or Edward as Headmaster of Eton, or Alfred as Colonial Secretary; but he would have been overjoyed to think of Hagley's filling up with children again; proud of Albert in far-off Africa exercising his priestly calling; tickled that Bob, the prospective land agent, had ended up a solicitor; and he might even have diverted Spencer, as his daughters had failed to do, from a life devoted to concerts and travel.

The dear old eight. What would Lucy have made of the warm but demythologising sketch of 'The Uncles' by Meriel's daughter Gwendolen Stephenson as she looked back from the 1940s? Charles: 'a remote and beautiful figure' who combined inaccuracy with dogmatism. Albert: eccentric and unworldy; unkempt in threadbare clerical clothes. Nevy: the only one of the uncles who played with children and enjoyed them. Spencer: 'a great shirker', whose private means meant that 'the Lyttelton inertia had no counterbalancing impetus'. Arthur: who had his father's scholarship, but somehow seemed to care more for *topics* than for the person he was talking to. Bob: an incompetent man of business but the most openly affectionate uncle. Edward: given to tiresome fads (anti-birth control, Jaeger sheets, co-education, vegetarianism), but sweet-tempered – an outstanding Christian. ('I think there was a good deal of the saint in him'). Alfred: 'To most of us . . . a dazzling stranger', whose spectacular popularity had made her parents shy of inviting him, out of a fear that he would be bored.

> Strange that to the world at large 'the Uncles' appeared to be a rather arrogant and mutually admiring phalanx, almost insolently self-satisfied. In reality most of them suffered from incapacitating diffidence . . . Their father left them each with only £200 a year so that with the exception of Spencer they all had to make their own living. This I think was an element in their success.

'But as I look back, I like to see again the expression in the eyes of each: an expression of innocence and of kindness unusual in middle-aged men and common to them all.'[29]

If Charles's marriage had given a fillip, in Lucy's eyes, to the old home circle, the General Election of 1880 did the same for politics: the Liberals won. She had thrown herself into electioneering with greater zest than ever before. 'I daresay your wicked people [Tories] are having their little pickings in the south and London', she wrote to Meriel, 'but I am ready to back the North to do great things the other way.'

> It's impossible not to enjoy myself, though I do feel a heartless wife for saying so when it is great nuisance and labour to F.; but he is speaking so capitally, and the receptions are so famous and the Yorkshire people so delightful, I can't help it![30]

As to hospitality, 'wine and salmon and sweetbreads and feather-beds abound', runs the diary, 'and all sorts and conditions of men are working like horses . . . at the canvassing'. There follow pages about the results: triumph on a scale which, she proudly noted, brought in *eight* of her relations as County Members. And more pages on the moral dilemma as to who should be Prime Minister: Uncle William (who had retired as Liberal leader after the defeat of 1874 but whose amazing Midlothian speeches had fired the Liberals to this huge success) or Lord Hartington (Fred's brother) who had had the job of leading the party through the great man's five-year retirement?

Gladstone not only became Prime Minister but chose to combine this with the Exchequer; and so, for the routine Treasury work, appointed Fred as Financial Secretary. 'Aunty Pussy told me he said he could not undertake the Exchequer without someone like him', Lucy wrote.[31] Though it meant late hours and uncertain dinner times, she was naturally over the moon; inclined, that 'lovely blossoming spring', to see good omens on every side. But for the one that she could never banish. To Meriel and Johnny, who had tried to console her the previous year by pointing out the drawbacks of having a large family, she had answered:

> Every word you may say about many children versus none is truth itself and what's more I believe I should be far less fitted than the dear old chief Crépin [Meriel] to cope with the burden. But these considerations somehow are accepted by one's sense without filling up the gap in one's heart.[32]

And the following year, when she was forty,

I *did* love your dear letter on my wizzy birthday, a day which brought me real pangs. It is a tremendous clock-striking, and to me, of course, a sort of knell of poor tired-out hopes; but that's only a small dark segment of my 'full-orbed' happiness.[33]

'The blessed satisfied sense of dependence on one who is as my own life to me', which she had expressed in the first year of marriage, can be glimpsed right through the years of grandeur and high politics which marriage brought her. Though the extent to which she could impose herself upon the ducal lifestyle was limited, and she was still not at ease with the Duke, yet in the brilliantly crowded diary there are endless little treats with 'my Fred': rides together and readings together. In town, 'a little junket with my Fred to choose him a library table'; in the country, 'a Darby and Joan walk', picking primroses and white violets. 'It is the having Fred that makes *home* to me', Lucy had declared at the start. And to him, who was the less brilliant and shyer, she brought that sense of domestic life which she had taken in from her parents, and then in his widowerhood, from her father. 'Take the word of a middle-aged wife,' she wrote to a newly-engaged friend, 'there is nothing in the whole world like this particular happiness.' In the aftermath of her father's death ('the most terrible experience of my life'), she had clung to the blessing of her own and her sisters' 'inner home sanctuaries' still safe and bright.[34] 'Freddy is with you', Lavinia had told her. And she had admitted that, without him, 'I don't know what would have become of me'.[35]

Fred held his Treasury post for two years. He liked the work and was very conscientious, so if Gladstone's judgement had been astray in adding the burdens of the Exchequer to the burdens of the Premiership, at least he had appointed a good lieutenant. Beyond that, there were genuine bonds of friendship and affection between the two; and on Fred's side, great admiration. As for Gladstone, he had made a Cabinet with a number of ambitious men in it, by no means all ready to pull together, and it can only have been agreeable to have had behind him such an unself-seeking and reliable lieutenant. This second government (unlike his first) came in with no distinct idea of the main issues that would have to be faced, and was thus 'a poor vessel for the weathering of storms', driven by events instead of shaping them.[36] As the new Ministers' names were announced, Lucy recorded in her diary, 'Every-one steps into a hash of difficulties, but I should think there was nothing to equal India with the Afghan war dragging on'.[37] Gladstone evidently thought the same, for he made Lord Hartington – one of the heavyweights – Secretary of State for India. Meanwhile, at his own back door, in Ireland, a Greek tragedy was in the making.

Gladstone's lack of foresight here may have stemmed from a blindspot over economics (as opposed to budgetary finance) which made him slow to appreciate the truly frightful impact on Ireland of the agricultural depression. Prices fell to nothing; more than 10,000 tenants were evicted for non-payment of rent in the year his government took office. A desperate peasantry responded with death threats, rick-burning and cattle-maiming. Gladstone's attempt to get through Parliament a compensatory land bill failed, and in 1881 W.E. Forster, now Secretary for Ireland and a hardliner, pushed through a new Coercion Act which suspended Habeas Corpus and gave unlimited powers of arrest. It provoked further extremes of terror. The next year Gladstone made a secret pact with Charles Parnell, the Irish Nationalist leader, to release him from prison in return for his support for new land measures. W.E. Forster resigned in protest; and so unconsciously opened the door to the horror that lay ahead.

Lucy's account of the next few days fits so well with the rest of the diary that it comes as a shock to realise that she wrote it after her husband's death.[38]

> May 2nd 1882. Mr Forster's resignation announced in the House . . .
> Mrs Grenfell came to tea with me and we wondered who would succeed
> him. I saw nothing of my Fred till dinner-time. We dined with the Miss
> Hollands . . . and on the way there he told me his name was among
> those to be considered . . . He was much disturbed and I was very much
> vexed, hating his being taken out of what he was doing so well.

Fred next day went to see Lord Granville (leader of the party in the House of Lords) to argue his own unsuitability, but unluckily without success. They dined with the Liberal Sir John Lubbock: 'My poor Fred all along in great perturbation, but dwelling not at all on interruption of his congenial and most successful work at the Treasury . . . but only on whether he could be the fittest man for such a difficult post.' It troubled him, she says, that the Duke was against it (unwilling to lose so much of him at Holker, or see him take on such a thankless task), though he agreed with her that personal preference ought not to outweigh public duty. He consulted various friends and associates. Nevy took the view that it was right to go. Lord Rosebery said, 'Are you going to your martyrdom?' The news of his appointment was badly received in the House of Commons and in the press, where he was dismissed as 'an unknown man'.

Lucy also canvassed opinion. Gladstone was reassuringly certain that
he had chosen the best man for the job. ('But what I am to do without
him I can't imagine.') Lady Cowper, whose husband had just resigned
the Lord Lieutenancy of Ireland, said 'I cannot congratulate you', and
spoke of the despairing state of things, the cold-shouldering of the
gentry, the isolation; but Charlotte Spencer, whose husband Earl
Spencer (Lucy's cousin) had just succeeded Cowper as Lord Lieutenant
(and had also held the post before), said that, though she knew how
bad things were, she liked being there and had spent in Ireland 'five
of the happiest . . . years of her life'. She was sure too that Spencer
and Fred would get on well in their work together.

The two men left London on Friday, 5 May 1882, catching the night
train to Holyhead. 'There was some hustle at the last', wrote Lucy, 'as
the servant was putting clean shirts into his portmanteau at the last
moment . . . and we laughed about it.'

> My Fred ran into his room and took some bank-notes out of his writ-
> ing-table drawer. I said, 'Have you money enough?' He said, 'O yes, I
> shall go free most of the way' (because he had a Director's pass). Then
> came our goodbye – our last kiss. There were no particular last words.
> I had not a feeling but that he was coming back on Sunday night: I
> called to him, 'Mind and send me word of your train, that I may send
> to meet you' . . . I heard afterwards that he all but missed the train.
> This was my last sight of my own darling.

Arriving in Dublin on the Saturday, Lord Spencer and Fred took
their oaths at the Castle. Walking that afternoon in Phoenix Park, Fred
saw Thomas Burke, his Under-Secretary, driving. Burke was a civil
servant whose whole career had been at Dublin Castle; latterly, of course,
under Mr Forster, when he had certainly attracted some of the odium
attached to the Coercion Act. Now, most tragically for them both, he
got down from his vehicle to talk to Fred. In broad daylight, and despite
the presence of others strolling about the park, they were set upon
from behind and hacked to death with surgical knives.

'Saturday, May 6th: I read a short prayer at Family Prayers for my
Fred, that he might be guided right and strengthened for his terribly
anxious work.' Nevy and others came to lunch. In the afternoon Lucy
went to Westminster Abbey and came in as the choir was singing 'Thou
shalt keep him in perfect peace whose mind is stayed on Thee'; 'and
I thought, "O these are the very words for my Fred".'

I knelt down and prayed for him with my whole heart, but not that he might be saved from peril (a mere idle thought crossed me once – what if the steamer should go down on the passage?) . . . but that he might have wisdom and strength and help.

She had a rather enjoyable evening. Word came through that Spencer and Fred had been well received in Dublin. Admiral Egerton and his wife (her much-loved sister-in-law, Lady Louisa) and her brother Alfred came to dinner. Meriel called later and they all chaffed Lucy about the entertaining she would have to do to help her husband in his new position, and how she must be smartly dressed and so on. Then the Egertons went off to an Admiralty party and Alfred left also. But Meriel stayed.

> I read her a nice letter of Uncle Billy's, raving of her children, whom he had been with at Falconhurst: and I said to her how sad it seemed that a character like Fred's should not be transmitted to children.

When Meriel left, about half past eleven, Lucy wrote letters and opened a parcel which Uncle William had had sent over with a set of his *Gleanings of Past Years*, accompanied by an affectionate note, 'begging me to ask Freddy to give them a place on his shelves, "in grateful memory on my part of what he has been to me these past two years".' She had just started on a reply 'when the door opened and Lou came in . . . As soon as I saw her face the terror seized me . . . She had the dreadful telegram in her hand'. But Louisa said at first that he was dangerously wounded; and Meriel (who now knew the worst), reappeared to hear Lucy saying, 'Oh I know he will pull through . . . he is in such fine health!' When from their manner she perceived the truth, she sank to the floor. 'It is cruel, so cruel'; and, 'Don't let them hate them, Freddy wouldn't like it'. 'I don't think they could have done it if they had known about me.'

She later recalled a muddled feeling that it would kill Uncle William, who had sent him.

> But then Uncle William himself came in with Auntie Pussy – I saw his face, pale, sorrow-stricken, but like a prophet's in its look of faith and strength. He came up and almost took me in his arms, and his first words were, 'Father, forgive them for they know not what they do'. Then he said to me, 'Be assured it will not be in vain', and across all my agony there fell a bright ray of hope, and I saw in a vision Ireland at peace, and my darling's life-blood accepted as a sacrifice . . . to bring this to pass.

Without any doubt or hesitation Gladstone assured her it was right to have sent him. Afterwards, Lucy said to Meriel, 'He is like an oak to lean against.'

'We took her upstairs and she undressed and lay down', Meriel wrote, 'and I lay down by her and we were alone for some hours.'[39]

> She cried a good deal, and talked to me – it was wonderfully natural; she never seemed bewildered, or to lose her balance. [She spoke] a great deal of Freddy's tenderness and their ways together, how they were just like lovers always . . . Sometimes, 'How *could* they do it – it was cruel . . . He never said one bitter word against Ireland. He always thought if the right remedy could be found, they would behave well'.

And then again she returned for comfort to the thought of the Christlike sacrifice.

> I see now, I see that our Saviour's death seemed a failure . . . and yet it was victory, and Freddy's will be like that; it will do more good than his life. And all the rest of the night she never quite lost hold of the thought, but dwelt on it and leant on it.

At this time they did not realise 'the dreadful *accidentalness* of it all': that he had been killed defending Mr Burke, by assailants who had no idea who he was.

Gwendolen Stephenson was only five when, with her younger sister, Peg, she came upon the grown-ups crying and learned that Uncle Freddy had died. 'Poor little things', her mother had said, 'they are too young to understand.' 'Your generation cannot picture the atmosphere of awful mourning which surrounded Aunt Lucy', Lady Stephenson wrote in 1943. Yet she remained tremendous fun, so full of interest in everything – 'even though we knew her heart was broken'.[40] The understanding of that came later.

'I think of having reached the *end* of my life with a sort of stupefied feeling', Lucy had written to her brother Alfred, in the autumn of 1882. 'There may be as many years again to live [there were forty-three] for I can't imagine what is ever to weaken my leathery health, but I have entered on the solemn last stage for all that.'

> The social delights, the absorbing Political life, and all the fun of shooting seasons, lawn tennis – riding – is gone by . . . and I am stranded on an awful quiet shore, in the loneliness that none of the dear loving hearts that so help and bless me can ever . . . relieve.[41]

From Holker she wrote to Meriel, 'The going on here from day to day is unspeakably sad and dreary work. I miss him more incessantly than in London', To Mary Gladstone, 'I am never ten minutes . . . without the full and aching consciousness of what has fallen upon me'. 'With "long patience" I must believe that . . . the blessed happiness of my past years will come to be shining joy to me', she told Lavinia in 1883. 'But as yet I *cannot* be comforted.' Life was unbearable, she explained to Meriel, not from intrinsic unbearableness 'but from the utter vanishing of all my old mainspring of joy and delight'. These were the early days. The pain she felt became less obvious as time went on. But Mary Gladstone was dismayed to find, some ten years later, that though in company she could be delightfully animated, 'alone with you and talking about her own condition . . . you feel she does not advance an inch'.[42] It was something Lucy had tried to explain to her brother Edward at the start.

> Being with you, my darling young belongings, with all present brightness and future hopes shining round you, is good and pleasant and helps me to have the *antechambers* of my heart cheerful. The pathetic thing is what someone calls 'the great motionless inner lake of sorrow', into which none of the sunshine can penetrate.[43]

This picture, sprung from an agony of grief, seems, in essence, never to have left her. Her father himself had put his finger on Lucy's dark side when he observed that she of all his children had 'to some extent' inherited his mental constitution.[44] Religion succoured them yet brought them both a sense of anxiety and sinfulness. ('A feeling came sadly over me that it would have been well if I had died after my first Communion, full of blessed faith', she wrote in 1870, 'and God knows the intense happiness of my life and how I shrink from giving it up.')[45]

But she did not dwell by the motionless lake. The antechambers of her heart were crammed with all the things she cared for and worked for. When Lady Stephenson pictured her, 'sitting writing far into the night, shaking her fountain-pen with a characteristic movement of impatience', the odds are that she was writing an appeal to the current Duke of Devonshire (her father-in-law, brother-in-law and nephew successively found themselves in that exposed position) for a subscription – or worse, a speech – on behalf of the Girls' Public Day School Trust, or the Yorkshire Ladies' Education Council, or the Parochial Mission Women. Any Prime Minister or Foreign Secretary known to her (and there were several) would be implored by Lucy as President of the Friends of Armenia to exert himself on behalf of the victims of Turkish atrocities. Temperance was another of her causes, though it never spoilt her sense of humour. ('At the first spoonful of soup, she announced, "there's alcohol in this", a niece relates; 'and after the second, "and how dreadfully good it is!".')[46] Her Church of England life filled an antechamber. And there was Ireland – and her hopes for peace. She had begun at once, after Freddy's death, with a letter to Lord Spencer, explaining her view of the sacrifice for Ireland: which she would not grudge, 'if only it leads to the putting down of the frightful spirit of evil in that land'. When the assassins had been caught and tried (they were members of a secret society called The Invincibles, and four were hanged), she sent the one convicted of killing Fred a letter of forgiveness, with a crucifix. She became an advocate of Home Rule, and when the Liberal Home Rule Bill was going through the Commons in 1913 congratulated Redmond, the Irish leader, on the size of the majority.

Had Lavinia been bereaved in her forties, and childless, one might imagine her having become head of Lady Margaret Hall, the women's college which she and Edward helped to found at Oxford, and which would have offered ample scope for her talent for administration. But this sort of thing was not for Lucy. When Mary Gladstone, in 1884, suggested she might let her name go forward as a possible Mistress of Girton, she dismissed the idea at once.

> I cannot see why because my sorrow came upon me in that tremendous way I should conclude that I am called to be dragged up into prominent mountain-tops. Dear Freddy would wish me rather to be useful in quiet natural ways.[47]

To her the most natural had always been bound up with her faith and her family. And so it went on. 'Among ourselves it is you, old soul', her brother Edward told her, 'who have done most to teach us to carry out the idea of love.'

> And perhaps more through all the great tragedy than ever before; and whatever happens you may feel sure that your eight brothers are still looking to you for a continuation of that teaching, although your love in the common sense of the word has been so broken.[48]

Nothing ever broke her sense of family. 'Oh dear!' she wrote joyfully in 1883, this time to Lavinia, 'there never was anything like old Nevy's head over-ears condition – it does one's heart good to see him'. He had just got engaged to Katharine Stuart-Wortley (a niece of Mrs Talbot), 'and sits in her pocket, holding her hand and stroking her arm and both look blissful'.[49]

Lucy's letters now were often a mixture of Irish politics and family problems – such as how they could help impoverished Albert to clear his debts. In 1888 she immensely enjoyed a visit to him in Kimberley, South Africa, writing of 'an atmosphere pure and light as it never can be in poor moist over-crowded be-smoked and be-gassed England'; of his little tin biscuit box of a church, his house where the sand came drifting in and she was always sweeping it out; and how she had improved it by painting a cupboard, making a *portière* for the kitchen door ('it was my bed cover, and I rigged it up with rings on a Kaffir knob-kerrie') and planting vegetables in the garden.[50] As for her relations with 'old Meriel', those went on in the same old style of deeply loving incompatibility. 'Mother was always liable to be unresponsive to her enthusiasms and despairs', wrote Lady Stephenson. 'It was in the middle of one of these that Aunt Lucy said, anxiously, 'Meriel dear, are you well? Your eyes are so glassy'. Of course she continued her (generally unsuccessful) attempts to wring letters out of Meriel or contrive their meeting. 'I believe,' she wrote in August 1883,

> nothing short of my deathbed could unearth you from the recesses of Falconhurst during the summer holydays, you poor old Mother of Millions; and I shall blame myself much if I ever *do* die further off than London in August.[51]

This problem was resolved by their dying on the same day – 22 April 1925 – and within two hours of each other.

# Appendix

## Lyttelton Asks Gladstone for an Earldom\*

### Lyttelton to Gladstone, 11 November 1873

Dear W.,

I am about to ask a question, implying a request about myself which I fear will appear to you preposterous. And it is fair to say, which I do with perfect sincerity, that if I was you I should without hesitation refuse it. It is, whether I might be made an Earl.

I have only one reason why I wish for this, which also, I fear, will appear a foolish one. But before mentioning it I will fairly say what appears sufficiently strong against the request.

I apprehend that since the Reform Act (though not before) Earldoms have not been given except on the ground of eminent public service or great wealth. The two have often if not always been separated [gives examples]. To the former of course I can make no pretence; nor to the latter at present . . . I may however add that I have heard persons of judgement say that there may be outward circumstances apart from wealth which might justify it; such as the possession of an estate of very great antiquity, and in some respects not without celebrity.

But I hope I need not say that it is an object for which in itself I do not care, and for which, without a particular reason, I should not think of asking.

The reason is, that I cannot keep off a certain promotion in this same line which will come to me or my successor without fault or merit of ours, without a shilling of income; and which would be extremely disagreeable to me. Unless the present Duchess of Buckingham dies,

\* British Library, Add. MS 44240, fos 237–40 and 242–43.

and the Duke marries again and has a son (unlikely events) I shall become – Viscount Cobham.

I greatly dislike the rank of Viscount. The title is ugly and ungainly; the historical avocations not good. The only two Lord Cobhams known in our annals, the one a great Lollard (unconnected with me, however) the other, through whom I should inherit, a bad and tenth-rate politician of the last century, now hardly remembered except as the subject of a lying panegyric by Pope.

Of course I do not mean to make much of all this; and you will not suppose that either I look for any sort of personal bias on your part, or should feel anything worth the name of disappointment if you refuse.

I need not ask that it be kept a dead secret.

Yr aff.
Lyttelton

*Gladstone to Lyttelton, 11 November 1873*

My dear George,

I have received and read your letter and I shall show it to my wife which I consider to be entirely *within* the limits allowed by your injunction of secrecy. I however put down my first impressions . . . They are to the effect that it would be best for you that the request should not be pressed.

1. The balance of considerations connected with money is against it.
2. The [? Dastroy] precedent was, I believe, looked upon as rather tainted with favoritism; and in the case of a near connection this charge would more readily revive.
3. As head of the Endowed Schools Commission you are engaged in fighting a gallant battle for the public, but the time when such battle is in progress is not the time for awarding honour to the combatants for the right cause.
4. I am sorry to say that your aversion to Viscounties is distinctly a reason against a request for an Earldom. It is our business to give as much value as possibly to the lower ranks of title and honour . . . to encourage personal depreciation of Viscounties is directly to lower that order of the Peerage . . .

I am afraid that Cobham impends but one can hardly say the danger is proximate.

Always affty yours
W.E.G.

P.S. Catherine concurs. I translated those few pretty lines of Aristophanes on the way to town, and will send you my version.

*Lyttelton to Gladstone, 12 November 1873*

Dear W.,

I do not doubt you are right . . . I was not so much actually making
the request as asking your opinion. On one point, however, it is notable
how many such promotions *have* skipped over one or even two grades
[gives examples]
    . . . Of course I expected you to tell Catherine though I have not
even told my wife, for I have a serious dread of the thing appearing a
'quiz' (This word may be added some day to the *Glynnese Glossary*) . . .
However, I beg you will not make me a Viscount, nor a Marquis, which
is about as bad . . . Finally I request you often to pray for the life of
the Duke of Buckingham, that Charles and not I may be Cobhamed.*

                                                      Yr. aff.
                                                      Lyttelton.

* Charles, who succeeded as fifth Baron Lyttelton in 1876, became eighth Viscount
Cobham in 1889.

# *Note on Sources*

This book is based on diaries and letters of the Lyttelton, Talbot and Gladstone families in the second half of the nineteenth century. John Bailey's abridged two-volume edition of Lucy Lyttelton's diary was published in 1927 as *The Diary of the Lady Frederick Cavendish*. The original manuscript is in the Archives at Chatsworth in Derbyshire. The diaries of Lord Lyttelton, Lavinia Lyttelton, May Lyttelton and Spencer Lyttelton are in the Archives at Hagley Hall, Worcestershire. Meriel Lyttelton's diary is in the Talbot Archive (general reference U 1612) at the Centre for Kentish Studies, Maidstone, Kent.

The Talbot Archive includes a substantial collection (sorted, but uncatalogued) of letters written to Meriel Talbot (née Lyttelton) and other members of the Talbot family (into which Lavinia Lyttelton also married). More purely Lyttelton correspondence (e.g. the many letters between Lord Lyttelton and Lucy) are in the Archives at Hagley Hall, also sorted and uncatalogued. There is correspondence between Lord Lyttelton and Gladstone in the Gladstone Papers at the British Library; and between various Lytteltons and Mary Gladstone in the Mary Gladstone Papers there, which also contain a copy of the family Record of Lady Lyttelton's death in 1857. Other correspondence with the Gladstone family is in the Glynne/Gladstone papers at Clwyd County Record Office at Hawarden. Queen Mary and Westfield College, London, holds a substantial Sir Neville Lyttelton Archive; while Lucy Cavendish College, Cambridge, has a small collection of Lyttelton letters.

On the few occasions where quotations are abbreviated, this is indicated in the note. All Lord Lyttelton's children were entitled to be called 'The Honourable'; to have referred to them as such would have been impossibly cumbersome.

# Abbreviations

Meriel, Lucy, Lavinia and May Lyttelton are referred to by their Christian names only.

| | |
|---|---|
| BL | British Library |
| GG | Glynne-Gladstone Papers, Clwyd County Record Office, Hawarden |
| GP | Gladstone Papers, British Library |
| Hagley | Hagley Hall Archives, Worcestershire |
| Lavinia, Diary | Lavinia Lyttelton (The Hon. Mrs Edward Talbot), MS Diary, Hagley Hall, Worcestershire |
| Lucy, Diary | Lucy Lyttelton, MS Diary, Chatsworth |
| May, Diary | May Lyttelton, MS Diary, Hagley Hall, Worcestershire |
| Meriel, Autobiography | Meriel Lyttelton (The Hon. Mrs John Talbot), MS Autobiography, Centre for Kentish Studies, Maidstone, Kent |
| Meriel, Diary | Meriel Lyttelton (The Hon. Mrs John Talbot), MS Diary, Centre for Kentish Studies, Maidstone, Kent |
| Sir Neville Lyttelton Archive | Sir Neville Lyttelton Archive, Queen Mary and Westfield College, London |
| Record | 'Record of the Death of Lady Lyttelton'. Copy by May Lyttelton and Mary Gladstone, Mary Gladstone Papers, British Library, Add. MS 46269 |
| TP | Talbot Papers, Centre for Kentish Studies, Maidstone, Kent |

# Notes

## Chapter 1: Hagley

1. William Howitt, *Rural Life in England* (London, 1838), ii, p. 126.
2. F. M. L. Thompson, *English Landed Society in the Nineteenth Century* (London, 1963), pp. 25–26.
3. Catherine and Mary Glynne to their brother Henry Glynne, 3.6.1839, quoted in Betty Askwith, *The Lytteltons: A Family Chronicle of the Nineteenth Century* (London, 1975), p. 57.
4. Parliamentary Papers, 72 (1874), *Return of Owners of Land, 1872–73* (known as 'The New Domesday Book').
5. Copy of letter to Lord Beauchamp (enclosed with letter from Lyttelton to Gladstone, 23.3.1857), in which Lyttelton expressed his thanks for money subscribed in the county and diocese of Worcester to pay for alterations to Hagley Church, in honour of his work as Lord Lieutenant. BL, Gladstone Papers [GP], Add. MS 44239.
6. Edward Lyttelton, *Alfred Lyttelton* (privately printed, 1916), p. 6.
7. General Sir Neville Lyttelton, *Eighty Years: Soldiering, Politics, Games* (London, 1927), p. 11.
8. Quoted John Bailey, ed., *The Diary of Lady Frederick Cavendish* (London, 1927), i, pp. 14,15.

## Chapter 2: An Eloquent Death

1. Lucy Lyttelton, Diary, 1.1.1857. The manuscript is in the Chatsworth Archives; John Bailey's abridged two-volume edition was published as *The Diary of Lady Frederick Cavendish* (London, 1927).
2. Lucy, Diary, 7.2.1857.
3. Sarah Lyttelton to Meriel, 7.4.1857. Centre for Kentish Studies, Maidstone, Kent, Talbot Papers [TP], U 1612, box 13.
4. Mrs Talbot to Meriel, 13.5.1857, TP 16.
5. Quoted in the 'Record of the Death of Lady Lyttelton' [Record], which was composed from the recollections of family members and copied out by different hands over the years. I have used a copy made in 1871 by May Lyttelton and Mary Gladstone, BL, Mary Gladstone Papers, Add. MS 46269.
6. Lucy, Diary, 1.6.1857.
7. Ibid., 8.6.1857.

8. Ibid., 10.6.1857.
9. Ibid., 19.6.1857.
10. Ibid., 7.7.1857.
11. 'Death of Lady Lyttelton: Account by the Dowager Lady Lyttelton', 20.7.1857, TP, U1612; F245.
12. Ibid., 20.7.1857.
13. Ibid., 27.7.1857.
14. Ibid., 29.7.1857.
15. Ibid., 31.7.1857.
16. Ibid., 10.8.1857.
17. Ibid., 10.8.1857.
18. Ibid., 14.8.1857.
19. Ibid., 14.8.1857.
20. Record, 16.8.1857, Gladstone's comment noted by Lord Lyttelton.
21. Mary Lyttelton to Meriel, 4.10.1851, TP 13. Lady Lyttelton's letters, quoted below, range from 1844 (when Meriel was four) to 1855 (when she was fifteen).
22. Mary Lyttelton to Meriel, August 1848.
23. Mary Lyttelton to Meriel, 4.10.1850. Aunt Lavinia (their father's sister) was the wife of the Reverend Henry Glynne of Hawarden (their mother's brother): a classic case of aristocratic intermarriage.
24. Record, 16.8.1857 (by Lucy).
25. Ibid. (by Mrs Talbot).
26. Ibid. (by Mrs Gladstone).
27. Ibid. (by Mrs Talbot).
28. Ibid. (by Lucy).
29. Ibid. (by Mrs Gladstone).
30. Ibid. (by Sarah Lyttelton).
31. Ibid. (by Lord Lyttelton).
32. Ibid. (by Mrs Gladstone).
33. Johnny Talbot to Mrs Talbot, 21.11.1852, TP 36.
34. Record, 16.8.1857 (by Lord Lyttelton).
35. Ibid., 17.8.1857 (by Lord Lyttelton).
36. Ibid., 17.8.1857 (by Lucy).
37. Ibid., 17.8.1857 (by Mrs Gladstone).
38. Ibid., 16.8.1857 (by Lord Lyttelton).
39. Ibid., 17.8.1857 (by Lucy).
40. 'Death of Lady Lyttelton', 19.8.1857.
41. Record, 16.8.1857 (by William Gladstone).

## Chapter 3: Lord Lyttelton

1. Lucy to Meriel, 11.9.1876, TP, U1612.
2. Lucy, Diary, 17.8.1857.
3. Mary Lyttelton to Emy Lyttelton, 7.4.1856, Lucy Cavendish College Archive.
4. Meriel to Mrs Talbot, 8.9.1857, TP 36.
5. Meriel, Autobiography, TP F104.
6. Edward Lyttelton *Memories and Hopes* (London, 1925), p. 1.
7. Meriel, Autobiography.

8. Meriel to Mrs Talbot, 17.9.1857, TP 36.
9. Mary Lyttelton to Meriel, 17.6.1850, TP 13.
10. Meriel to Mrs Talbot, 13.9.1857, TP 36.
11. Meriel to Mrs Talbot, 16.9.1857.
12. Meriel, Autobiography.
13. Meriel to Mrs Talbot, 13.9.1857, TP 36.
14. Meriel to Mrs Gladstone, 21.11.1857, Clwyd Record Office, Glynne/Gladstone Papers [GG] 793.
15. Meriel to Mrs Talbot, 6.9.1857, TP 36.
16. Lucy, Diary, 3.12.1857.
17. Lord Lyttelton to Meriel, 29.12.1848, TP 13.
18. Meriel to Mrs Talbot, 16.9.1857, TP 36.
19. Lord Lyttelton to Mrs Gladstone, 29.8.1857, GG 791.
20. Mrs Talbot to Mrs Gladstone, n.d. (autumn, 1857), GG 804.
21. Lord Lyttelton to Mrs Gladstone, 21.9.1857, GG 791.
22. Quoted John Bailey, ed., *Diary of Lady Frederick Cavendish* (1927), i, p. 14.
23. Mrs Talbot to Meriel, 1.10.1857, TP 16.
24. Meriel to Mrs Talbot, Michaelmas Day 1857, TP 36.
25. Lord Lyttelton to Mrs Gladstone, 19.11.1857, GG 791.
26. The Reverend J. W. Blakesley to Lord Lyttelton, 10.1.1839; quoted in Betty Askwith, *The Lytteltons: A Family Chronicle of the Nineteenth Century* (London, 1975), p. 52.
27. Lord Lyttelton to Gladstone, 4.1.1846, BL, GP, Add. MS 44238.
28. Lord Lyttelton to Gladstone, 7.7.1846, BL, GP, Add. MS 44238.
29. Caroline Lyttelton to Meriel, 5.5.1876, TP 10.
30. Roy Jenkins, *Gladstone* (London, 1995), p. 8; Edward Lyttelton, *Alfred Lyttelton*, pp. 7–9.
31. The Spencer connection came through Sarah, his mother: daughter of the second Earl Spencer and sister of the third and fourth Earls.
32. Meriel, quoted Edward Lyttelton, *Alfred Lyttelton*, p. 8.
33. Lord Lyttelton, *Address at Hagley Hall on the Death of Mr and Mrs Firmstone by Lord Lyttelton* (1874).
34. Record.
35. Lord Lyttelton to Mrs Gladstone, 3.11.1855, GG 791.
36. Mary Lyttelton to Billy and Emy Lyttelton, 29.9.1854, Lucy Cavendish College.
37. Lord Lyttelton to Mrs Gladstone, 12.9.1857, GG 791.
38. Lord Lyttelton to Mrs Gladstone, 27.7.1866, GG 791.
39. Mary Lyttelton to Mrs Talbot, 27 June 1856, TP 16.
40. Quoted John Bailey, ed., *Diary of Lady Frederick Cavendish* (London, 1927), i, p. 42.
41. See Askwith, *The Lytteltons*, p. 146.

## Chapter 4: Meriel

1. Meriel to Mrs Gladstone, 30.12.1857, GG 793.
2. Meriel to Mrs Talbot, 4.8.1858, TP 36.
3. 'New Zealand and the Canterbury Colony', read at Hagley by Lord Lyttelton,

11 January 1859. The Irish barrister, John Robert Godley (1814–61) took the lead in founding the colony.

4. *Memorials of Hon. Mrs John Chetwynd Talbot*, privately printed 1876.
5. Johnny Talbot to Meriel, 8.8.1857, TP 18.
6. W. E. Gladstone to Mrs Wellesley, 9.8.1882: copy-letter attached to the fly-leaf of the British Library's copy of the *Glynnese Glossary*.
7. Johnny Talbot to Mrs Talbot, 20.8.1853, TP 36.
8. Quoted, Gwendolen Stephenson, *Edward Stuart Talbot* (London, 1936), p. 7.
9. *Memorials of Hon. Mrs John Chetwynd Talbot*.
10. Mrs Talbot to Meriel, 27.4.1857, TP 16.
11. Mrs Talbot to Meriel, 9.2.1856, TP 16.
12. Mary Lyttelton to Mrs Talbot, 21.6.1856, TP 16.
13. Mary Lyttelton to Mrs Talbot, 17.7.1856, TP 16.
14. Mary Lyttelton to Mrs Talbot, 22.7.1856, TP 16.
15. Mary Lyttelton to Mrs Talbot, 5.6.1856, TP 16.
16. Mary Lyttelton to Mrs Talbot, 4.8.1856, TP 16.
17. Mary Lyttelton to Mrs Talbot, 3.6.1856, TP 16.
18. Mrs Talbot to Meriel, 11.9.1857, TP 16.
19. Meriel to Mrs Talbot, n.d. (September 1857), TP 36.
20. Edward Talbot to Meriel, 10.10.1857, TP 16.
21. Meriel to Mrs Gladstone, 11.3.1859, GG 793.
22. Meriel to Mrs Talbot, 16.9.1857, TP 36.
23. Meriel to Mrs Talbot, n.d. (probably September 1857), TP 36.
24. Lucy, Diary, 5.6.1856.
25. Lucy, Diary, 7.4.1859 and 8.5.1859.
26. Meriel, Diary, 22, 26 and 30 June 1858.
27. Meriel to Mrs Talbot, 8.9.1857, TP 36.
28. Meriel to Mrs Gladstone, 10.7.1858, GG 793.
29. Sarah Lyttelton to Meriel, 22.6.1858, TP 13.
30. Sarah Lyttelton to Meriel, 19.11.1857, TP 13.
31. Lucy to Mrs Gladstone, 6.9.1858, Hagley Hall, Worcestershire, Archive [Hagley], 23.
32. Mary Lyttelton to Emy Lyttelton, 7.4.1856, Lucy Cavendish College.
33. Sarah Lyttelton to Meriel, 19.11.1857, TP 13.
34. Lucy to Lord Lyttelton, 10.12.1873, Hagley 25.
35. Lord Lyttelton to Mrs Gladstone, 22.6.1858, GG 791.
36. Lucy, Diary, 21.9.1858.
37. Lord Lyttelton to Gladstone, 24.9.1858, BL, Add. MS 44239.
38. Lucy, Diary, 20.6.1859.
39. Meriel, unpublished Autobiography, TP F104.
40. Lucy to Emy Lyttelton, 27.5.1859, Hagley 'Oddments'.
41. Lucy, Diary, 7.6.1859.
42. Lucy, Diary, 11.6.1859.
43. Lucy, Diary, 9.7.1859.
44. Lucy to Emy Lyttelton, 27.5.1859.
45. Mary Lyttelton to Meriel, 11.5.1855, TP 13.
46. Lucy, Diary, 29.5.1859.
47. Lucy, Diary, 29.7.1859.

48. Lord Lyttelton to Mrs Gladstone, 22.6.1858, GG 791.
49. Lord Lyttelton to Meriel, 5.7.1858, TP 13.
50. Meriel to Mrs Talbot, 16.8.1858, TP 36.
51. Lord Lyttelton to Meriel, 21.7.1858, TP 13.
52. Sarah Lyttelton to Mrs Talbot, 2.8.1861, Hagley 8
53. Edward Lyttelton, *Memories and Hopes*, p. 6

## Chapter 5: Lucy

1. Miss Smith to Lord Lyttelton, 29.5.1860, Hagley 3.
2. Mrs Talbot to Meriel, 8.12.1856, TP 18.
3. Johnny Talbot to Meriel, 22.7.1857, TP 18.
4. Johnny Talbot to Meriel, 13.11.1857, TP 18.
5. Lord Lyttelton to Gladstone, 23.12.1857, GP, BL, Add. MS 44239.
6. Johnny Talbot to Meriel, 31.12.1857, TP 18.
7. Johnny Talbot to Meriel, 4.2.1858, TP 18.
8. Johnny Talbot to Meriel, 3.7.1858, TP 16.
9. Johnny to Mrs Talbot, 22.4.1860, TP 36.
10. Lucy, Diary, 26.5.1860.
11. Lord Lyttelton to Meriel, 30.5.1860, TP 13.
12. Lucy, Diary, 19.7.1860.
13. Ibid., 12.6.1860.
14. Quoted Askwith, *The Lytteltons: A Family Chronicle of the Nineteeth Century* (London, 1975), p. 145.
15. Meriel, Autobiography, TP F104.
16. Meriel to Mrs Talbot, 23.7.1860 and 3.8.1860, TP 13.
17. Lord Lyttelton to Meriel, 20.7.1860, TP 13.
18. Sarah Lyttelton to Meriel, 20.7.1860, TP 13.
19. Lucy to Meriel, 20.7.1860 and 21.7.1860, TP folder.
20. Adelaide, Countess Spencer, to Lucy, 25.7.1860, GG 998 (abbreviated).
21. Sarah Lyttelton to Lucy, 26.3.1861, Hagley 8.
22. Lucy to Meriel, 18.8.1860, TP folder.
23. Lord Lyttelton to Meriel, 27.11.1860, TP 13.
24. Lucy to Meriel, 19.10.1860, TP folder.
25. Lord Lyttelton *Address to Young Men at the Wordsley Institute*, November 1875 (on the sin of impurity).
26. Edward Lyttelton, *Alfred Lyttelton*, p. 17.
27. Undated draft, Worcester County Record Office, bulk accession 5467 (ref. 705; 658; parcel 73, i). Similar letter in Queen Mary and Westfield College, London, Sir Neville Lyttelton Archive [Sir Nevillle Lyttelton Archive].
28. Lucy to Meriel, 5.2.1861, TP.
29. See Askwith, *The Lytteltons*, p. 165.
30. Sarah Lyttelton to Meriel, 25.8.1860, TP 13.
31. Lucy to Meriel, 31.8.1860, TP.
32. Lord Lyttelton to Meriel, September 1860, TP 13.
33. Lord Lyttelton to Gladstone, 13.11.1860, GP, BL, Add. MS 44239.
34. Undated draft, Worcester County Record Office, 5467
35. Lord Lyttelton to Meriel, 26.12.1860, TP 13.

36.   Sarah Lyttelton to Meriel, 18.9.1860, TP 13.
37.   Letter quoted Askwith, *The Lytteltons*, pp. 149–50 (abbreviated).
38.   Mrs Talbot to Mrs Gladstone, 2.11.1860, GG 804 (abbreviated).
39.   Lucy to Meriel, 13.11.1860, TP.
40.   Mary Lyttelton to Emy Lyttelton, 3.12.1855, TP 13.
41.   Meriel to Mrs Gladstone, 12.11.1860, Hagley 23.
42.   Edward Talbot to Meriel, 25.3.1858, TP 16.
43.   Mrs Talbot to Meriel, 2.2.1861, TP 16 (abbreviated).
44.   *Memorials of Hon. Mrs John Chetwynd Talbot* (privately printed, 1876).
45.   Johnny Talbot to Mrs Talbot, 21.7.1860, TP 36.
46.   Meriel, Autobiography.
47.   Lucy to Meriel, 17.4.1861, TP.
48.   Lucy, Diary, 11.2.1864.
49.   Lucy to Meriel, 12.8.1861, TP.
50.   Lucy to Neville, 1.4.1862, Sir Neville Lyttelton Archive.
51.   Lucy to Meriel, 4.4.1862, TP.
52.   Lord Lyttelton to Meriel, 14.4.1862, TP 13.
53.   Lucy to Meriel 19.4.1862, TP.
54.   Lavinia, Diary, 1862 passim.'That' means menstruation.
55.   Lucy, Diary 16.9.1863.
56.   'Lady Frederick Cavendish: A Note on Her Early Life by Her Sister, Lavinia',
      in John Bailey, ed., *Diary of Lady Frederick Cavendish* (London, 1927), ii, pp.
      350–52.
57.   Lucy to Lord Lyttelton, 19.11.1862, Hagley 25.
58.   Lucy to Meriel, 25.11.1862, TP.
59.   Lucy, Diary, 24.21.1862.

## *Chapter 6: Coming of Age*

1.    Lucy, Diary, 7.6.1862 and 9.6.1862.
2.    Lord Lyttelton to Gladstone, 22.7.1866, GP, BL, Add. MS 44240.
3.    Lord Lyttelton to Gladstone, 12.4.1864, GP, BL, Add. MS 44239. 'Hodiest'
      from Latin *hodie* = today.
4.    Lord Lyttelton, during second reading of his *Subdivision of Dioceses Bill*, House
      of Lords, 14 March 1861.
5.    Lord Lyttelton to Gladstone, 31.8.1861, BL, Add. MS 44239.
6.    Sarah Lyttelton to Meriel, 16.10.1863, TP 13.
7.    Lord Lyttelton to Lucy, 14.7.1862, Hagley 25.
8.    Lucy to Lord Lyttelton, 12.2.1863, Hagley 25.
9.    *A Master's Address to his Domestic Servants on the Subject of the Holy Communion,
      by George William, Lord Lyttelton*, SPCK (London, 1844).
10.   Lord Lyttelton to Lucy, 18.2.1860, Hagley 25.
11.   Lucy to Meriel, Monday in Holy Week 1863, TP.
12.   Lord Lyttelton to Lavinia, 12.2.1863, Hagley 25.
13.   Lord Lyttelton to Lucy, 4.3.1863, Hagley 25.
14.   Lucy, Diary, 8.6.1863.
15.   Lavinia, Diary, 23.6.1863.
16.   Lucy, Diary, 19.6.1863.

17. Ibid., 10.9.1863.
18. Ibid., 11.9.1863.
19. Ibid., 13.9.1863.
20. Ibid., 18.9.1863.
21. Lord Lyttelton to Mrs Gladstone, 23.11.1864, GG 791.
22. Lord Lyttelton to Mrs Gladstone, 25.9.1863, GG 791.
23. Lucy to Lord Lyttelton, Letters September and October 1863, Hagley 25.
24. Lord Lyttelton to Lucy, 13.10 1863, Hagley 25 (abbreviated).
25. Lucy to Lord Lyttelton, 14.10.1863, Hagley 25.
26. Lucy, Diary, 27.10.1863.
27. Lucy to Lord Lyttelton, 10.11.1863, Hagley 25.
28. Sarah Lyttelton to Meriel, 16.10.1863, TP 13.
29. Lucy to Meriel, 8.12.1863, TP.
30. Lucy, Diary, 4.12.1863.
31. Lucy to Meriel, 14.12.1863, TP (abbreviated).
32. Lucy to Meriel, 16.12.1863. TP (abbreviated).
33. Sarah Lyttelton to Meriel, 16.10.1863, TP 13.
34. Lucy, Diary, 15.6.1863.
35. Lord Lyttelton, 'On Bringing Nonconformists into Unity with the Church', in *Ephemera* (1865–72).
36. Lord Lyttelton to Gladstone, 2.1.1864, GP, BL, Add. MS 44239.
37. Sarah Lyttelton to Meriel, 2.2.1864, TP 13.
38. Lord Lyttelton to Lucy 10.1.1864, Hagley 25.
39. Ibid.
40. Julia Cartwright, ed., *The Journals of Lady Knightley of Fawsley, 1856–1884* (London, 1915), p. 69.
41. Lucy to Meriel, 14.12.1864, TP.
42. Lucy, Diary, 17.1.1864.
43. Lucy to Lord Lyttelton, 26.1.1864, Hagley 25 (abbreviated).
44. Lucy, Diary, 25.1.1864 and 29.1.1864.
45. Ibid., 11.4.1864 (abbreviated).
46. Lucy to Lord Lyttelton, 14.4.1864, Hagley 25.
47. Lucy to Meriel, 16.4.1864, TP.
48. Lord Lyttelton to Lucy,18.4. 1864, Hagley 25.
49. Lucy, Diary, 22.4.1864.
50. Sarah Lyttelton to Lucy, 3.5.1864, Hagley 8.
51. Lucy to Meriel, 17.5.1864, TP.
52. Lord Lyttelton to Gladstone, 19.10.1863, BL, Add. MS 44239.
53. Lord Lyttelton to Gladstone, 31.10.1865.
54. Lord Lyttelton to Gladstone, 26.3.1866.
55. Mrs Gladstone to Lucy, 19.5.1864, Hagley 23.
56. Lucy to Emy Lyttelton, 3.6.1864, Hagley 'Oddments'.
57. Lord Frederick Cavendish to Lord Lyttelton, 9.6.1864 (abbreviated).

## Chapter 7: Lavinia

1. Lavinia, Diary, 7.6.1864.
2. Lavinia, Diary, passim.

3. Lavinia to Meriel, 2.1.1865, Hagley 21.
4. Lavinia to Meriel, 4.10.1864, Hagley 21.
5. Lavinia, Diary, 31.7.1864.
6. Ibid., 9.7.1863.
7. Edward Lyttelton, *Memories and Hopes* (London, 1925), p. 6; idem, *Alfred Lyttelton* (privately printed, 1916), p. 11.
8. Edward Lyttelton, *Alfred Lyttelton*, pp. 13–14.
9. Lucy to May, 25.5.1863, Lucy Cavendish College.
10. Lavinia, Diary, 7.12.1864.
11. Lucy, Diary, 7.7.1864.
12. Sarah Lyttelton to Lucy, 4.9.1864, Hagley 8.
13. Lucy, Diary, 26.10.1864.
14. Lucy, Diary.
15. Lucy to Meriel, 5.1.1865, TP.
16. Ibid.
17. Lavinia to Meriel, 2.1.1865, Hagley 21.
18. Lucy to Meriel, 23.1.1865, TP.
19. Sarah Lyttelton to Lucy, 24.1.1865, Hagley 8.
20. Sarah Lyttelton to Lucy, 18.1.1865, Hagley 8.
21. Lavinia, Diary, 13.3.1865.
22. Lucy to May, Good Friday 1865, Lucy Cavendish College.
23. Lavinia, Diary, 3.5.1865.
24. Lucy to Lavinia and May, 20.8.1865, Hagley 25 (quoting Order of Baptism in *Book of Common Prayer*).
25. Lavinia, Diary, 18.10.1865.
26. Meriel to Neville Lyttelton, 25.10.1865, Sir Neville Lyttelton Archive.
27. Now in the possession of Mr Charles Talbot of Falconhurst, Kent.
28. Lucy to Meriel, 31.12.1864, TP.
29. Account (privately printed, *c.* 1903) by Meriel's daughter Gwendolen Stephenson of family nurse 'Toody' (Harriet Fuller), TP F254.
30. *Parochial Mission Women*, Mrs Talbot's account of the origin and work of the Mission, was published in 1862.
31. Sarah Lyttelton to Meriel, 25.8.1861, Hagley 8.
32. Gwendolen Stephenson, Account (typescript 1943) of Talbot family, TP F3. She had, however, no personal experience of Ganma's reign since she was not born until 1876, the year in which Mrs Talbot died.
33. Mrs Talbot to Meriel, 11.4.1870, TP 16.
34. Mrs Talbot to Mrs Gladstone, 31.12.1863, GG 804.
35. Edward Talbot to Meriel, 14.2.1865, TP 16.
36. Lucy, Diary, 16.12.1864.
37. Edward Talbot to Meriel, 28.1.1866, TP 16.
38. Ibid.
39. Sarah Lyttelton to Meriel, 19.1.1864, TP 13.
40. Lord Lyttelton to Meriel, 25.1.1865, TP13
41. *Transactions of the National Association for the Promotion of Social Science* (1864), pp. 394–404.
42. Lucy to Meriel, 5.1.1865, TP.
43. Meriel, Autobiography, TP F104.

44. *Transactions of the National Association for the Promotion of Social Science* (1864), pp. 402–3.
45. Lavinia, Diary, 4.1.1866.
46. May to Lucy, 9.3.1866, Hagley.
47. Lavinia, Diary, 4.1.1866.
48. Lavinia, Diary, 13.5.1866.
49. Lavinia to May, 3.12.1871, Hagley.
50. Lord Lyttelton to Mrs Gladstone, 27.7.1866, GG 791.
51. Lucy to Meriel, 14.11.1866, TP.
52. Lavinia to Meriel, 7.11.1866, Hagley 21 (abbreviated).
53. Lucy, Diary, 7.11.1866 and 4.22.1866.
54. Lucy to Meriel, 14.11.1866, TP.
55. Lucy, Diary, 18.2.1866.
56. Ibid., 16.11.1865.
57. Ibid., 21.2.1867
58. May to Lucy, January 1867, Hagley.
59. Lavinia to Meriel, 2.3.1867, Hagley 21.
60. Lucy to Meriel, Low Sunday 1867, TP.
61. Lavinia to Meriel, 18.11.1867, Hagley 21.
62. Lucy to Meriel, 14.11.1866, TP.

## Chapter 8: Courting

1. 'New Zealand and the Canterbury Colony', read by Lord Lyttelton at Hagley, 11.1.1859.
2. Lord Lyttelton to Meriel, 18.10.1867.
3. Lord Lyttelton to Lucy, 5.9.1867, Hagley 25.
4. Lord Lyttelton to Mrs Gladstone, 7.9.1865, GG 791 (abbreviated).
5. Lord Lyttelton to Gladstone, 8.10.1867, GP, BL, Add. MS 44240.
6. Lord Lyttelton to Lucy, 1.12.1867, Hagley 25.
7. Lavinia to Meriel, 29.12.1867, Hagley 21.
8. Ibid.
9. Lavinia to Lucy, 17.2.1868, Hagley 25.
10. Lavinia, Diary, 30.3.1868.
11. Ibid., 30.4.1868.
12. Ibid., 3.5.1868.
13. Caroline Lyttelton to Meriel, 11.5.1868, TP 13.
14. Lavinia, Diary, 24.6.1868 (abbreviated).
15. Lavinia, Diary, 17.7.1868.
16. Lavinia to Meriel, 22.7.1868, Hagley 21 (abbreviated).
17. Lord Lyttelton to Gladstone, 14.8.1868, GP, BL, Add. MS 44240.
18. Sarah Lyttelton to Meriel, 12.12.1866, TP 13.
19. Edward Talbot to Meriel, 6.4.1869, TP 16.
20. Lavinia to Meriel, 2.12.1868, Hagley 21.
21. Lord Lyttelton to Meriel, 8.12.1868, TP 13.
22. Lord Lyttelton to Meriel, 13.12.1868, TP 13.
23. Lord Lyttelton to Meriel, 15.11.1868, TP 13.
24. Lord Lyttelton to Meriel, 17.12.1868, TP 13.

25. Lord Lyttelton to Meriel, 24.22.1868, TP 13.
26. Quoted Askwith, *The Lytteltons: A Family Chronicle of the Nineteenth Century* (London, 1975), pp. 154–55.
27. *Transactions of the National Association for the Promotion of Social Science* (1868), p. 70.
28. Sarah Lyttelton to Lucy, 10.12.1868, Hagley 8.
29. Lucy to Meriel, 31.12.1868, TP (abbreviated).
30. Edward Talbot to Meriel, 6.4.1869, TP 16.
31. Lord Lyttelton to Meriel, 29.1.1869, TP 13.
32. Lord Lyttelton to Lucy, 2.4.1869, Hagley 25.
33. Lucy, Diary, 27.4.1869.
34. Lavinia, Diary, 27.4.1869; 28.4.1869.
35. Edward Talbot to Meriel, 28.4.1869, TP 16.
36. Lucy, Diary, 28.4.1869.
37. Lavinia, Diary, 28.4.1869.
38. Lavinia, Diary, 3.5.1869.
39. Quoted in Penelope Gladstone, *Portrait of a Family: The Gladstones* (Kendal, 1989), p. 94.
40. Lord Lyttelton to Meriel, 8.5.1869, TP 13.
41. Lord Lyttelton to Lucy, 10.6.1869, Hagley 25.

## Chapter 9: Inevitable Change

1. Edward Talbot to Meriel, 10.5.1869, TP 16.
2. Lavinia to Meriel, 19.5.1869, Hagley 21.
3. Sarah Lyttelton to May, 25.5.1869, Hagley.
4. Lucy, Diary, 14.6.1869.
5. May, Diary, 18–25.5.1870.
6. Quoted in Betty Askwith, *The Lytteltons: A Family Chronicle of the Nineteenth Century* (London, 1975), p. 171.
7. Lord Lyttelton to Lucy, 26.6.1869, Hagley 25 (abbreviated).
8. Lavinia, Diary, 28.6.1869.
9. Quoted Askwith, *The Lytteltons*, p. 171.
10. Lucy, Diary, 15.6.1869.
11. Lavinia to Meriel, 17.7.1869, Hagley 21.
12. Edward Talbot to Meriel, 17.7.1869, TP 16.
13. May to Lucy, 16.8.1869, Hagley.
14. Edward Talbot to Meriel, 7.8.1869, TP 16.
15. Edward Lyttelton, *Alfred Lyttelton* (privately printed, 1916), p. 11.
16. Lucy to Meriel, 24.22.1869, TP.
17. Edward Talbot to Meriel, 7.8.1869, TP 16.
18. Lord Lyttelton to Gladstone, 15.6.1869, GP, BL, Add. MS 44240.
19. Lord Lyttelton to Gladstone, 12.4.1865, GP, BL, Add. MS 44239.
20. Lavinia to Meriel, 9.9.1869, Hagley 21.
21. Sarah Lyttelton to Lucy, 14.9.1869, Hagley 8.
22. Lavinia to May, 20.9.1869, Hagley (abbreviated).
23. Lavinia to May, 25.9.1869, Hagley.
24. May to Lucy, 7.10.1869, Hagley.

25. Lavinia to May, 29.9.1869, Hagley.
26. Lavinia to Meriel, 16.10.1869, Hagley 21.
27. Lavinia to Meriel, 28.10.1869, Hagley 21; Lucy to Lavinia, 1.11.69, Hagley 25.
28. Lavinia to Meriel, 26.12.1869, TP 13 (abbreviated).
29. Lavinia to Meriel, 4.11.1869, Hagley 21.
30. Lucy to Meriel, 28.10.1869, TP.
31. Edward Talbot to Meriel, 7.11.1869, Hagley 21.
32. Account (privately printed, *c.* 1903), by Meriel's daughter Gwendolen Stephenson, of family nurse 'Toody' (Harriet Fuller), TP F254.
33. Stephenson, Account of family, TP F3.
34. Lucy to Meriel, 28.10.1869, TP.
35. Lucy to Meriel, 20.4.1868.
36. Lucy to Lavinia, 4.8.1869, Hagley 25.
37. Sarah Lyttelton to Lucy, 4.9.1868, Hagley 8.
38. Sarah Lyttelton to Lucy, 5.11.1869 Hagley 8.
39. Lucy to Lord Lyttelton, 20.3.1870, Hagley 25.
40. Lavinia to Meriel, 3.4.1870, Hagley 21 (abbreviated).
41. Lucy to Emy Lyttelton, 14.3.1870, Hagley.
42. May, Diary (abbreviated).
43. Edward Talbot to Meriel, 9.1.1870, TP 16.
44. Lavinia, Diary, 17.6.1870.
45. May, Diary, 25.6.1870.
46. Ibid., 21.6.1870.
47. Ibid., 28.6.1870.
48. Lavinia, Diary, 29.6.1870.
49. Lavinia to May, 30.6.1870, Hagley.
50. Ibid., 3.7.1870.
51. May, Diary, 27.7.1870.
52. Ibid., 1.9.1870
53. Quoted in Askwith, *The Lytteltons*, p. 161.

## Chapter 10: May

1. Lavinia to Meriel, 13.10.1870, Hagley 21.
2. May, Diary, 20.10.1870 and 24.10.1870, Hagley.
3. May to Lucy, 12.11.1870, Hagley.
4. Mrs Talbot to Meriel, 5.11.1870, TP 16; Lucy to Lavinia, n.d., Hagley 25.
5. May, Diary, 17.12.1870.
6. Ibid., 11.12.1870.
7. Ibid., 8.1.1871.
8. Lavinia to Meriel, 9.1.1871, Hagley 21.
9. Lavinia to May, 14.11.1870, Hagley.
10. Lavinia to May, 28.4.1871, Hagley.
11. May, Diary, 26.1.1871.
12. Ibid., 8.3.1871.
13. Ibid., 20.3.1871.
14. Ibid., 12.4.1871.

15. Ibid., 20.3.1871.
16. Ibid., 25.7.1871.
17. Ibid., 30.6.1871.
18. Ibid., 12.8.1871.
19. Lavinia to May, 3.12.1871, Hagley.
20. Lavinia to May, 11.3.1872, Hagley.
21. May, Diary, 15.3.1872.
22. Lucy to Lavinia, 9.5.1872, Hagley.
23. Lavinia to May, 8.5.1872, Hagley.
24. Lavinia to May, 8.9.1872.
25. Lucy to Meriel, 4.11.1872, TP.
26. Lavinia to May, 30.11.1872, Hagley
27. Lavinia to May, 1.11.1872.
28. Lavinia, Diary, 6.7.1872, Hagley.
29. Lavinia to May, 1.11.1872, Hagley.
30. Lavinia to May, 3.12.1871 (abbreviated).
31. Lord Lyttelton to Meriel, 13.11.1872, TP 13.
32. Lord Lyttelton to Meriel, 10.11.1872, TP 13.
33. Lucy to Meriel, 4.11.1872, TP.
34. Lavinia to Meriel, 18.11.1872, Hagley 21.
35. Sybella Lyttelton to Meriel, 5.1.1873, TP 10 (abbreviated).
36. Lord Lyttelton to Lucy, 4.1.1873, Hagley 25.
37. Lucy to Lord Lyttelton, 6.1.1873, Hagley 25 (abbreviated).
38. *Bedford Times*, 29.8.1871.
39. Archdeacon Denison to Lord Lyttelton, 27.4.1873, Worcester County Record Office, bulk accession 5467.
40. Lucy, Diary, 3.3.1873, Chatsworth.
41. *Parliamentary Debates*, 221: 1124–31 (3.8.1874).
42. Lord Lyttelton to Lucy, fragment August 1873, Hagley 25.
43. Sybella to Meriel, n.d (probably Oct. 1873), TP 13.
44. Lucy, Diary, 17.7.1874.
45. *Parliamentary Debates*, 221: 1124–31 (3.8.1874) (abbreviated).
46. *Bedford Times*, 29.8.1871.
47. Lord Lyttelton, evidence to Select Committee, *British Parliamentary Papers* (1873), viii.
48. Lavinia to May, February 1874, Hagley.
49. *Parliamentary Debates*, 221: 1124–31 (3.8.1874)
50. May, Diary, 1.10.1873.
51. Sybella to Meriel, n.d. (probably 23.10.1873), TP 10.
52. Lucy to Meriel, 8.9.1873, TP.
53. Lord Lyttelton to Meriel, 14.9.1873, TP 13.
54. May, Diary, 21.7.1874
55. Ibid., 17.8.1874
56. May to Meriel, 12.9.1874, Hagley.
57. May to Lucy, 1.1. 1875, Hagley.
58. Lord Lyttelton to Meriel, 22.1.1875, TP 13 (abbreviated).
59. Lavinia, Diary, 26.1.1875.
60. Ibid., 28.1.1875.

61. Lavinia to Mary Gladstone, 13.2.1875, Mary Gladstone Papers, BL, Add. MS 46236.
62. Mrs Talbot to Mrs Gladstone, n.d. (early 1875), GG 804.
63. Lucy to Meriel, 26.2.1875, TP.
64. Mrs Talbot to Meriel, 6.2.1875, TP 16.
65. Lord Lyttelton to Meriel, 13.3.1875, TP 13.

## Chapter 11: A Fall

1. Spencer Lyttelton, Diary, 25.3.1875.
2. Lord Lyttelton to Rev. Williamson of All Souls, London, 21.3.1875.
3. Extracts from appraisals of May Lyttelton, Mary Gladstone Papers, BL, Add. MS 46269.
4. Lord Lyttelton to Neville Lyttelton, 22.4.1875, Sir Neville Lyttelton Archive.
5. Meriel to Neville Lyttelton, 30.4.1875, Sir Neville Lyttelton Archive.
6. Lucy to Neville Lyttelton, 30.4.1875, Sir Neville Lyttelton Archive.
7. Lavinia to Meriel, 10.1.1873, Hagley 21.
8. Mary Gladstone to Neville Lyttelton (note added to Lucy's letter of 30.4.1875), Hagley 21.
9. Arthur Lyttelton to Mary Gladstone, 18.4.1875, Mary Gladstone Papers, BL, Add. MS 46235.
10. Edward Talbot to Illingworth (abbreviated).
11. Mrs Talbot to Meriel, 22.3.1875, TP 16.
12. Regular courses of Ladies' Lectures were started in 1873 by Professor T.H. Green and others eager to advance women's higher education. They marked the beginning of the movement (in which Edward and Lavinia Talbot were involved) to found women's colleges at Oxford.
13. Lavinia to Meriel, 12.9.1875, TP 16.
14. Edward Talbot to Meriel, 14.5.1875, TP 16.
15. Lord Lyttelton to Meriel, 2.4.1875, TP 13.
16. Lord Lyttelton to Neville Lyttelton, 22.4.1875, Sir Neville Lyttelton Archive.
17. Lord Lyttelton to Lucy, 15.1.1876, Hagley 25.
18. Lucy to Lord Lyttelton, 26.4.1875, Hagley 25.
19. Lord Lyttelton to Mrs Gladstone, 18.5.1875, GG 791.
20. Lucy to Meriel, 11.8.1875, TP.
21. Lucy to Lord Lyttelton, 8.9.75, Hagley 25.
22. Lord Lyttelton to Lucy, 2.2.1876, Hagley 25.
23. Charles Lyttelton to Mary Gladstone, 25.3.1876, BL, Mary Gladstone Papers, Add. MS 46235.
24. Lavinia to Meriel, 12.2.1876, TP 16.
25. Sybella Lyttelton to Meriel, 13.4.1876, TP 10.
26. Edward Talbot to Meriel, 12.4.1876, TP 16.
27. Lavinia to Lucy, 11.4.1876, Hagley 29.
28. Edward Talbot to Meriel, 14.4.1876, TP 16.
29. Lavinia, Diary, 15.4.1876.
30. Ibid., 16.4.1876.
31. Edward Talbot to Meriel, 16.4.1876
32. Edward Talbot to Meriel, 17.4.1876.

33  Lavinia, Diary, 17.4.1876.
34.  Lucy to Meriel, 17.4.1876, TP.
35.  *Birmingham Daily Post*, 21.4.1876, 'Tragical Death of Lord Lyttelton'.
36.  Edward Talbot to Meriel, 19.4.1876, TP 16.
37.  Caroline Lyttelton to Meriel, 5.5.1876, TP 10.
38.  This and the other extracts below from letters relating to Lord Lyttelton's death come from a collection at Hagley ref. 32012.
39.  Lucy, Diary, 17–23.4.1876.
40.  Lucy to Neville Lyttelton, 19.4.1876, Sir Neville Lyttelton Archive.
41.  Meriel to Neville Lyttelton, 24.4.1876, Sir Neville Lyttelton Archive.
42.  Mrs Talbot to Meriel, 24.4.1876, TP 16.
43.  *Guardian*, 26.4.1876.
44.  *British Medical Journal*, 29.4.1876, pp. 542–43.
45.  *Times*, 24.4.1876, p. 9.
46.  See note 39 above.
47.  *Journal of the Women's Education Union*, 15 May 1876.

## Chapter 12: The Last Chapter

1.  Lucy, Diary, 24–30 April 1876.
2.  Sybella Lyttelton to Meriel, 26.5.1876.
3.  Lavinia to Meriel, 18.10.1873, Hagley 21.
4.  Sybella Lyttelton to Meriel, 26.5.1876, TP 10.
5.  Lucy to Meriel, 28.4.1876, TP.
6.  Lavinia, Diary, 28.4.1876.
7.  Lucy to Meriel, 28.4.1876, TP.
8.  Charles Lyttelton to Meriel, 1.11.1876, TP 13 (abbreviated).
9.  Lavinia, Diary, 8–12 May 1876.
10.  Lucy to Neville Lyttelton, 12.5.1876, Sir Neville Lyttelton Archive.
11.  Edward Talbot to Meriel, 9.1.1870, TP 16.
12.  Lavinia, Diary, 18–19.4.1876.
13.  Mrs Talbot to Meriel, 24.4.1876, TP 16.
14.  Neville Lyttelton to Meriel, 28.5.1876, TP 13,
15.  Bob Lyttelton to Mary Gladstone, 7.5.1876, Mary Gladstone Papers, BL, Add. MS 46235.
16.  Lucy to Meriel, 11.9.1876, TP.
17.  Meriel to Lucy, 14.8.1876, Hagley.
18.  Lavinia to Lucy, 12.10.1876, Hagley 25.
19.  Ibid.
20.  Lavinia to Lucy, 14.11.1876, Hagley 25.
21.  Lavinia to Lucy, 12.10.1876
22.  Lucy to Meriel, 2.8.1878, TP.
23.  Lucy to Meriel, 23.8.1878.
24.  Lavinia to Edward Lyttelton, 6.9.1878, Hagley.
25.  Lucy to Meriel, 26.8.1878, TP.
26.  Lavinia to Lucy, September 1878
27.  Sybella Lyttelton to Meriel, n.d., TP 10.
28.  Lucy, Diary, 19.10.1878.

29. Gwendolen Stephenson, 'The Ucks, Aunt Lucy and the Uncles', unpublished memoir, TP F3.
30. Lucy to Meriel, Easter Tuesday 1880.
31. Lucy, Diary, 19–25.4.1880.
32. Lucy to Meriel and Johnny Talbot, 11.9.1879, TP
33. Lucy to Meriel, 16.9.1881.
34. Lucy to Meriel, 30.6.1876, TP.
35. Lucy to Meriel, Easter Day 1877, TP.
36. Roy Jenkins, *Gladstone* (London, 1995), p. 442.
37. Lucy, Diary, 26.4.1880 to 2.5.1880.
38. The account which follows is based on John Bailey, ed., *The Diary of Lady Frederick Cavendish* (London,1927), ii, pp. 302–21.
39. 'Another Account of the Night of May 6th, 1882', ibid., pp. 330–32.
40. Stephenson, 'The Ucks, Aunt Lucy and the Uncles', TP F3.
41. Lucy to Alfred Lyttelton, 26.9.1882, Lucy Cavendish College.
42. Mary Gladstone to Lavinia, 1892, quoted in 'Lucy Cavendish: A Memoir' by Lucy Masterman (Neville Lyttelton's daughter), typescript, Lucy Cavendish College.
43. Lucy to Edward Lyttelton, 5.10.1882, Lucy Cavendish College.
44. Lord Lyttelton to Meriel, 17.12.1868, TP 13.
45. Lucy, Diary, 24.4.1870.
46. Lucy Masterman, 'Lucy Cavendish: A Memoir'.
47. Bailey, ed., *The Diary of Lady Frederick Cavendish*, i, p. xxviii.
48. Edward Lyttelton to Lucy, quoted Cyril Alington, *Edward Lyttelton* (London, 1943), p. 6.
49. Lucy to Lavinia, 17.7.1883, Lucy Cavendish College.
50. Lucy to Constance Lyttelton (Uncle Billy's second wife), Epiphany 1888, Hagley.
51. Lucy to Meriel, 25.8.1883, Lucy Cavendish College.

# Index

*Illustrations are shown in bold*